Biggins
My Story

Biggins
My Story

Christopher Biggins

JOHN BLAKE

First published by
John Blake Publishing Limited
3 Bramber Court, 2 Bramber Road
London W14 9PB

www.johnblakepublishing.co.uk

www.facebook.com/johnblakebooks 🖪
twitter.com/jblakebooks 🖪

First published in hardback, as *Just Biggins: My Story*, in 2008
This updated paperback edition first published in 2015

ISBN: 978-1-78418-766-8

British Library Cataloguing-in-Publication Data:

A catalogue record for this book is available from the British Library.

Design by www.envydesign.co.uk

Printed in Great Britain by CPI Group (UK) Ltd

1 3 5 7 9 10 8 6 4 2

Papers used by John Blake Publishing are natural, recyclable
products made from wood grown in sustainable forests. The manufacturing
processes conform to the environmental regulations of the country of origin.

Every attempt has been made to contact the relevant copyright-holders,
but some were unobtainable. We would be grateful if the appropriate
people could contact us.

National treasure **Christopher Biggins** was born in Oldham and raised in Salisbury, the elder of two sons. His television work has encompassed everything from drama to presenting, both in the UK and the USA. He has played leading roles in the theatre all over the world, not to mention more than forty years as Britain's most loved pantomime dame. Biggins is also a respected director, and has written numerous articles for British newspapers and magazines. After winning *I'm a Celebrity…Get Me Out of Here* his feet hardly touched the ground, and he continues to star on stage and television. He lives in London with his partner Neil.

To my parents, Pam and Bill;
and to Neil Sinclair

Acknowledgements

Thanks to Neil Simpson for his help with writing the book. Thanks also to Lesley Duff and Charlie Cox at Diamond Management.

Contents

Prologue

Waiting and Worrying

Five men and five women face the cameras at the lavish Versace Hotel on Australia's Gold Coast. After just one day of luxury, they are divided into two groups, put in helicopters and boats, then led off into the jungle. It's November 2007, time for the latest series of *I'm A Celebrity... Get Me Out Of Here!* and these ten faces will soon be the most talked-about people in Britain.

I wasn't one of them.

I didn't even know who any of them were.

When Malcolm McLaren got cold feet – and Janice Dickinson and Lynne Franks had their first fabulous row – I was locked away in a sky-high suite in another, slightly less glitzy Australian hotel. I was in seclusion. No television. No internet. No newspapers and no phone calls home.

A charming assistant – or was she my jailer? – seemed to be outside my room at all times. She even vetted the room-service staff, so I didn't get any clues about events in the jungle. I was going to be the surprise late arrival in that year's *I'm A Celebrity*. And I was absolutely terrified. In little over a year's time I would be 60. Why on earth had I agreed to spend up to three weeks sleeping in a hammock, showering in a stream and eating food from a bonfire? This was not the Biggins way.

Shame about that no-telephone rule. Good job I'd smuggled in a spare mobile. So for a few glorious moments I thought I might get some vital information from the UK. I rang my partner, Neil. 'Has it started? Is it on? Who are the celebrities?' I asked, desperate for an idea of what might lie ahead of me.

'There's a real monster of an American woman,' Neil told me. Who could that be?

'And then there's the girl from...'

There was a loud, angry knock on my door. My assistant had heard my whispered conversation. The mobile was confiscated, my knuckles were rapped and my last link to the outside world was removed. 'The girl from where?' I asked myself. And it would be a while before I found out the monster's name.

I gazed out over the golf course from my hotel suite for two long days and nights. By now I imagined that the other celebrities would all have bonded and be living happily in their camp. I wasn't sure they would want a late arrival. Would I be welcome? Would I know who anyone was?

The more I thought about the show the more I worried. And the more I was told about the jungle the worse it got. Dr Bob and his team certainly didn't sugar-coat the pill when they came round to tell me about the hazards I might face. It was all poison this, bite that, danger the other. Looking back, I think I can see why Malcolm headed home. It's suddenly made very clear that this is no sanitised television studio. Serious things can happen.

'Are you ready?' my minder asks.

I'm smiling. 'As I'll ever be.'

And off we go for my one, very brief spell at the Versace. I do some photos, give some final interviews, then it's back into a blacked-out van for an hour and a half's drive to a grimy little motel in the middle of nowhere. As instructed, I've got my regulation three pairs of underwear and two pairs of swimming trunks, and I'm given the pack of other clothes that I'll have to wear from now on.

It's very, very early in the morning, though I don't know the exact time. My watch has been taken from me, and the crew who lead me into the jungle have theirs covered with masking tape. The mind games have begun. No words are spoken. I follow when the crew indicate that I should. I stop when they hold up their hands. All I know is that it's prime time back in Britain and that I'm doing a live trial. The crew leave me behind a tree and after a few moments I hear familiar voices. Ant and Dec.

Then I hear something else.

The dulcet tones of one Ms Janice Dickinson.

When I'm told to, I leave the safety of my tree and walk in front of the cameras.

This is it. But what have I done? In the next few moments everything is hysterical and fabulous and terrifying in equal measure. I realise, in one moment of absolute clarity, that I have given up all control of my life for the duration of the show.

I was on the *I'm A Celebrity* rollercoaster, the public could chuck me off at any moment and there was nothing I could do except be myself.

I hugged Janice, shook hands with Ant and Dec and took a very deep breath.

Would I be able to cope? What would the public think? Was I making the biggest mistake of my life?

1

A Boy from Oldham

I t is fair to say that my earliest reviews weren't good. 'He won't make old bones,' pronounced my grandmother, looking down on the little lad in his mother's arms. There was none of the traditional 'Oh, what a beautiful baby' messing around for good old Grannie Biggins. I've always been a straight talker. No prizes for guessing who I get it from.

And Grannie B wasn't the only critic to think I was in for a very short run.

'He's so tiny he'll be blown away in the wind when you take him home,' the maternity nurses told my mother, perhaps a little too cheerfully for her liking. Then came the worst review of all. 'If you don't get your son out of Oldham, he'll die,' said the doctor. It's hard to ignore a closure notice like that.

Like all bad reviews, it seemed a little unfair. Despite

the nurses' comments, I was actually a pretty healthy weight – a decent 9lb, thank you very much. The problem was my constitution. I wasn't strong. I had bronchitis, gastric problems and the staff seemed to think I was at risk of pneumonia.

'It's all the smoke in the air,' the doctor explained after another examination. 'His lungs are too weak to cope with it and he won't ever be able to breathe around here. Isn't there somewhere else you could go, at least for a while?'

That was all the encouragement my mother needed. She had been up north for less than a year. On balance she felt it had been a year too long. We made the move in January 1949, when I was just three weeks old. I was wrapped up in a big, soft nest of cotton wool and set down on the passenger seat of a huge Pickfords lorry.

'We're going south,' said my mother with a very broad smile. South was her idea of civilisation. Oldham, it's fair to say, was not. She had been happy enough to give it a go. But the initial signs hadn't been good. The first time my father came home from work on his motorbike, his face had been so covered in black soot from all the cotton mills, the coal mines and the factories that she hadn't recognised him. She likes to call herself a Hampshire hog. The Lowry lifestyle simply didn't suit her.

She tells me she sang all the way down the old A6 when we left town that cold January day. All except for the bit of the journey where we knocked over a water hydrant and left a brand-new fountain in our wake. As an actor I've always known the value of making a big entrance. At three weeks old it was nice to have made such a spectacular exit.

Fortunately, my dad was more than happy to give up his job and start a new life down south. He was Oldham born and bred but he'd seen the world in the Royal Air Force, where he'd met my mum before being posted out in Africa. So he was prepared to see a bit more of England now he had a sickly little lad to consider as well.

Our removal van dropped us off in the gloriously beautiful town of Salisbury. I always joked that I didn't need to be in a Merchant Ivory film (though it might have been nice to be asked). Instead I got to grow up in one. The buildings are picture-postcard perfect. We had the river, the cathedral, the parks, the half-timbered houses, you name it. Trouble was, beautiful surroundings don't pay the bills – a lesson I would need to learn and relearn many times in the years ahead. Nor did the fresh southern air solve all my medical issues overnight.

The first problem was that I had proved to be allergic to cotton wool. So being wrapped up in the stuff for half a day on the journey south hadn't been a great idea. It took quite a while for those rashes to pass, Mum says. And I still come out in blotches if I touch the stuff.

And while the doctors in Salisbury weren't quite as negative as the ones up at Boundary Park Hospital in Oldham, they too thought I needed a lot of work. My main doctor was a man who became a dear friend of the family. Dr Jim Drummond visited us up to three times a day when I was at my weakest, and he saw all of us through a lot of tough times. He helped me build up my strength and let my lungs develop at their own pace. It's probably because of him that I *have* made old bones.

Mum and Dad had met in the sergeants' mess at RAF Colerne near Bath in 1943. My dad, Bill, was a Leading Aircraft Man or LAC, while my mum, Pam, was a Leading Aircraft Woman or LACW. I remember seeing photos of them, proud and young in their forces uniforms. Back then the world was a frightening place. If you found love, you grasped it fast in case the war snatched it away from you. So, when something clicked at RAF Colerne, my parents didn't hang around. They were married in St Paul's church in Salisbury within three months of meeting. But wartime love affairs weren't easy. They tried to have a honeymoon – though going to a home for retired priests in Fleetwood hardly sounds the most romantic of destinations. And the holiday was interrupted by my father's call-up, which may well have been for the best.

Dad was sent out to Africa. Mum stayed in the forces on the home front, but, although they were both demobbed in 1946, they were left half a world apart. My mother headed back to Salisbury to look for work, and Dad was left nursing an injury in Cape Town while he waited for a space on a boat that could bring him home. Or would a boat take Mum out to him instead? Servicemen could take their wives out to Africa for £100 and get leave to stay for 12 months to see if they liked it. Dad could easily have got a job in a garage out in the sunshine of the Cape but my mother said no. If only she had known that the alternative to Cape Town would ultimately be Oldham.

They moved north for one simple reason: to find work. The krugerrands my father had brought back with him didn't last long. And his first job, in a post office in Southampton, wasn't for him. So after less than a year

4

they were on the road. Dad was going to work at Middleton Motors in his native Oldham. My mother was going to have a baby. Everything was going to change.

I was born on 16 December 1948. It was just three years after the end of the war and the country was still coming to terms with how tough victory would be. Mum and Dad were grafters. They didn't take charity. But, like everyone, they struggled. The ups and down that have always been a feature of my life were already a feature of theirs.

When we arrived back in Salisbury, we were doing well. We moved into a tiny flat above a tailor's shop. It was perfect because all we had were a few borrowed pieces of furniture from Mum's family. But even that got lost when a fire in the shop spread upstairs.

Our next stop should have been better. We had a house – Mum's parents' old home – on Devizes Road on the edge of town. But it looked to have been a leap too far. Mum and Dad both worked all hours: Mum in hotels and bars, Dad in garages and petrol stations. But it was never enough to keep up the payments, so after a couple of years we moved out of there as well.

This time the three of us were going down the housing ladder. We moved out of town and into a caravan propped up on bricks in the corner of a muddy farmyard. It was a cold, crowded place and we stayed for two cold and crowded years. I don't remember a lot of it – though putting my hand on a red-hot electric grill and saying, 'Is this on?' seems to stand out. My hand bubbled up like an omelette and out came the dreaded cotton wool to patch it up and make a bad job even worse. Outside the van I also remember finding a rat trap. But looking at it wasn't enough. I had to put my hand in it, to see what it did. 'It traps you, Biggins, it traps you.' One of the farm workers heard the screams and rushed over to help release the spring. To this day my fingers don't quite sit straight.

Self-inflicted injuries apart, the time we spent in that caravan did teach me some pretty important lessons. One was that you can never expect your life to run in a straight line. Another was that life is what you make it. Living in a caravan with a small child is no party. But Mum and Dad did at least try to keep up appearances. Our caravan was clean and we certainly didn't starve. We made the most of what we had. We survived.

I learned how to put on a show in that draughty old caravan. My mum taught me. I watched her get ready for work at a clothes shop in town and at the High Post Hotel just on the outskirts. She got into character for each role. Every day she put on the performance of her life. She was a glamorous, sparkling woman. Money and make-up were still pretty scarce in the early 1950s. But when my mum was serving behind her counters you would never have known she had got ready in a caravan. She dressed well and knew how to charm the customers. Showbusiness is all about smoke and mirrors, painting on a smile and carrying on with the show. I learned that early. I had a feeling I would end up being pretty good at it.

Dad's lessons were just as important. He simply never gives up. When his garage work didn't bring in enough cash during the week, he manned petrol pumps at another one at the weekend. When the River Avon rose six feet, burst its banks, flooded his first premises and destroyed most of his equipment, he just started all over again. And he put on a performance as well. He's the best salesman I know. He can talk the hind legs off a donkey and win jobs with charm alone. That's another useful skill in showbusiness.

'Christopher, I need you to help me pack. We're moving.' Mum's smile was as wide as I had ever seen it. Dad's was just as broad. It was 1953 and we were heading back into Salisbury, to a two-up, two-down house backing on to the railway line on Sidney Street. It's a stretch to say the good times were going to roll. But we were certainly on the up.

Having people my own age around was a revelation in our new home – in fact, having any neighbours at all was a little different after the farmyard. But I wasn't actually that keen on all the other kids. I think I was already getting to like being the centre of attention. Sharing the limelight with other children was never going to be my thing. So I didn't mix that well during our first few years back in town. Mum remembers me playing with the rest of the so-called Sidney Street gang, but I only really remember playing with one of the kids from the newsagents' shop opposite, Noyce & Sons. Kay, the owners' daughter, was that one early pal. We played Doctors and Nurses, the way you do. That's when I discovered the female form, though strictly as an observer.

Where I did have fun was Southampton with my other grandparents. Lil and Jack Parsons had a little flat there and I was always desperate to visit. Lil was very theatrical, which I already loved. She was always singing and she could play the piano by ear. She also gave me my first taste of real theatre. She had a huge extended family and one of her brothers was a leading light in amateur dramatics. I never got the chance to see him in a play – at this point I'd never even been inside a village hall, let alone a theatre. But I listened when he talked about his rehearsals and performances. It all sounded so thrilling, so magical. I wanted some of that excitement to rub off on me. So, while Grannie cooked a meal and Granddad sat around in his long johns and vest chain-smoking untipped cigarettes, I set up my own little fantasy world.

I would hang a sheet up in my bedroom to look like a theatre curtain. And I would put on little shows for the Southampton branch of the family.

Back in Salisbury our family's only other very loose link with the entertainment world was a friendship with the Neagles, a trio who sang on cruise ships and had moved to Florida before I had even met them. Dad missed them and didn't just talk about them all the time – he tried to talk like them as well. The head of the Neagle family had given him a Star of David as a keepsake. So Dad put on a cod-Jewish voice that made me laugh and drove Mum mad. 'I don't know what he's talking about. He's not even circumcised,' she said after one particularly long impression.

'I won't take my coat off. I'm not stopping.' That's what Grannie B would always say when she arrived from Oldham. Then she would stay for weeks. Sidney Street always seemed to be crowded. Yes, it was a lot bigger than the caravan. But it wasn't exactly a palace. We had an outside toilet – everyone did back then. And our toilet was never empty. We had a very big resident spider. I was terrified, quite terrified, of spiders back then, which meant going to the toilet as a boy was all a bit of a nightmare. Now, after the jungle, I have learned to take both spiders and outside toilets in my stride.

Monday night was bath night on Sidney Street. Dad dragged out the standard-issue tin bath and Mum filled it up with water boiled up on the fire in the front room. Then I got in for my weekly wash. Now, having a bath in front of your parents is bad enough. But I had a bigger audience. Every Monday, every single one for around 16 years, my mum's friend Maisie came round. The regularity of it drove Mum mad. The embarrassment of it nearly did the same to me.

Maisie's husband Les would go out to the pub with my dad and she would settle down for the night as I got undressed and began my ablutions. Yes, I already liked having an audience and being the centre of attention. But this was ridiculous. Couldn't Maisie arrive later or leave earlier? Did her visits always have to happen on a Monday? Some weeks when my bath water had been drained away, Mum would change into her nightdress and put her curlers in to try to persuade Maisie it was time to leave. But she never got the hint. I was so pleased when we finally had enough money to have an indoor bathroom put in. Maisie still came round every Monday night until I was well into my teens. But at least I was no longer the main attraction in the middle of the living-room floor.

Monday must have been one of my mum's rare nights off. She had a new job in a cocktail bar at the Cathedral Hotel on Milford Street in the middle of town. Today it's a sad and tired-looking place. But in its heyday, in Mum's day, the hotel and its main bar absolutely glittered. People dressed up to drink there. Nights out were few and far between, so everyone felt a sense of occasion when they enjoyed them. And the job could hardly have suited Mum more. She was so glamorous, so gregarious.

The place suited me just as well as it suited my mum. The hotel manager and his family lived upstairs and I would hang around with their daughter, Pam, while our parents worked. I think Pam and I were supposed to do our homework and play games. But we found something else. We discovered the wonder of room service. We rang down for whatever we wanted. Beans on toast. Strawberry milkshakes. Cheese sandwiches. A matter of minutes later, as if by magic, our orders would arrive. Men and women in uniform would bring them, on trays and trolleys, the white china plates covered in shiny silver domes and resting on starched white cloths. It was divine. And there was something else. Pam and I were kids. She was the manager's daughter. So we never had to pay the bill. For many, many years I don't think I realised that with room service there was a bill. The pattern of my life was already beginning to emerge.

Food aside, I wasn't just in love with being treated like a king at the hotel. I loved having free run of the place. I could walk through all the doors that were off limits to the guests. I saw the way the hotel worked, saw how different things were in the staff corridors, the kitchen, the laundry rooms. Our guests were shown a calm, clean and elegant world. But I knew how different it was behind the scenes. This was my first taste of going backstage. I adored it.

When Mum was working day shifts and Pam wasn't around I would be left in the Chelsea Tea Rooms at the Red Lion Hotel opposite. It was almost as much fun as ordering free room service. Mum says I sat and charmed all the ladies in their fine hats – they would feed me tiny little sandwiches and elegant little cakes off their serving towers. I would listen to the chink of the china tea cups and the soft chatter of conversation. It was an awful long way from a farmyard caravan. It was bliss.

Sitting in the tea rooms, I also got to watch my mother a little closer. In the evenings I watched her even more from the back of the hotel bar. It was like watching a command performance. All good waiters and waitresses put on a show. My mother was up with the best. She practically danced as she flitted between tables. Watching her serve drinks was like watching a ballerina. Watching her charm the customers was like watching an award-winning actress. And the set wasn't too shabby either.

I've always said that, if I could, I would happily live in a hotel. Coco Chanel lived at the Paris Ritz for 30 years and Elaine Stritch put down roots at the Carlyle in New York – the same hotel where I would one day meet a certain Ms Joan Collins. Back in the late 1950s and early 1960s, I would have happily moved into the Cathedral Hotel. I loved the place and I loved the cast of characters that were constantly flitting through its doors. That was just as well.

One of mother's best friends at the Cathedral Hotel was a pretty waitress called Christine who was dating a fellow worker there called Jock. He lost his room at the hotel when he quit his bar job to go and work in a local wine shop.

'Can he lodge with you? Just for a few months till he finds a new place?' Christine asked.

Mum and Dad said yes, and Jock stayed for the next 11 years.

He was a good man. It was like having a new live-in uncle. And once more I was happy to be with another adult. It was when someone my own age moved in that things went wrong.

To their huge credit, my parents decided to foster another child as I grew up. We might not have had much money, or much room, but we could still offer someone a chance. Trouble was, the boy in question didn't want to take it. Some bad things happened between us, things I was determined to keep from my parents. But while I could keep that secret, I couldn't hide how often I was physically thrown into the rubbish bin in our backyard. So, after one incident too many, this troubled lad was moved on.

Life had changed completely by the time I approached secondary school age – because Dad's business had started to boom. He had moved on from selling motorbikes to selling cars. He bought and built up the first of his own garages. And he began to take on staff.

Dad had always been doing deals. He always had the gift of the gab and was always joking as he wheeled and dealed. I got all of that from him. He's a born storyteller. He can talk to anyone about anything. And he's always looking for the next big chance. He started work cutting up and selling planks of wood at just 13 years old – though he says the Manpower Board put a stop to his little enterprise, just as Health and Safety might do today. He then tried to get rich with a horse and cart – but he reckons he ended up with the laziest horse in town. He never gave up, though. All the time he was in the Air Force he was trying to come up with new schemes and business ideas.

That's why when he wasn't at the garage he always had some other deal on the go. Fifty years before eBay, he was busy trading coins, antiques and junk with American collectors. And if anyone closer to home was ready to pay for anything, as far as Dad was concerned they could have it.

My mother and I knew that to our cost. One wet afternoon we were sitting having a pot of tea and watching a black-and-white film on television when Dad rushed in.

'I need the television,' he said, switching it off and unplugging it.

'What's the matter? We were watching that,' I wailed.

'I've sold it. I'll get you a bigger, better one tomorrow.'

And he did. The Artful Dodger in Dad always managed to replace what he had sold with something bigger and better – and still left himself quids in on the deal. Amazing. Though I've still never seen the end of that film.

2

Finding My Voice

Next in the cast of characters of our family was Great-Aunt Vi – the biggest snob I ever met. She lived in Faversham in Kent, where she and her husband, Arthur, owned a seed shop in one of the most beautiful buildings in the town. Auntie Vi taught me how to lay a table properly, how to place napkins and how to make a wonderful Victoria sponge. When I went to stay, or she came over to ours, I got bedtime stories in the bath with a glass of ginger wine. I thought it was the height of sophistication.

As far as Mum, Dad and I were concerned, Great-Aunt Vi was a woman with a mission. She hated my Wiltshire burr – Mum had it too – and Dad's voice annoyed her even more. It had a touch of the north, a touch of cockney and even that joking, Jewish lilt in it for good measure. So good old Great-Aunt Vi paid for the elocution lessons that would turn the Oldham-born, Wiltshire-bred boy into the Christopher Biggins whose voice can boom so loudly today.

Mrs Christian was my elocution teacher. She was a fantastic, wonderful woman and I saw her once or twice a week for private classes at my new school and at her home. These were my *My Fair Lady* moments. The rain in Spain falls mainly on Salisbury Plain and all that. As the weeks passed, my Wiltshire burr began to fade. But my lessons went on. I think Mrs Christian saw something other than just a strong voice in me. She also taught drama and English at school and was the first to really get me interested in theatre. And she had help. If she had lit the theatrical flames, Mr Lewis, soon to be my music teacher at school, would be the one to fan them.

He was one of the biggest gossips I had ever met. All we did was gossip. To this day all I can play on the piano is 'Daffodil Dell' (and I'm not very good at that). But what I missed out on in terms of scales or harmonies I gained in terms of confidence and simple *joie de vivre*. Mr Lewis was probably a bit effeminate, but I didn't spot that then and it wouldn't have made any difference even if I had. There was certainly no element of impropriety in our long, funny theatrical chats. I think Mr Lewis simply saw me as a kindred spirit – albeit a much younger one. Those were lonely times for confirmed bachelors of a certain age. I think I just brightened some of my teacher's darker days. I let him forget how isolated he might be.

I had started at the private St Probus School for boys at 11. And it had all been a bit of a mess. Much to my dad's disappointment, I had failed my 11 Plus and so didn't qualify for the local grammar. Or did I? My father had been talking to some other parents and found out that, because I'd only been ten when I'd taken the exam, a loophole meant I could do a retake. If I passed I would be educated for free and, like I say, Dad loves a bargain. But the timing was all wrong. The day that Dad rushed home to tell us the news, Mum and I were busy buying my brand-new St Probus uniform and paying my fee for the first term.

'Too late now,' Dad said when he saw me in all my new finery.

So St Probus it was. And it served me well. I enjoyed school. We were neither a hugely academic nor a hugely sporting place. Just a very relaxed place. And we had a theatre. That would change everything for me.

My first proper stage performance at school was as the Pirate King in *The Pirates of Penzance*. I was in heaven. I took on as many other roles as possible after *Pirates*. And at 14 I enjoyed my first, campest, triumph. I played the Ethel Merman part in *Call Me Madam*. Yes, I think the clues were all there had anyone bothered to look for them. And if my choice of roles didn't raise eyebrows, my clothes certainly did. For quite some time I insisted on wearing a full-length blue kaftan when my poor mother took me shopping. To this day I can't remember where on earth I got it from. Sleepy old Salisbury, in the early 1960s, had hardly ever seen the like before. No wonder my mum always wanted to walk a few paces ahead or several paces behind me. No wonder she was mortified when I decided I wanted to stop in a shoe shop one day to see if I could get footwear to match. The girls there barely batted an eyelid. But Mum? She was mortified. Looking back, I can see her point.

My good fortune as a boy was to avoid the total isolation felt by anyone who grows up feeling a little different. I did that because I had a pal called John Brown at my side. We met in my first year at St Probus and were friends from the very start. We're still friends today, though we see each other far less frequently than we should.

As kids, John and I always had a hoot at theatre rehearsals – and every other moment of the day as well. Neither of us was especially sporty and in particular we both hated cross-country runs. We decided to turn them into cross-country walks. The two of us would amble around picking up flora and fauna and get back to the smelly locker rooms laden with wild flowers and berries.

'Biggins, come on!'

'Brown, get running!'

'Where have you two been?'

Everyone would be yelling for us to hurry up, because the games master said no one could leave until we were all finished. But there was no question of bullying at school, and no taunts about anything other than our lack of athletic skills. This sense of decency and respect came from the top, as it always does.

Our head teacher, Mr French, was very firm but very fair. Yes, he used the threat of the belt to keep us all in line, but I truly don't see the harm in that. We all learned the boundaries between good and bad behaviour from Mr French. Today we've probably gone too far the other way, giving kids too much freedom and not making it clear how they should behave. Mr French never made that mistake. Though I do remember a few oddities. Once he gave us a lecture on gingivitis and dental hygiene. The next day, for reasons I can't recall, we all rebelled over our school lunches. We threw all the food into the bins. And then in walked Mr French. He made every one of us get a spoon and eat at least a spoonful from the bins. Not exactly hygienic, or great for the gums. But it taught us to keep our rebellions on a smaller scale from then on.

Thinking laterally helped on the cross-country runs as well. John and I realised that we couldn't keep our classmates waiting every week. And I suddenly found a new way to avoid the run but still get to the finish line on time. Maisie's house was just outside the school playground, where the races began and ended. So John and I would pop in for a cup of tea and a gossip and emerge when the front-runners headed back past the front door. It was payback time for all those embarrassing bath times.

At the weekend John and I used to spend all our time together as well. We would sit for hours at the Red Lion Hotel having a cheese scone and a thick, milky coffee. We thought of it as utter sophistication. By now I knew a lot about the way you were supposed to behave in hotels. I had my mum's example, of course. But I had also lapped up all the glamorous stories from my grandmother. She had been a silver service waitress in the Red Lion back at a time when you had to pay the head waiter to get a shift.

'Always leave a tip,' she would tell me, remembering how tough it had been when others hadn't.

'Always leave a tip,' my mum would repeat when she

knew I was off out with John. But I didn't always take it seriously. One afternoon, when we really couldn't make our scones and coffee last any longer, I got a piece of paper and a pen out of my pocket.

'Tip: Back the first horse at Aintree,' I wrote, thinking I was hilarious and the first person to come up with a line like that. And if I was wrong on those points I was certainly wrong to think I would get away with it. The waitressing scene in Salisbury was as tight as the acting profession. Mum found out what I had done straight away and I got the biggest bollocking and the hardest slap of my life.

I left school at 16 without, I'm a little embarrassed to say, a single O Level. I've no regrets at all in my life. But if I was pushed I'd say I do almost regret not going on to some kind of college. I'd perhaps like to have seen how much more there was to know. I'd like to have learned more, though I don't know about what. Today I swear that if I won the Lottery and never needed to work again I would fill at least part of my time with study. I'd soak it up in my sixties. All the opportunities I let slip in my teens.

So what would I do for a living?

'I think I might want to be a vicar.'

That was a bit of a conversation-stopper back at home. My parents took it well and would have helped make it happen if I'd been serious. But I think I was just casting around for something that involved dressing up in costumes and reading things out in front of people.

Before I hit upon the other, blindingly obvious way to make a career out of those activities, I carried on doing odd jobs for my father. I'd always loved watching him work just as much as I loved watching my mother. He was at the top of his game in the mid-1960s – making money right and left, buying, selling, driving and even racing flash cars. He inspired me because it was so clear that he didn't just do the selling because of the money. It was also for the challenge and the thrill of the game. He always liked to see just how much he could get away with.

He taught me that you don't get much if you don't gamble and you don't get anything if you don't ask. Throughout my school days my father and I were a great combination at work. No, I wasn't exactly cut out to be a mechanic in his garage. But I happily tried to drum up extra business elsewhere.

'Don't drink and drive. But take a drink home from us.' That was the snappy advertising slogan I came up with for the local paper when we offered a free bottle of champagne on every car we sold for more than £150. And because our lodger Jock was still working in his wine shop I got a deal on the bubbly as well.

The wheeler-dealer in me was out. I've loved a bargain ever since. And I've never lost my taste for champagne. The tragedy for my poor father was that, like so many small businesses, his was killed off when VAT was introduced in the 1970s. Funny how life goes. My career was just about taking off at that point. My father was on the edge of bankruptcy. After so many years of being lent and given cars by him, I had just bought one of my own. I remember driving down to Salisbury to show it off. 'Dad, it's yours,' I said, handing over the keys and taking the train back to town.

It was Mrs Christian who pointed me in the right direction when I left school. Over the years we had read so many play texts in our elocution, drama and English lessons. We had talked so much about all the great actors and the wonders of the stage. She gave me the confidence to believe that I too could become a professional actor.

So after one final chat with her I went to the only place I could think of to look for work: the Salisbury Playhouse.

It wasn't an easy visit.

I had been to see plays there many times with the school and my family. And every time the lady in the box office had terrified me. Her name was Pauline Aston and she was a big, imposing lady, with heavily dyed hair piled up high on top of her head. To me she was a dragon, though like most people who have scared me throughout my life she ended up a close friend and a wonderful person. Her husband, Stan, the cantankerous but wonderful electrician, handyman and stage manager, scared me too – but we ended up getting on like a house on fire.

'Please don't let the dragon be there. Please don't let the dragon be there,' I mumbled to myself as I walked up to the theatre. The dragon was there.

'Can I see Mr Salzberk,' I said, mispronouncing the theatre manager Mr Salsberg's name because I was so nervous.

'Wait over there,' the dragon said, clearly unimpressed, and pointed to a bench on the other side of the theatre foyer.

But for some reason I hadn't understood exactly where she meant. And I was too scared to risk her wrath by asking again. So I waited, for more than an hour, on the other side of a wall in completely the wrong place. When

I ventured out, who should I find but Mr Salsberg, who, bless him, was still looking for me.

'I want to be an actor,' I blurted out. Six incoherent words. Not even a 'hello' or a 'how do you do?' I was the nervous little boy from nowhere. The boy who knew no one and nothing. Mr Salsberg should have laughed me out of town. Instead he looked me up and down and gave me my in.

'Well, I'm doing *She Stoops To Conquer*. You can come to that.' Two sentences in the man's lovely, low nasal voice. It was enough. It proved that if you don't ask you don't get. As usual, I thank my wheeler-dealer father for giving me the confidence to learn that lesson.

As I left the theatre I wasn't quite sure what the manager had meant. Was this a part in a play? Was I just being asked along to watch? Or was it a job? When I turned up at the theatre the next day I found it was the latter. I was in. There is a small comedy role as a servant in *She Stoops To Conquer*. It was mine. In truth, it was just a glorified walk-on part. But it did have a few lines. And that was enough. I was on my way. Within a few weeks I had signed a proper contract with the Playhouse. I started out on £2 a week as a student assistant stage manager. I would stay there for two years. It was just the most wonderful period of my life.

The theatre was on Fisherton Street near the river and the railway station. In truth, it wasn't a real theatre at all. The building used to be a Methodist hall, then something else, until finally it was turned into a theatre with a proper stage and seating. I'd been in the audience a few times with my parents and on school trips. I'd always adored the glamour of the lights, the thick velvet curtains, the plush carpets and all the trappings of theatre. I had also always dreamed that to go backstage would be like going to some kind of Narnia. And so it was – only in reverse.

'Mind that!'

'Careful!'

'Coming through!'

It was chaos. Backstage certainly wasn't quite the magical world of glamour and beauty that I had imagined. Salisbury Rep was falling apart. There was a tiny set of different stairs and rooms and corridors but there was nowhere to pick up a cat, let alone swing one. And yes, there was the high, intoxicatingly rich scent of make-up and hair spray. But there was also the smell of mould, mildew and damp. The roof leaked all over and most of the buckets were used to protect the seats in the auditorium. Backstage water just drained away wherever it could. Water soaked into almost everything and, however much heat our big old radiators banged out, it was never enough to dry it all out. Backstage the light bulbs died and weren't always replaced. Old sets, old costumes, long-forgotten props piled up in corridors and corners. Who knows what crawled among them. But who cared?

I always thought of that recruitment scene in *Oh! What A Lovely War* when the prospective soldiers are mesmerised by the radiant image of Maggie Smith. They all rush forward and find that when they got up close and personal she was a hideous, ravaged old hag. Salisbury Rep was my Maggie Smith. I rushed towards her with all the passion and idealism of youth. But I never ran away again when I saw the ugly truth. I loved her close up just as I had loved her from afar. I wasn't going to let a little bit of reality get in my way. I never have. It was clear from day one at Salisbury that I was so much younger than everyone else in the company. But for me, of all people, that wasn't a problem. I'd been around older people all my life. It suited me.

So did my role. As a student assistant stage manager, I was everyone's general dogsbody. I helped research, track down and collect the props. I was on the book, ready to prompt at each performance. I swept floors, picked up rubbish, even cleaned the toilets in the auditorium. And I barely had time to think. We worked on a fast, tough regime, putting on new plays every second week. Cast, read through, rehearse, perform, repeat. It was relentless. It was intoxicating.

My parents came to most of the shows, especially when I had a role. And we had fun. It was like a little game to see how many items from around their home they would see on stage in each production.

And my magpie tendencies were only one part of my poor mother's problems. If I wasn't 'borrowing' things for my latest production, Dad was still selling them to make a quick buck and enjoy the fun of the deal. No wonder Mum always had to check before she sat down in her own front room. We'd both take the chair from underneath her given half a chance.

'Excuse me, son. Do your parents know you're out in the middle of the night?'

Being stopped by the local bobbies at 2am was another

regular part of my new routine. At the end of each play's short run, I got lumbered with much of the get-in and get-out process. I would start packing up the props and pulling the scenery apart in the wings while the actors were still on stage out front. Then I would put down the screwdrivers and join them for the curtain call before getting on with the job. Most times the clear-up took well into the early hours, hence my moonlit walks home.

What an innocent age that those walks should attract the attention of the police. How grown-up I felt when I told them about my job.

'I work in the theatre,' I would say. What a wonderful phrase. I wasn't even 17 but I had already found my calling.

At the Rep I wasn't just learning how to put on plays. I was getting a master class in the whole theatrical experience. I loved it. Lesson one came when our passionate stage manager, Jan Booth, told me off for the way I had addressed our star, the marvellous Stephanie Cole, who is a dear friend to this day.

'Here's your script, Stephanie,' I had said as I bounded on to the stage.

'It's Miss Cole to you,' Jan told me in a fierce whisper afterwards. And so it was – at least during working hours. I liked the hierarchy. I could see that luvviness only lasts so long. Being in rep taught me that theatre is a business and that, if something goes wrong, backstage or on stage, then someone has to be held accountable. Everyone needs to know what their roles and responsibilities are.

Unfortunately, I didn't always get to grips with all of mine. One of our early plays was a murder mystery set in deepest Devon. When the curtain rose, the first thing the audience heard was a carriage clock (from my parents' house) strike midnight. The second thing they should have heard was the ringing of a phone. I was on props one night and was watching from the wings as the sole actor on stage listened to the clock and then froze. I froze with him. I had forgotten to put the phone on the table. And I had absolutely no idea what to do about it.

Once again Jan showed me the way.

She picked up the phone from the top of a pile of boxes backstage, walked to the back of the set and knocked on the door.

'Who is it?' our lead actor asked, with no idea what might be coming next.

'I'm here to install your telephone,' replied Jan.

'Do come in.'

'I'll put it here.' On stage, in her ordinary clothes, Jan walked to the table, placed the phone on top, tucked the wire under the carpet and turned to leave.

'Goodnight, sir.'

'Goodnight.'

Then the phone rang and the play began. What class.

Fortunately I wasn't the only one to mess up occasionally. Dear Jane Quy, one of our assistant stage managers, was 'on the book' in my place one night. For us this meant raising and lowering the curtain as well as being ready to prompt. It's not the most exciting job in the business, so you really need a hobby to help pass the time. Jane's hobby was to knit. She was a champion knitter and would work away – fortunately in total silence – while the performance went on to her left. She never once missed her place in the script.

But it did all go wrong one night when she was finishing a stitch as the end of the first act approached. Her knitting, her needles and two balls of bright-green wool all got caught in the curtain's pulley system. For some reason this short-circuited the whole contraption. The curtain itself barely moved. But Jane's colourful knitting made a slow procession all the way around our makeshift proscenium arch and all the way back again.

It got us the biggest round of applause of the night.

I don't think I could have stayed an actor for the next 50 years if I hadn't had that grounding backstage in Salisbury. I don't think my love affair with theatre would have survived if I hadn't seen all its warts from the start. But at the time the props, the curtains and the book weren't enough.

I wanted to learn how to act. And fortunately I was in very good company. Stephanie – sorry, Miss Cole – was an inspiration. I would watch her in rehearsal, and from the wings in a performance. She could grab an audience. She made bad writing sound good. And, oh God, did she make us all laugh.

She became a true pal, despite her lofty position at the top of the Salisbury tree. I think I first fell in love with her when she was in rehearsal for Mrs Hardcastle in that first production of *She Stoops To Conquer* when I was still a nervous little new boy in the company. She had to go down three steps while reciting three key lines. But that first rehearsal she tripped. 'Oh, f**k, c**t, shit,' she spluttered as she tried to regain her balance. I was such a little baby I barely knew what the words meant. I certainly didn't know that a woman could use them.

But I think I realised that Stephanie would be great company in the years ahead. I was certainly right about that.

Stephanie wasn't my only teacher, of course. Oliver Gordon, the Rep's director, gave me some tough love lessons from the start. His message was pretty simple: 'Don't muck about. Go on stage left, say your lines, then piss off stage right.' That was pretty much the way he saw it. In rep there was no faffing around, no rocket science and no method-acting silliness. Oliver's message was that if you're good you get re-hired. If not, try working in a shop. It was sink or swim. Oliver was a real Arthur Askey type and he was also a perfect pantomime dame. His Widow Twankey in *Aladdin* was a template of mine for years. And we were such a close, tight ship in Salisbury. Oliver's brother wrote lots of our pantomimes, was married to Stephanie and was another big influence on me.

Everything we did in Salisbury was on a shoestring, but the audiences would never have known it. If she had been asked, I swear that our wardrobe mistress, Barbara Wilson, could quite literally have made a silk purse out of a sow's ear. In fact, she could probably have made six. We pulled together and it all felt fantastic. For me, the lonely boy who had always felt just a little bit different, it was a revelation. I was in the world I had dreamed of. I was in my element.

For pretty much the only time in my life I also felt as if I was in the money. My £2 a week was pretty paltry. But I was living at home and in my second year at Salisbury my wage rose to £8 a week. After a few more months I hit £12 a week when I was made a full stage manager, while still living at home and paying next to nothing to my parents. Dad's garages were all doing well and he was always giving me cars and vans to drive. Life was just wonderful.

Staying at home protected me from a lot. It stopped me from growing up too fast and from getting into trouble. But it didn't entirely shield me from reality.

My sexuality was still pretty much a mystery to me in the late 1960s. I wasn't in denial and I wasn't tortured by any sort of sexual angst. I simply had too many other things whizzing around my mind to think about that side of life. But it seemed that plenty of people were prepared to think about it for me.

The wonderfully outrageous Raymond Bowers was clearly one of them. 'There's that Christopher Biggins. He's so queer he could be a lesbian,' he roared out above the crowd as I walked into the coffee shop at the Playhouse one afternoon. Robin Ellis, who would one day be Ross Poldark to my Reverend Ossie Whitworth, was in the coffee shop with Ralph Watson and his girlfriend Caroline Moody, who died so tragically young. The whole room seemed to fall about laughing at Raymond's words. I blushed so deeply I nearly fainted. Queer? Lesbian? I didn't know what any of the words meant, let alone understand the overall sentiment.

But, public embarrassment aside, Raymond turned from someone who could – and indeed did – scare me, into a close pal. He also proved to be a useful role model in an age when visibly gay people seemed few and far between. He lived in The Close in Salisbury with a chic older man called Geoffrey Larkin. Their big town house had a room painted entirely in yellow and contained nothing but a black grand piano. I thought it was the peak of sophistication. Maybe it was.

Raymond and Geoffrey upgraded Great-Aunt Vi's table manners for me. Serviettes became napkins and the living room itself became a drawing room. The pair were top-notch entertainers and threw the most wonderful dinner parties – or was I supposed to call them supper parties? I forget. Either way I would head home from the events reeling that such stylish and elegant people existed, let alone existed in Salisbury. I was just thrilled to be part of that world. While Geoffrey has sadly died, Raymond is still very much here, working at the National Theatre. I still smile every time I think of him.

Back at the theatre we put on so many productions. We had so many different directors, who all taught me new skills. I was 17 ½ when I got my Equity card, which was essential back then. It was only a simple piece of cardboard. There was no photograph on it and it wasn't even laminated. But it had my vital Equity number. It was easily the most precious object I had ever owned. After two amazing years I felt I was doing all the right things. But was I learning enough? Was I going in the right direction?

'You need to go to drama school,' said Stephanie one day – and I do hope that she meant it in a nice way.

'You mean in London?'

Something about that scared me. I was too young. Too confused about who I was.

'It doesn't have to be there. You should try the Bristol

Old Vic Theatre School. They're as good as anywhere in London but you won't be distracted by being in the big city and we'll still be able to see you. Try Bristol,' she said.

And so I did. But would I get in?

'Auditions will take place over the course of a weekend and you should be prepared to take part in a variety of exercises throughout your time with us.' I was floored by the first word of the instruction on the application form and don't think I ever made it to the end of the page. Auditions? Plural? These would be the first formal auditions I had ever done. A weekend of them would be a little different to collaring dear Mr Salsberg in the foyer of his theatre and saying I wanted to join his company. I feared auditions back then and I loathe them to this day. Do they ever really work? Can't you spend years perfecting one four-minute piece but be lousy at everything else you are called upon to do? Maybe that's why Bristol did ask so much more of us all.

Over the two-day assessment we all danced, sang, did our key audition piece and any number of other readings. Six or seven of the theatre school's people were watching us all the time, scratching things down on note pads, building up the tension with each stroke of the pen. I think it was the first time I'd ever been really nervous. My subconscious must have known how important this was. But after a few weeks of agony I got the acceptance letter. I'd made it past dozens of other keen candidates. I was on my way.

'I will never, ever experience anything as good as this again.' Excuse the drama, but that was what I felt. It was what I kept saying, through a ridiculous amount of tears, when I said my goodbyes at an end-of-season party at Salisbury Rep. I remember a few moments when everyone else left me alone in the back of the stalls – a sensible move on their part. I looked around. Yes, it was only a converted church hall. It wasn't the West End, it wasn't Broadway. But it had been so good to me.

I would even miss the damp and the smell of all the mildew. I blubbered so much that night I probably added quite a bit to the problem. I left my mark on that place in tears, if nothing else.

But more seriously I was right about it being the end of an era. Actors starting out today miss out enormously now that the old repertory system has passed. I needed that place where I learned so much from other people's experience. I needed a refuge where I could fall in love with drama. Putting on a new show every few weeks isn't for the faint-hearted. It's a hard slog. But it's worth it. In Salisbury I found out that in the theatre anything can happen, and it usually does. A bit like my life, as I had just discovered.

3

Stage School

'Christopher, I need to talk to you. I'm pregnant.' No, it wasn't a girlfriend talking to me – that really would have been a story. It was my mother. But bearing in mind that I was 18 and my mother was 40 it was still a pretty newsworthy event.

'How can you be pregnant?'

And why did I ask that question? Obviously I wasn't *that* naive. Though the thought of my mother and father still at it wasn't something I liked to dwell on.

Maybe what I meant to ask was: 'Why are you pregnant?' Although that didn't really sum up my feelings either. All told, it was all something of a shock. Mum and Dad had called me into the living room in my final few months at Salisbury Rep.

'You're going to have a baby brother or sister,' my

mother added. Yes, thanks for clearing up what 'I'm pregnant' means, Mother.

Of course, if I was in shock, you can imagine what my poor parents themselves thought. With me getting ready to go to Bristol they had probably been looking forward to having the house to themselves. I know Dad was particularly stunned by Mum's news. But he had a second surprise coming.

'Can Pam really be pregnant? It's been 18 years since she had Christopher,' he asked our long-time doctor, the still wonderful Jim Drummond.

'She certainly can be pregnant, and she's not the only one,' Jim said. It turned out that his wife was having a baby 19 years after her last. There must have been something in Wiltshire's water supply back then.

All things considered, it was probably a good thing that I was ready to fly the nest just as the new chick arrived. I like my sleep. And like most teenage boys I wasn't keen on the idea of changing any nappies. I was also a bit of a worrier – and I didn't like worrying about my mother's health. Giving birth after such a long gap wasn't easy for her. And this birth wasn't an easy one. It turned out that my mother had a fibroid as big as a grapefruit that needed to be removed. She had a Caesarean section to deliver her baby and the surgeon threw in a hysterectomy for good measure.

But she and my baby brother both came back from hospital safe and well. Little Sean was soon the new prince of Sidney Street. And he's turned out to be a real treasure. With an 18-year age gap, he and I were never going to be like ordinary brothers. Technically speaking I was easily old enough to be his father – when we were out in the street together I think a lot of strangers assumed that's what I was. Fortunately, as we hardly ever lived in the same house at the same time we never had any sibling rivalries either. And today I'm proud to say that we've always been good friends.

I cried on my first night at theatre school. I moved into digs in Bristol, for a taste of the full theatrical experience. I had a room high up in an attic in a house shared with half a dozen or so other students.

My mother and father had dropped me off, I had offered shy greetings to some of my fellow residents and then, upstairs and alone, the tears had begun to fall. This was the first time I had ever been on my own and everything felt so alien. All the confidence I had built up with all those talented, older people in Salisbury faded away. How would I cope on my own? More importantly, how would I cope among people of my own age?

Until I got to Bristol I think my peers had scared me. No, I'd never been bullied in school. Yes, I had dear John Brown and a handful of other pals from my various classes. But in the main I felt more comfortable with adults. I think it's because of that nagging feeling that I was different. Not having a sense of belonging can be quite horrible. If you're different you always worry that you might come under attack at any time. My thinking had always been that older people were less likely to lash out at me. I wanted them wrapped around me, just like the cotton wool that had made me itch all those years ago as a baby.

Bristol taught me so much. But the first lesson was that no one lashed out at anyone. Being different was fine – in fact, it was something to be applauded if not actually encouraged. Within weeks I realised that I loved being with my own age group. And maybe that's because we were the most extraordinary group in the theatre school's history.

Jeremy Irons was one of the first of my fellow students to say hello. Then I met the others. There was Simon Cadell, who came from a real dynasty of actors, Tim Pigott-Smith, Ian Gelder, John Caird, Tony Falkingham, the fantastic Gillian Morgan, who became Gillian Eton, Sheila Ferris, now married to Poirot himself David Suchet, the lovely mad girl Hazel Clyne and so many more. We were a fantastic group and we were in a fantastic place.

The theatre school – opened just after the war by none other than Laurence Olivier – was in a big old Victorian house right on the edge of Clifton Downs at the end of Blackboy Hill. You got to it by sweeping up a grand driveway – it was all very *Brideshead Revisited*, so Jeremy had a head start when he got into his role as Charles Ryder all those years later.

There were probably only about two dozen students in a year and a couple of years of students at the school at any one time. But the building was always buzzing. Groups were constantly rushing around – and unlike at an ordinary school we were all desperate to learn. We had a focus. We wanted to perform.

Best of all was the fact that we were all pretty much able to concentrate on our classes. Forget part-time jobs. These were the best of times to be students. I got a grant, as did almost everyone else. And my parents were always ready to top things up if I ran short some months, bless them. So I often did run short some months. That, too, has been a story of my life.

Our principal was a marvellous man called Nat Brenner. He was thin, wiry and hairy with a striking face and a good line in smart sports jackets. He and his lovely wife Joan lived in the flat on the top floor of the house and beneath them a warren of ten or so rooms were converted into different types of rehearsal studios and performance spaces.

Dear Nat was a hugely talented and wonderful character. It was because of him that we were so young in 1967. It was an experimental year at the theatre school, with so many of us aged just 18 and 19. They had never gambled on young talent like this before. But look where so many of us got to. And I think we all grew to be one of Nat's favourite intakes. He was incredibly supportive and I found him very approachable – so approach him I did. He knew theatre. Peter O'Toole was one of his best pals. So I guessed he might be good for a gossip and I was right.

Maybe not every 18-year-old newcomer would have been comfortable spending so much time with their principal. But it didn't seem strange to me. I also bonded with Nat's wife, Joan. I sensed that she could feel a bit excluded because Nat was so dedicated to his school and his students. So Joan and I would have coffee together and gossip in their flat. Again, I never thought for a minute that there was anything unusual about a new student sitting having coffee with the principal's wife in her drawing room. I never saw why some people were supposed to be off limits to others. If two people want to become friends, why shouldn't they? I didn't see why age, status, wealth, looks or anything else should get in the way. That's why I've had so many wonderful friends. And why they've all been such a fabulously mixed bunch.

'All right, class. Imagine you're squeezing a lemon between your buttocks. Now walk around the room without letting it go.' Rudi Shelley boomed out the instruction in his rich and wonderfully exotic accent from somewhere out in middle or Eastern Europe. Rudi was a small man with big presence. He had long hair, an extraordinarily rubbery face and, of course, perfect posture. He taught us all to stand tall and to walk properly. I'm six foot one and I do still stand and walk properly. I'm proud of that. It's kept me in good stead and it's largely thanks to Rudi. His deportment lessons were only the start of our background education. The lovely Lynn Britt, with her scraped-back black hair and angular dancer's face, gave us two hours of classical ballet instruction every week. It may seem ridiculous, really, to teach us all that. And even then I was no sylph-like ballerina. But ballet is a surprisingly useful skill. So much stems from all that training, all the breadth and depth I acquired in Bristol. It meant I could turn my hand to anything in the years ahead. Just as well, the way my feast-and-famine career would turn out.

But squeezing a lemon between my buttocks and doing a bit of ballet lost their thrill after a while. What I wanted to do most was act. Central to everything at the school was, of course, the dream of playing in the Bristol Old Vic itself. The theatre, a couple of miles away on King Street, is a most wonderful Georgian building. It had it all – an incredibly rich history, a cast list of almost all the greats you could care to name. It even had a theatre ghost, though my booming voice must have scared her away as she never turned up when I was around.

The first time I walked into the theatre I felt its embrace. It was so different to Salisbury Rep. This was a proper theatre, not a converted church hall. This was the real thing, with deep colours, rich brocades and row upon row of seats. But the place didn't fool me. I loved the fact that backstage everything was just as crowded and chaotic as it had been in my home town. Maybe that's what I like about theatre: the gap between artifice and reality. The different roles that theatres themselves can play. The magic we can make.

Of course I also liked the outrageous characters I met in them. And the Bristol Old Vic certainly provided them. It had a great front-of-house manager, a fittingly camp and theatrical man called Rodney West who loved the enthusiasm of all us young students. It was just as well because he ended up seeing an awful lot of us.

The marvellous Jacqueline Stanbury and I got the ball rolling. We decided to organise first-nighters for each new performance. Our gang would dress up, the boys in black tie, the girls in long dresses. Most of us might have had to rely on charity shops for our finery. But we made it look a million dollars. Rodney helped make sure we always got the seats we wanted. The theatre has a horseshoe gallery where you sit in a narrow row of seats on the side edge of the balcony. They're not the best seats in the house by any measure – the view was badly restricted and you had to lean at a worryingly wide angle to see the whole of the stage. But they were where we loved to be. When you sat there you were almost on display yourself – I could always sense it when people in the posh seats of the stalls were looking our way. We loved the attention.

It was in those seats that it dawned on me that theatre itself would be one of the great loves of my life. The company was extraordinary in those years, great plays, wonderful performances. Thelma Barlow, still a dear friend, was at the Bristol Old Vic back then and I remember being dazzled by her performances – she was like a lovely china doll. A lovely china doll who could set the stage on fire when her play demanded it. And leading the company was the marvellous Peggy Ann Wood, the first person I ever saw to get an entrance round when they walked on stage. I was stunned by the thrill of it as I joined that applause. Now, whenever I get an entrance round, I thank Peggy for showing how it's done.

Today I'm known as an avid first-nighter and I'm sad that it's often misconstrued. It's not about being at the opening of an envelope – though I've done my fair share of that as well. No, my first nights are about the love of theatre, of the excitement, nerves and magic of an opening. It's important to me to keep seeing more actors in more plays. I don't understand some other actors who seem proud of the fact that they never go to the theatre. Shouldn't they be ashamed of it instead? To me, the theatre is where we learn. It's where we find new passions. That was instilled in me in Bristol.

So I was a worthy, hard-working, theatre-obsessed pupil, then? Well, not quite. I loved the life of a drama student just as much as I loved the drama itself. I loved the camaraderie, the in-jokes, the tricks we played and the stupid things we all did. Tim Pigott-Smith and Simon Cadell were in the serious set, they were dedicated to the craft, and I respected that. But I had fallen for the whole ambience, the joking, the laughing that went on when the audience wasn't looking.

Maybe that was my downfall: not to be seen as a serious actor. I ultimately beat a lot of those serious players into the Royal Shakespeare Company. But I never quite made it stick.

Funnily enough, Jeremy Irons was the other person in our year who was widely seen as insufficiently serious for the classic roles. He was so handsome, a clear leading man with extraordinary presence. He was so social, so gregarious, and that's why we got on so well. He was also very sporty, and he loved his horses and country life. Academically speaking, neither of us was exactly the brightest of people at Bristol. But we laughed the most. Jeremy's reputation today is far more serious. At the time, though, we both just wanted to have fun.

He and I sat in the Blackboy Cafe once to have a laugh over the latest industry gossip, the way we always did. The Australian Coral Browne, Vincent Price's wife and surely the world's campest actress, was a heroine of ours. We had just heard the probably apocryphal story of her hailing a cab one rainy night outside the Haymarket Theatre in London. As she climbed in through one door, another soaking-wet passenger climbed through the other.

'I'm sorry, sir, I'm afraid the lady is first,' said the cabbie.

'Which lady?' asked the man.

'This fucking lady,' she snapped.

Jeremy and I just knew that she was our type of girl.

'We should write to her. Just be honest and say we're two drama students out in Bristol and that we'd like to have lunch with her,' I said.

'Do you really think she would come?'

'I think she will. She'll be a hoot.'

Shame on the two of us for chickening out. Coral's no longer with us. But I'm still convinced she would have joined us if we'd ever had the guts to post the letter.

When we weren't in school, my new gang all had a home from home in the cafe on Blackboy Hill. You could get a full roast lunch and pudding for practically nothing. It was like a common room, for us kids from an earlier *Fame*. Though I don't think my mother – let alone my grandmother – would always have approved of the service. You had to write your order on one half of a raffle ticket and kept the other half while you waited for your number to be called.

'Number 472!'

When the call came, you got up to get your plate from the counter. And day after day the other half of your ticket would be swimming on top of the gravy. Silver service it wasn't. Sorry, Mum, but I don't think I always left a tip.

Our group was always ready for an adventure. But we always seemed to be totally unprepared. One day we decided to go on a big day out on the beach at Weston-Super-Mare. None of us had any idea about distances or timings, so we decided that to make a real day of it we would have to leave early. We hired a huge van and all piled in at 6.30 in the morning. We arrived at our destination at precisely 6.45. It was still dark and nothing was open. Why had none of us realised that Weston was only just down the road? Hungry and sleepy but laughing like drains at our own stupidity, we piled back in the car and set off again. In the end we had our day out in Devon, but we got it wrong again as it turned out to be a lot further than any of us had expected.

I lasted my full first year in my garret room in the student digs. Then Tony, Tim, Michael Hadley and I shared a rented house in Clifton. And not just any house. Our digs had a ballroom! No wonder I started to get ideas above my station. They were great times. Tim was the most anal of us all and wanted everything to be very tidy and clean. I seem to remember rotas for cleaning different rooms on different days. But I don't remember paying much attention to them. Nor do I remember ever doing the washing up. Sorry, Tim.

It was in that second year that I first met Nat's pal Peter O'Toole. He was in his late thirties then (how old that seemed!) and had already immortalised Lawrence of Arabia, been nominated for two Oscars and scored some amazing reviews on stage. Nat had invited him over to Bristol to talk to us and inspire us. He succeeded. Peter was by far the most famous man I had ever met. I loved him then. He was charismatic, very theatrical, dry and witty. Theatrical gossip was already my drug of choice and I was thrilled to try to get a bit of a fix of it from him. Such a shame that when I worked with the great man on *Masada* so many years later it turned out to be such a terrible experience. But I will get to that story in a while.

As well as being a wonderful man, Nat's great strength was in spotting talent. He could see beyond four-minute audition spots and somehow grasp what actors were truly capable of. In a strange sort of way I think he helped push Jeremy and me together and cement our friendship. I think he adored me, and he adored Jeremy as well for quite different reasons. He saw the talent Jeremy had as an actor. He saw the talent I had as a personality. There was a wildness about Jeremy back then that Nat also respected. It was the same wildness he responded to in Peter O'Toole. Nat loved a challenge. He loved to bring the best out of people and I think we were both touched by his genius. He didn't always create great actors. But he always created great people.

For all our laughs and jokes, Jeremy and I weren't entirely inseparable. He had asked our fellow student Julie Hallam out on a date. Then he fell in love with her and she fell in love with him. It was the great romance of our gang. I'd barely kissed anyone, let alone been in love at this point, so I was beside myself with excitement at having front-row seats for this love story. After about a year we practically forced them to get married because we were all in love with the romance of the situation. Talk about living through others.

Julie's family were well-off, so the ceremony was marvellously grand. It was held in a gorgeous country church and all us students – mostly in some variation of our first-night finery – crammed in and then headed over to the reception. I was best man, which I saw as an enormous honour and responsibility. I adored making a best man's speech – being the centre of attention and making people laugh was quite wonderful. And I didn't feel as if my duties as best man should end there. After helping to manage the whole ceremony, I joined the happy couple on their honeymoon as well. I'm not sure the concept of being a gooseberry had been fully explained to me.

The happy couple sat in the front, while I lounged on the back seat of their Citroen 2CV as we raced down through France to Denia, then a little village on the coast near Alicante in Spain. We had the roof down all the way and had glorious sunshine right from Calais. Though it turned out to have been a little bit too glorious for my liking. Our little villa was called Los Pinos (no sniggering at the back, please) and when we arrived I was burned almost from head to toe. Then the actual sunstroke kicked in. I was so sick I couldn't leave my room for days. I could hardly bear to have a sheet on my skin and for quite a while thought I might actually die. It gave the honeymooners some privacy, I suppose. But I made sure they took frequent breaks from their marital bliss so I could tell them how much I had been vomiting.

Funny how things turn out. Everyone saw Julie as the huge talent of our class. She was the one we would all tip for greatness. Jeremy, meanwhile, was the fun-lover, like me, who didn't always take it too seriously. And when their marriage broke up after a year or so, she became a doctor's wife and has barely acted again, while he went on to win an Oscar.

The course lasted two years and for our end-of-term shows we got to tread the boards on the Bristol Old Vic's stage itself. These performances were the ultimate showcases. You never knew who might be watching. As news got around about the depth of young talent in Bristol in both our years, we attracted a lot of agents, casting directors and other powerful industry figures.

I can see now that I should probably have taken more advantage of all that. Trouble was, I never felt the competition or the rivalry that ran to the core of some of my fellow students. Maybe I should have done. Some of my peers fought for every role. They schmoozed people to within an inch of their lives. They were desperate to get the big parts. They talked constantly of all the roles they thought they had been born to play. I didn't. I just waited for life to happen to me. Maybe it's because I was never an easy actor to categorise. I was never a classically handsome leading man – so how odd that I ended up a leading woman in panto. And, while I wanted to be in *Hamlet*, I never saw the need to actually be Hamlet. I was in my element in the minor roles. I just wanted to be in the company. I could have made a lot more money and enjoyed a lot more respect if I'd had that killer instinct. But maybe I wouldn't have had so much fun. Besides, my strange belief that life would happen to me anyway seemed to be coming true. I did get good roles. And they got noticed.

My first big break came in a play I can barely remember today. I've had to struggle even to track down its title. I think it was *The Life of Tom Paine*. But it could well have been *The Rights of Man* by Tom Paine. Or possibly something else altogether. What I do remember is that it was a marvellous role. British-born Tom Paine was a hero in 18th-century America, an Everyman figure who took part in the country's Revolution. The play was a modern take on life in the USA and it was a huge coup for me to be offered the lead.

Throughout our course, Nat brought in a stream of talented directors to work with us on different performances. For *Tom Paine*, we had David Benedictus and we performed the play as a showcase in one of the studios in Clifton. An invited audience from the industry was watching, and among them was David Jones, director of the Royal Shakespeare Company. It seems that he saw something good in either my performance or my personality, or both. It would be quite a few months before I found out what it was.

The tears when I left Salisbury Rep were nothing compared with those we all cried when our Bristol years ended. Breaking up our little gang seemed almost criminal. We were so close. And for me there was one extra thing to worry about as reality beckoned.

'Come on, Christopher, enough's enough,' my father said to me after I had moved back from Bristol to Salisbury and was planning my theatrical takeover of the world. 'You've got the theatre out of your system now. You should come and work in the business with me. You can make £100 a week.' And Dad, ever the gentlemen, was prepared to change the business to suit me. I was passionate about antiques and bric-a-brac – not least because I had spent so long in antique shops when I was propping in Salisbury. I had become a regular face in most of the local shops, always trying to do a deal and borrow some furniture or fittings for our next production. Two years on and most of those shopkeepers still remembered me, which may or may not be a good thing.

'Let's open a bric-a-brac shop of our own,' my father said. And we did – I seem to think that we called it 'Biggins'. It was a lovely shop, I'll admit that straight away. But working there was just as dull as I had expected. We were bang in the middle of Salisbury but some days several hours would go by before I saw a single person. And when that sole customer did come in I could hardly follow them around the shop and pepper them with questions just to get a conversation started.

Always leave a tip. Going back to my mum's old rule, my tip would be that, if you love people and you're always up for a laugh and a gossip, don't work in an antique shop.

'Sorry, Dad, but I can't stay. Will you be able to run it without me?' I'd been in our new shop for less than six weeks. It felt like six years. And by now I had an escape route.

4

On the Boards

Roger Clissold had been one of my early heroes at Salisbury Rep – not least because he hadn't shouted at me too much when I ruined one of his performances.

Disaster had struck in the middle of Thornton Wilder's *Our Town*.

'Yup, it was a real smart farm,' was the line Roger should have delivered in the cemetery scene. I was one of the 12 extras on stage holding umbrellas painted with headstones and instructed to be as still as the grave. 'Yup, it was a real fart smarm,' was what I swear Roger said one fateful performance.

My umbrella was the first to start shaking. Then the one next to me began to shake, and the next. Soon all 12 of us were laughing out loud and rolling around the stage. I suppose if you're going to corpse on stage you might as well do it in a cemetery scene. But at the end of the night I was ready for a bollocking for my bad example. Roger, to his credit, had seen the funny side. And our friendship grew from there. Today I'm godfather to his son and I've been with him through a lot of the ups and downs of his life.

By 1969, Roger had moved on from Salisbury and become artistic director of a new company he had formed in Derby. He asked me to join the cast in *Lysistrata* and then join his Rep full-time. He said he could afford to pay me something like £30 a week – so much less than I could have got if I'd stuck with my dad's antique shop. But I could just about survive, so I said yes without a second thought. At least in the theatre I had people to talk to pretty much 24 hours a day.

In Derby I moved into a classic theatrical digs. I had a tiny single bed in a boxroom, shared the family bathroom and had to be up and out just after breakfast each morning. As soon as I shut the front door I would head off to meet a fellow company member who lodged nearby. We would gossip away as we headed to the theatre together. But our journey didn't always go smoothly. Does anything?

One morning an old female tramp leaped out at us as we turned a corner. I nearly had a heart attack with fright. 'Can you spare something for some food, sir?' she asked me as I tried to breathe normally. I found a few coins.

'Ow, Gawd bless you, sir. You're a true gentleman. I won't forget you,' she squawked. 'Your lady friend is blessed to have you.'

One week later the same grubby little lady popped up again. 'Sorry, love, I don't have any change today,' I said, with a relaxed smile.

'You shit. You horrible fat man. You're a disgrace, you should rot in hell,' she spat out in fury as we scuttled away.

It was a good lesson for the rest of my professional career. You can be hot one week, ice-cold the next. No one remembers your last review. You truly are only as good as your last performance.

In Derby I met another set of marvellous people, and worked on ever more powerful plays. I also learned another life lesson, this time without the aid of abuse in the street. I learned the old chestnut that it's not what you know but who you know – and most importantly of all it's who knows you.

Another old pal from Salisbury knew me. He was the actor and writer David Wood and he asked me to come to London to do a musical play he had written. *The Owl and the Pussycat Went to See...* was based on Edward Lear's poem and was moving to London after a tryout in Worcester. It was a wonderful opportunity and Roger Clissold agreed that I should take it. So two weeks later I moved out of my digs, left Derby Rep and headed south. It was 1969 and *The Owl and the Pussycat* was opening at the Jeanetta Cochrane Theatre in the strange no man's land of Holborn. Our audiences were vast, noisy crowds of school kids. I played Head Jumbly and a bluebird. No, it wasn't *King Lear*. But it was London. It was bliss.

I celebrated my 21st birthday in that company. Patsy Rowlands, the wife of our musical director, made me laugh, and nearly made me cry, when she presented me with a cake. 'You're lucky to get it. This was my seventh attempt and if it hadn't worked I would have gone to the shop,' she said as she lit the candles. All the others had burned, failed to rise or fallen prey to some other kind of culinary disaster. I was in tears that someone had taken so much trouble over my birthday. And I was thrilled that my parents could see how well I was being looked after. My parents had come up to town for the big day. They had seen our latest show, and then a big group of us went for dinner in a restaurant in Earl's Court.

As I had given up Dad's shop for this, it was important to me that he saw me as a success. And it was pretty clear I was falling on my feet. I was surrounded by friends and laughter. There's no nicer place to be. When Mum and Dad came to see where I was living, they got another indication of how well I was doing. The boy who had lived in a caravan for two years and had been brought up in a house with an outside toilet and no bath had already adapted brilliantly to living in a house with a ballroom in the Bristol days. Now in London I acquired even more expensive tastes. I was offered a room – well, two rooms – with two other old pals from Salisbury Rep, the marvellous aristocratic Jonathan Cecil and his wife Vivien Heilbron. They lived in a beautiful house in Fulham, on Ifield Road, and frankly I blame them for reinforcing in me the standard of living I had already started to grow accustomed to. I had two rooms of my own, a bedroom and a sitting room. But I also had the run of the whole amazing house. And I paid only £4 a week. I was 21, and I could live the life of Riley. I developed a keen taste for luxury living. Some things never change.

Now here's a surprise. Shortly after moving into Ifield Road I took a girl back to my rooms. She was a fellow actress from *The Owl and the Pussycat* and something about her had caught my attention from the very start. Beatrice Aston was a bright-red-haired Australian with a bright Australian sense of humour, and she was playing a Jumbly Girl to my Head Jumbly. We hit it off after our very first rehearsal. That very first time we found ourselves in some local dive until late, and after that we seemed to be back there night after night. We had lunches, dinners, whole days together whenever we could. We laughed and we plotted and we planned. I remember how wonderful it felt to have someone entirely on my side. And how wonderful it was to have someone who was always there, someone you could accept joint invitations to parties with, someone you could always have beside you.

Have I always been in love with the idea of being in love? I think I may have been. And as the months passed I felt, so strongly, that I was in love with Beatrice.

'We should get married.'

It wasn't a proposal as such. It was more of a conversation. And it ended with Beatrice saying yes. So our plotting and our planning moved up a gear and led to a wedding ceremony at Chelsea Register Office, with her good friends Willie and Dorgan Rushton as our witnesses. We were all dressed in colourful, fun clothes and we had a colourful, fun day. The four of us went out for lunch afterwards and we just carried on laughing.

Beatrice moved in with me in Ifield Road. I was 21 years old and a married man – a happily married man. Wonders never cease.

Today Beatrice carries a heavy load for having married me. She was terrorised by the press when I was in the jungle in 2007. All of them were desperate to dig up a story which simply isn't there. For the truth about our marriage is very simple. We were happy together for all the time that we were together. We were still very naive about life back then. But we were happy. And it was only much later that we both started to accept that something wasn't quite right.

When those cracks began to show, we never rowed and we never said anything we now regret. We just followed slightly different paths and wanted different things as the months went by. And after a couple of years we faced up to things and agreed to split. We had got married in a low-key way. We moved on from our marriage in exactly the same fashion. Nobody ever got hurt and I have promised that I will never say more than this – because there's absolutely nothing else to say. What happened was entirely right for us both at the time. Our marriage didn't last but our friendship has. And Beatrice deserves to have it left at that.

Back on the work front, like every other jobbing actor back then, I tended to work on short-term contracts – six weeks tended to be the most security you ever got. But who cares about security at 21? Who cares if there are times when you're out of work and need to borrow a little from pals to scrape by? You do the same for them in their fallow patches. That was the way of the theatrical world. And I was lucky. Bits and pieces of work always came in. I always felt I was moving in the right direction. And I loved having the chance to branch out.

My first piece of television was for a detective series called *Paul Temple* with Francis Matthews in the lead role. I played a gentleman thief and my job was to break into a safe while eating a chicken leg. Classy stuff.

I got my first agents, Gillian Coffey and Harry Harbour, who had lovely crowded old offices just off Brook Street near Grosvenor Square. They had all the good old variety people on their books and were incredibly well respected in the theatrical world. Gillian had seen me perform in Bristol and left me a note saying I should get in touch if I ever needed representation. I jumped at the chance and never regretted it. Over the years Gillian became a close friend – one year she even joined my dad and I on a week's holiday. Mum doesn't like to fly, so Dad and I were off to a Greek island and Gillian had the time to come too. We had tiny, clean rooms in one of those classic whitewashed houses on – wait for it – Mykonos. It is probably the gayest island in the world and I swear I had no idea when we booked. Nor, needless to say, did my dad. But we had a lovely week. As I looked around at our fellow sun-worshippers out there, I was starting to realise just why I felt 'different'. I was starting to think it wouldn't turn out so bad after all.

Despite my theatrical roots, Gillian got me plenty of TV work over the years. And I loved that new challenge. Television was a whole new world for me. On set everything seemed small, intense and serious. I took a while to work out how to act for the cameras. It was so different. These huge machines totally hid the cameramen (and back then they were all men) behind them. I felt lost without the wide open spaces of a theatre and I hated not having the noise and atmosphere of a live audience. But I buckled down. I know some of my theatre pals from Bristol looked down on television. They thought it was beneath them.

But I just wanted to work. I think it is only the very young and the very beautiful who can pick and choose their jobs. They are the only ones who can declare that they're going to Hollywood or that they'll only play the classics. People like me had to say yes to every offer we were made. So I said yes to *Doctor at Sea*, part of a set of comedy series filmed in studios near Wembley. It was tacky, low-brow stuff. But I had a strange feeling that other, far grander projects were still in store for me. It turned out that I was right.

5

The RSC

I got that call from David Jones after I had been in London for less than three months. 'Come to see us at the RSC,' he said. I nearly fell over.

'The Royal Shakespeare Company wants me! The RS bloody C!' This was what Tim, Simon, Ian and all the serious players from Bristol had craved. But it was me that the RSC asked along for an audition. Life would never stop surprising me.

'I saw you as Tom Paine and I think you have a quality that will be perfect for our next play,' David explained when I met him. The play was Dion Boucicault's *London Assurance*, which the RSC was putting on at the Aldwych Theatre. Right alongside the Waldorf Hotel on the edge of Covent Garden, it's a beautiful, turn-of-the-century theatre with a handful over 1,000 seats. And the RSC's residency was the theatrical event of the season. Judi

Dench, Donald Sinden and Elizabeth Spriggs were just some of the names in the company. We could hardly have promised a starrier night.

My role was small but perfectly formed, though I say so myself.

The maid, played by Janet Whiteside, had a lover called Jenks who was talked about throughout the play. That was me. It was a non-speaking role, but I had three entrances and three exits towards the end of the second act. I made the most of them.

'We want someone with personality. Someone who can bring the house down,' David said when he explained the role. I wasn't going to let him down. 'Christopher, we're also going to need you to be an understudy on some other plays as well,' he added.

'Absolutely. Of course,' I said, a fixed grin on my face. What the hell's an understudy? I was thinking. Hard to believe, but I had absolutely no idea. At theatre school they hadn't really taught us much about that sort of thing. They hadn't wanted to put us off, I suppose. Almost as soon as I found out what the role involved I hated it. You have to be word-perfect and know the part backwards, but you can't put any of your own personality into it. You need to play the role just like the principal, so that if you do go on stage you don't throw the other actors. But so often, of course, you don't go on. So often you just sit there. You are so near, yet so far. You are in the theatre, but not on the stage.

Fortunately, I made the most of this professional limbo – I would ultimately be given small parts and understudy duties in everything from *Twelfth Night* and *Henry VIII* to

Pericles. But my big moment looked set to come a whole lot sooner.

'Christopher, we need you on stage.' I got the call while we were still rehearsing *London Assurance*. I was in the wings waiting for my second-act entrances and exits as Jenks. But we had a gap in our cast. Barrie Ingham, the comic genius who was playing Dazzle, had called in sick. So I went on stage for all the rest of our rehearsals. At 21 years old, I, Christopher Biggins, acted for the RSC, alongside Judi, Donald, Elizabeth Spriggs, Roger Reece and all the others. OK, so our first night was still a week away. But it was all still truly terrifying and truly fantastic.

So would I make it into the production proper? Dazzle is a big part and, while I knew that Barrie would almost certainly be back for the opening night, I was desperately hoping he might stay away. So many understudies are always the bridesmaid. I might get the chance to be the bride. I stayed up all night learning the part. But I never had my moment. By the time the previews began and we had an actual audience in the theatre Barrie had made a miraculous recovery from whatever had ailed him. I was left in the wings. But I coped. I still had my three entrances and exits as Jenks to look forward to. And I just kept thinking how happy I was. 'It will all come good next time,' I told myself. 'This is where I belong. This is what I want to do for the rest of my life.' When I wasn't in the wings or on stage at the Aldwych, I never strayed far. London's theatreland was a treasure trove of an area for me. I had a lot of London to explore and a lot of new friends to make. Night after night you would find me in the much-missed Luigi's on Tavistock Street alongside the back of the Strand. Back then you got a big bowl of pasta, a coffee and a glass of wine for a pound and ten shillings. Not bad as I was making £30 a week and paying just £4 in rent. If life was like that today I would be dining out even more often than I do.

The RSC did warp my sense of financial priorities. I blame it for all my personal extravagances in the years ahead. Back then it had a huge grant and there seemed to be money to burn. *London Assurance* was in rep with several other plays, each with a vast budget. For *Henry VIII* we were all measured up for bespoke thigh-high leather boots, for example. But when they arrived someone decided that they didn't go with the rest of the costumes, so the top halves of them were simply cut off and thrown away. Then there was the time they wanted the box to be carpeted – and that no cheap or second-hand carpet would do. We had thick new Axminster. As if anyone would have noticed, even from the front of the stalls.

I got swept away in the unreality of it all. I vowed to live my life the RSC way. My poor bank manager.

London Assurance opened to amazing reviews. It was my first, intoxicating taste of success. And I was part of it. As the weeks went by, that sense of belonging – something so important to me – intensified. I made firm friends in the RSC company. David Dundas, the pop star turned actor, was one of the first. And I also had plenty of very talented people to learn from. Peggy Ashcroft – Dame Peggy to the likes of me – was the best example. They don't make them like that any more, more's the pity. I remember that she was hugely grand. Her dresser (who now I come to think of it was almost as grand as the lady herself) wasn't allowed in her employer's dressing room unannounced. So hour after hour she sat motionless on a chair outside, waiting for a call. I was mesmerised. And I was childishly thrilled to find out that this lady did the great lady's laundry. Imagine washing Dame Peggy's smalls! It was another age.

It was also fabulous fun that not everyone in the company shared my sense of reverence about Dame Peggy. In *Henry VIII*, where Dame Peggy was playing Katherine of Valois, I was on stage alongside Derek Smith and Michael Gambon, one of the naughtiest men I'd ever met. 'I wonder if she's wearing any knickers,' Michael whispered to me as Peggy began her big speech. How I got through that scene without corpsing completely I don't know. But how wonderful of Michael to share the joke with me: the new boy and pretty much the youngest player in the company. I was always thrilled to be treated like an equal – and after Michael the next person to give me a lift like that was Judi.

'Let's take all our clothes off,' she whispered one afternoon as we rehearsed a new scene with the wonderful, if idiosyncratic, director John Barton. John directed us with his head in the script – quite literally. He paid so much attention to the text it seemed he didn't even look up at the stage.

'Come on, I dare you. Take your clothes off,' whispered Judi again. So I did. And so did the rest of the cast. And so did Judi. Right down to our underwear. Then, as the read-through continued, we all got dressed again. 'That's marvellous. Let's move on to scene three,' John called when we got to our final lines. He never saw a thing.

I remember Judi with a naughty-girl twinkle in her eye. She was never what you could call classically beautiful. But she mesmerised people. You could look at her and just know she was a star. She was also incredibly kind. She loved leading her company, just as I would love leading mine when I finally got to the same position. Judi helped people. She was supportive and always there to listen if people had any problems. She mothered us when we needed it and, as the youngster and new boy, I needed it most of all.

Judi also knows how to make the time fly backstage. The boys in the cast had a set of tiny, shared dressing rooms up three flights of stairs from the wings. Night after night Judi would be up there with us, playing games, sharing jokes and gossiping. Then she would dash down the three flights for her cue, act her part and then run back up to her boys as soon as she came off stage. Up and down, up and down. Joking, laughing, never missing a cue. And yes, giving the most thrilling, incandescent performances on stage.

I'm not sure if I can always claim such professionalism. One unusually quiet night backstage, I'm mortified to admit, I actually fell asleep and missed one of my three entrances as Jenks. Judi laughed so much she fell over.

When *London Assurance* was well into its run, my mum brought my brother up to town for a matinée performance. It was a big day. Sean was only about seven and it was the first time he'd been to the theatre, so he was a little bit nervous about the whole thing. We went to Luigi's for lunch and I was desperate for them both to have a wonderful time. 'Where are we sitting?' Mum asked as we waited for the meal.

This was where I could really show off to my baby brother. 'I've got you great seats in a box,' I told him.

'Oh,' he replied, and went very quiet for the rest of the meal. When we left Luigi's there was a still a frown on his face. 'Christopher,' he asked as we headed over to the Aldwych, 'will there be holes in the box for us to breathe?'

Call me a soppy old romantic, but I love the fact that theatre people can't stop falling in love. That's why I was so keen to push Jeremy and Julie together at Bristol, I suppose. And romance was certainly in the air at the RSC. Judi and dear Michael Williams were inseparable – and clearly made for each other. They were both such open, attractive people. They fitted like a glove.

I think that season was one of the highest points in Judi's life – and this includes all her Oscars and film acclaim that has come these past few years. She was madly in love and producing electrifying performances on stage. It's a combination you can't beat. We were doing *Twelfth Night* when Judi and Michael got married. I loved it. When she took her curtain calls we threw confetti over her and the crowd went even more wild than normal. Judi loves animals and we had created a frieze of animals on all the walls from her dressing room to the stage door for her to see when she left for the night.

Still the good times rolled. So much, so young and it all seemed so easy. Was there anything better than being in such stellar company at the Aldwych Theatre? Yes there was – *London Assurance* was transferring to the West End.

We decamped to the Albery Theatre in St Martin's Lane, near Leicester Square. John Gielgud, Sybil Thorndike, Laurence Olivier and so many other great names had acted there. Now I was moving into one of its tiny dressing rooms. I was so thrilled I could barely breathe.

After six more glittering months, Judi was getting to leave the show. I was still the youngest there, so I was picked to organise her collection and get her leaving card signed. But was I really the right person to present it to Judi herself? Sure, we had been half-naked together in our rehearsal with John Barton. Sure, we had shared a thousand jokes in the dressing rooms by now. But I still didn't feel I could presume to hand over her gift. I turned to Donald Sinden for advice.

'Donald, do you mind me asking if you would do the speech for Judi tonight? I've got the card and the gift all here.'

'I don't mind you asking at all, young man. But I won't do the presentation. I've got someone in tonight who will do it far better.'

'Who is it?'

'I'll have to swear you to secrecy.'

'I swear.'

'Then come here.' And he whispered the name in my ear – which wasn't easy for someone with such a resonant, booming voice. It was my turn to nearly fall over.

'You mustn't tell a soul,' Donald repeated.

So I spent the rest of the day, and all of that night's performance, tied up in knots of excitement and anticipation.

'Come on in!' We all crowded into Donald's dressing room after the curtain calls. Everyone was giggling, joking, drinking and high on the occasion, the way actors always are. 'Be quiet! Now, we all know why we're here. Judi, it has of course been absolutely marvellous working with you and it is terribly, terribly sad you are leaving us. We all want to wish you the absolute best on this new adventure you are embarking upon.' Everyone cheered. 'And we look forward to having you back on stage as soon as possible.' More cheers. Then we got to the secret.

'Now, Biggins came to me today and asked me to arrange a presentation for you,' Donald said. 'But I don't feel that I am the right person to hand over our little gift. I'd like a dear friend of mine to do it instead.'

And at that moment none other than Princess Grace of Monaco stepped out of Donald's tiny lavatory to hand over Judi's card and flowers. Everyone went wild.

The Princess was like a porcelain doll, so radiant, so beautiful and so much fun. We all knew the rumours of what a marvellously naughty girl she had been in Hollywood. But she had got her prince and she looked every inch the princess. She flattered us all, saying how much she loved the show. And I think she truly did. I got a sharp and sudden sense that she missed showbusiness a lot more than she was letting on. Perhaps life in a palace couldn't quite compete with life in a theatre dressing room. Or even a dressing-room toilet.

I can't leave this part of my story without telling one anecdote about the other woman in Donald's life: his equally wonderful wife, Diana. I loved the fact that she had her husband's voice. The same rich, booming, unmistakable tone. And if it amazed me, it had even more of an effect overseas. Diana loved telling the story of a trip to Disneyland when her husband was filming in LA. She saw some alarm clocks with Mickey Mouse on the front in the gift shop and decided that if she could buy enough of them they would make great presents for their children and other relatives. 'I love those clocks. Do you have many?' she boomed at the assistant.

'I'm sorry, Ma'am, we only have Mickey,' came the reply.

It was 1975 and Sinead Cusack took over from Judi in *London Assurance*. And love was still in the air. The Albery is practically attached to the Wyndham's Theatre, so it's wonderfully easy to flit between the two. I loved the set-up, mainly because it gave me two sets of theatre people to gossip and joke with rather than just one. Better still, Jeremy Irons was in *Godspell* at the Wyndham's, so we were able to catch up before and after almost every performance. It was like Bristol all over again. But with bigger audiences and better wages.

After one performance I introduced Sinead to Jeremy and knew, in an instant, that they would hit it off. They married a couple of years later, though this time I felt it was best not to join the happy couple on their honeymoon.

I didn't fall in love in those Covent Garden days. But I did meet one quite incredible man. My dear friend, the soon-to-be leading lady Gay Soper made the introductions at a party. 'Christopher, you must meet my friend Peter Delaney. He knows everything about theatre.'

I liked the man's smile from that first moment. We talked about theatre for the rest of that night. We have never stopped.

Peter had a theatrical background but had moved on to become the resident vicar of the University of London. He was – and is – an extraordinarily inspirational man. He believed that drama could help get people into church and be a power of good in even the worst of lives. I joined up when he did productions in his church in Old Hallows, putting a makeshift stage in the centre of the nave, leaving his local parishioners gobsmacked – but impressed. Our first productions included *Pudding Lane*, *The Woodland Gospels According to Captain Beaky and His Band* and *Narnia*. It was great, eclectic stuff.

In the years ahead Peter and I would take mystery plays on tour on the back of a lorry through the City of London, and we linked up with a church on Park Avenue in New York to put on similar performances there. Peter was such an influential man. And he had a thrillingly starry past – featuring none other than Judy Garland. No wonder we got along.

My favourite story was of how Judy had called him one afternoon in Los Angeles. 'Pick me up at 6.30. We're going to have dinner with a friend,' she had said. The friend was Marilyn Monroe. They went to her apartment and she had made them a hotpot.

Peter's links with Judy ran deep and wide. He had officiated at Judy's final marriage and did the same for daughters Liza and Lorna as well. And with tears in his eyes he conducted the service at Judy's funeral. Then, after all those highs and lows, all that glitz and glamour, he became a vicar for a bunch of students over in London. Today he is Archdeacon of London. Peter is the ultimate proof that we can all live many lives – and that you can never guess what, or who, life may throw at you next.

6

Roman Holiday

My agent, Gillian, took the call. Apparently, my show-stopping entrances and exits as Jenks had been noticed. 'Can we see him?' she was asked. The 'we' in question was Roman Polanski. And he wanted to see me in Rome in two days' time.

'Do you think you could get out of the play and get to Italy for the night?' I was asked.

The actor in me said, 'Yes, yes, yes.' But the well-brought-up boy in me said, 'No.' I knew I wouldn't get permission. You just didn't in the theatre and at my level. And I agonised over the thought of calling in sick and letting my friends in the company down.

But, really: Roman Polanski.

I took the sickie. I might be well brought up. But I'm not stupid.

Plane tickets arrived. Gillian and I were beside ourselves

with excitement and I jetted out to Rome on the Friday. A car was waiting for me at the airport and I was whisked to a hotel in the centre of the city. It was the most glamorous time of my life. I was Cary Grant, Clark Gable, Spencer Tracy, all in one. With a little Katharine Hepburn and Grace Kelly thrown in for good measure.

At 7pm, I was sitting nervously on the edge of my bed when the phone rang in my room. 'Roman would like you to come to join him for dinner,' I was told.

So another chauffeur-driven car zipped me out to the director's villa. It was a hot, still night and scent from the trees hung heavy on the air. Light bounced off the marble terraces and candles lit up the most glamorous of scenes. There must have been two dozen people squeezed around the dinner table. To be precise, there were around two dozen very beautiful people squeezed around the table – this was Italy, after all. But Roman leaped up the moment I walked towards them all.

He introduced me to every one of his other guests, all of whose names I promptly forgot, I was so dazzled by the glamour. Then he sat me down, with him on one side and none other than Marcello Mastroianni on the other. Conversation was frank, to say the least. 'I cannot find any actress who will play the lead who will fuck me,' was Roman's wonderful opening gambit.

Sex – or the quest for it – dominated a lot of the early conversations. But things did get darker as the night wore on.

'Why did you use so much blood when you filmed *Macbeth*?' someone shouted across at Roman at one point.

'When you have seen your own wife's blood on the ceiling and dripping down the walls you can never see worse gore ever again,' said the man who had lost Sharon Tate – and their unborn child – less than two years before filming began. Sidestepping that sort of downer took all the social skills Great-Aunt Vi had tried to teach me all those years ago. But I pride myself on my ability to keep a party light. I came up with some line or other and somehow we all started to laugh again.

As the conversation turned to Roman's big new project, I realised that the decision to cast me had already been made. It didn't seem as if they wanted an audition, a screen test or anything. The whole thing was surreal. 'When you are filming you must come and stay on my boat,' the hugely animated Marcello told me. I was the 23-year-old boy from Oldham. I nearly fell off my chair. This was a fairytale.

'Can I ring my mother?' I asked Roman towards the end of the evening when we had popped into his villa for some reason. How embarrassing my request seems today.

'What's the number?' he asked.

'Salisbury 2589,' I told him, a little Englander personified. But somehow Roman managed to track down the correct dialling code and get through. Though my dear mother was not as impressed as she could have been.

'I've just had dinner with Roman Polanski,' I told her.

'Raymond Huntley? Oh, I love Raymond Huntley.'

'No, Mother. Just go back to bed,' I told her.

I got back to my hotel in the early hours and was called for a meeting by the pool later that morning. How Hollywood was that? This was when the talk about my part in the film got more serious. 'You'd be perfect,' Roman told me.

But it wasn't to be. Apparently Roman had needed extra funding from the Italian government and part of the deal he struck was to use more Italian actors. Elocution lessons meant I had long since hidden my Oldham roots, but even I couldn't become Italian overnight. My great European film career went on temporary hold. Where it remains to this day, funnily enough.

From dinner at Roman Polanski's villa in Rome to lunch at the BBC canteen in East Acton. Life soon taught me to take the rough with the smooth. And anyway, the transition wasn't as bad as it sounds. However much the Two Ronnies and all us luvvies might have joked about it, the BBC canteen was a fine place to be. I thought I was in the old star system in a Hollywood studio when I first ate there. In those days almost all the BBC's big shows were filmed in-house at Television Centre. So on every table there seemed to be someone yet more famous than on the one before. It was the ultimate place for table-hopping, and I'm pretty certain that's where the phrase was first coined.

When *London Assurance* closed, I had been in and out of work like every other jobbing actor. I had done a few short tours in the provinces. And I was doing my fair share of television, even though I could be in awe of my surroundings and sometimes unaccountably nervous in front of the cameras. In *Man of Straw*, directed by Herbert Wise, who would also direct *I Claudius*, I was alongside Derek Jacobi – who, incestuously enough, would also be in *I Claudius*. We were all playing students and the costume department gave me a pair of small, wire-framed glasses to wear. They didn't have any lenses in and as I'm short-sighted I tended to keep them in my pocket and wear my own glasses right up until the last moment.

Except that on one important take I forgot to do the switch.

'Brilliant. On to the next scene,' called Herbie.

As we all got ready to move I realised that I had been wearing the wrong specs. Should I tell someone? Could I? I felt like a little boy again. There were so many people involved in every scene. The unions were all-powerful and everyone lived in fear of wasting precious minutes and forcing the producers to pay the crews overtime rates if you did too many retakes. So I kept my mouth shut. So far I've never seen the show included on any of these 'continuity disaster' compilations. But I expect it will soon pop up now. At least I wasn't wearing a wristwatch. Or at least I hope I wasn't.

After passing my first anniversary of living in Fulham I felt I'd really put down roots in London. I had even made up some fancy printed cards with my name and address on to make me seem professional, successful and older. It turned out they were nearly the downfall of me. Ifield Road was an inconveniently long one-way street. Driving out to the Fulham Road, which you needed to do to get almost anywhere, was a real pain. So I always did an illegal turn and headed down the wrong way, trying to feign ignorance at any angry motorists who tooted at me. This normally worked. Until one day the angry motorist in question was a policeman in a panda car.

'Did you realise that this is a one-way street, sir?' he asked.

'A one-way street? Really? I'm not from around here and I had absolutely no idea, officer,' I replied shamelessly. It was worthy of an Olivier Award.

'Do you have any identification on you?' He could hardly have been more stern-faced. I was in serious trouble.

'Here's my card,' I said, spotting in the instant that I passed it over that it had my address, 142 Ifield Road, London SW10, on the front. Not so easy to pretend I was a stranger in town now.

'Put both your hands together and out in front of you, sir.' Oh, God, he's going to arrest me. I'm going to be handcuffed in the street. What will the neighbours say? What will my mother say? But there were no handcuffs. Instead, the policeman looked me in the eye, tilted his head and slapped me on both wrists. It was pretty much the campest thing I had ever seen – and, trust me, I've seen a lot. Two minutes later I was back on my way again. Don't you love the British bobby?

I've never lived a racy enough life to have a tabloid-style 'drugs hell'. For all the laughs, I was brought up to be a grafter. I would never have had time for six months in rehab. Apart from anything else, I've always had too many parties to go to, too many restaurants to visit. But that's not to say I haven't had a few extraordinary moments.

The first came way back when I was living above my means in Ifield Road. Two old pals from drama school, Gillian Morgan, who had been on a celebrated world tour with the RSC, and Hazel Clyne, were taking *A Midsummer Night's Dream* around the world and I could barely be more jealous. They performed in some of the world's greatest theatres. And wherever they went the Royal Shakespeare Company's reputation swept all before them. No bean counter should ever underestimate the value of that name. I said before that the RSC's vast subsidy was often misspent. Even so, it was worth every penny. It makes me proud to be British.

Gillian called me from Chicago. She had met a man called Randy Eaton. Later I would see first-hand that he was spectacularly handsome. He was also one of the richest and most charming men I had ever met. Yes, you really can have it all – or at least Gillian could. She was so in love that she quit the RSC and didn't work under Trevor Nunn again. But for a long time it seemed as if all's well would end well. She married Randy and they raised two fine boys. Back in the 1970s, though, we were all thick as thieves. It was on one of the pair's transatlantic visits, before their children arrived, that Randy made the proposal.

'Christopher, I'd like you to join me on a trip,' he said.

'Lovely, where to? Brighton?' I asked, though I was secretly hoping for Florence, Venice or somewhere equally glamorous.

'No, I want you to do LSD with me,' he laughed.

And I said 'OK' without a moment's hesitation. There was always something in Randy's manner. He was what counts in America as old money. His family owned a string of newspapers in Chicago and the Midwest. That gave him confidence. And he made it infectious. You always felt that whatever he suggested would come out right. When you were with Randy it always felt as if nothing could go wrong. So off I went on my little trip.

I met Randy at my house in Fulham. Both of us had a little flake put on our fingers. It looked so tiny, so silly. I was convinced that it wouldn't do a thing to me. So after putting it on my tongue and sitting around for a while I got bored. I started doing some tidying up.

Later, I sat on the back doorstep and looked around the garden. How absolutely incredible, I thought. 'In all the years I've lived here I've never noticed that island before. I've never seen how the ocean laps up at the walls of the house. Why have I never sat here before? It's so beautiful, so peaceful, sitting in the sun listening to the lapping of the waves.' I loved that house in those moments. I was so pleased I had chosen to live there, right up beside the sea in Fulham. Oh dear, oh dear.

We left the house and I dozed off on a tombstone in Brompton Cemetery. I was desperately hungry and thirsty, so I tore off to the corner shop I used every day. I knew, with complete clarity, that I had to choose food by colour. So I picked the most colourful things I could see. Scouring pads. Dish cloths. Even a big red bottle of floor cleaner. I piled it all on to the counter in front of the dear Indian owner, who got his wife to very carefully put it all back.

Now, if I'm being serious, I'll say I know all too well the horrors of drug addiction. I've seen the destruction that drugs have done to some theatre pals' looks, their lives and everything from their family to their finances. But that day in Fulham was innocent and wonderful. It was one of the most extraordinary experiences of my life. And there would be one more to come.

The next one took place in Fort Lauderdale in Florida. Again I was with Randy. His fortune was still intact at this point and he had paid huge sums to buy and renovate a vast boat. 'Come with me. We'll go to the Caribbean,' he said. I could hardly get to the marina fast enough. This was the kind of life I was desperate to enjoy. These were the kinds of people I wanted to be with.

On board there was a mad character, who I'll call Freddie, who sailed the boat while his equally off-beat girlfriend was there to cook and make us drinks. Well, that was the idea. Everyone except Freddie and I got horrifically seasick. Possibly he escaped it because he was stoned. All I know is that most of the time I seemed to be the only fully conscious person on deck. And hour after hour we never seemed to get that far from the Florida coast. 'Do you think everything is all right with the boat, Freddie?' I asked towards sunset.

'I'll go check, dude,' he told me. And everything turned out to be very wrong. The engine room was full of water. Freddie turned on some pump or other but it made matters worse.

'Isn't that supposed to be taking the water out?' I asked, an expert all of a sudden.

'Sure is, dude.'

'Doesn't it look to you as if it's sucking the water in instead?'

'Looks like it.'

There seemed to be an unnecessarily long pause.

'What does that mean?' I asked finally.

In Freddie's considered opinion, it meant we were going down.

'Should we get help?' I asked, not entirely clear how I, of all people, had become the captain of the ship.

But getting help was a problem too. The radio hadn't been fitted properly. We could hear people, but they couldn't hear us. Presumably the same people who had done the pump had done the radio. In the end the Miami Coastguard spotted us and headed over to find out why we weren't moving. My last memory of that boat is of us all treading dirt and oil and seaweed through the sodden, brand-new cream carpets as we abandoned ship. It may well have sunk, I don't remember.

'Biggins, we feel terrible. But I'll make it up to you. Let's go down to the Keys.' Randy's good old American hospitality knew no bounds. I felt it would be impolite to decline the offer. And when we got there I had my second and last tab of LSD. This time we were by the sea, but I didn't see it. Instead I mainly saw food, fish and animals.

I walked down to the beach. I became a huge fish eye. We decided to go tenpin bowling. (Why? Why on earth was that ever going to be a good idea?) And it was a disaster. Everyone there was a fish to me. One handsome bald man was a seal. Someone else was a frog. They started to kiss.

It was all Disney's *Fantasia* writ large. And even without the drug the whole trip was surreal. This fabulously wealthy man and me, his soon-to-be famously easy-living and theatrical friend, weren't staying in some bijou boutique hotel or some five-star palace with hot and cold running waiters. We were camping. In one of Florida's biggest electrical storms. My tent collapsed in the early evening but I didn't even notice. Randy said all he could see was my not inconsiderable outline, tightly wrapped in tarpaulin-like clingfilm. Apparently I looked like a vast, oven-ready chicken. I could have been barcoded and sold in Safeway.

7

Living Large

Back in Britain I was developing ideas above my station. Living in a gorgeous house in Fulham, then spending time with American millionaires, had been a very bad idea. That would be the story of my life. Most people get led astray by bad company. I was always led astray by good company. I never noticed when I was out of my depth.

Anyway, my old love of antiques and bric-a-brac had pretty quickly developed into a love of art. When I was on a brief tour to the Watermill Theatre in Newbury, Berkshire – one of the most picturesque theatres in the country – I saw a painting at an art fair for £80. My weekly wage back then was just £40. But still I bought it. Pictures really do tell stories, for me. They trigger wonderful memories, because I buy them when I'm in a good place, physically or mentally. It's a testament to how many good times I've had that I've got thousands of paintings now, far more than I ever have room to hang. I really should stop buying, I know. But I can't. After leaving the jungle, Neil and I bought a lovely Anne McGill picture of a couple dancing to remind us of those lovely days. The sad thing about life is that events can sometimes get in the way of these simple pleasures. When I was young and careless I could buy luxuries like paintings whenever I got a new job. Now when I get some good new work, all I think about is the mortgage and the taxman. Or at least that's what I say.

I was still in Fulham when a group of us went to the first night of *Company*, easily my favourite Sondheim musical. It was a big night and the show had a huge American cast, hot over from Broadway. Clearly it was the kind of night you dress up for. So I did. I wore a vast, desperately ornate silver kaftan. And in the process I made an important (but fortunately temporary) enemy. Across the theatre Cameron Mackintosh apparently took an instant dislike to me. 'Who on earth is that fat geezer wearing that horrible outfit?' he asked his suitably stylish, black-clad friends.

'Biggins,' came the one-word reply. And my card was marked.

Meeting Cameron again in a professional capacity could have been a disaster. That happened when the director Veronica Flint-Shipman, a very important lady in my life, was producing *Winnie the Pooh* with Bob West. No prizes for guessing that I was Pooh. We toured the show, then Cameron took over as producer. And did he remember me as the fat geezer in the ridiculously gaudy kaftan? Oh yes. But this time we clicked. Soon we were the very best of friends.

Over all the years to come I would gravitate back to Cameron whenever I was out of work. I'd help him out behind the scenes on his productions or even in his makeshift offices. Those were his early days, when we had to transfer funds from one bank account to pay another if we wanted the shows to stay on the road. It was high-wire stuff, but it was thrilling. As usual, there were some incredible laughs. Some of the best came with *Rock Nativity*. I was watching the dress rehearsal in Newcastle – and everything, absolutely everything, was going wrong. At that time there weren't any wireless mikes you could attach to your face or hair. This show had traditional rock mikes – all of which had long leads attached. By the end of Act One, there was a spaghetti junction of wires knotted up over the front of the stage. Some of the performers had to kneel down to sing because they couldn't get any more slack to pull their mikes more than a foot from the floor.

'At least it can't get much worse,' I whispered to Veronica. How wrong I was.

In a moment of sheer frustration the Virgin Mary let out a roar of anger and tried to throw the baby Jesus into the audience. She missed. The doll slammed against the proscenium arch of the theatre and fell, in pieces, to the floor of the stalls. As a moment of pure theatre it was hard to beat. And once we had all stopped laughing – and untangled the microphone leads and glued baby Jesus back together – *Rock Nativity* did go on to open well. Veronica and I looked after the show for quite a while. And looked after means doing whatever it takes to keep it on the road.

Up in Scotland we were in the middle of a flu epidemic and our cast fell like flies. By the time the evening's performance was due to start we had a real problem.

'Biggins, you've got to go on.'

Desperately trying to remember the lines I joined the chorus and had my Peggy Sawyer moment from *42nd Street*. I was going on a nobody, hoping to come off a star. Though not everyone really noticed. My old pal and dance legend Dougie Squires happened to be in the audience that night. He called me the next day. 'Christopher, I don't know who he was and I couldn't find his name in the programme, but there was an actor in *Rock Nativity* last night who could have been your double.'

Going on tour with a show can be one of the most fun – and most gruelling – things any actor can do. It's a hard slog. New digs, new theatres, new faces, week after week. Sometimes you play to full houses and feel like the king of the world. Sometimes you come off stage and cry.

I've done my share of both.

Playing Pooh, for example, was a surprisingly physical task. The show was adapted, with music, by the lovely Julian Slade. As Pooh my costume was hotter than hell. I had a tight hood, a vast thick suit and, unaccountably, a set of long johns to wear. At the interval I had to wring the sweat out of all of them into a bucket. Ah, the glamour of theatre.

To make matters worse, with *Pooh* our first theatre wasn't a theatre at all. It was a tent. The Royal Ballet was about to use this supposedly mobile construction for its tour, but we were the guinea pigs to test it out down in

Plymouth. The whole structure was innovative and exciting. But it's fair to say we had a few teething troubles.

'Biggins, I need a word,' Bob West, the company manager, called me over one night when the clouds above Plymouth were rumbling with thunder and alive with flashes of lightning.

'Will the audience be able to hear us over all this?' I asked as the rain lashed down on our canvas roof. But that was the least of our problems.

'Just put the word out to the rest of the cast not to panic but not to touch anything metal during the performance,' Bob said. During the interval he came up to me again. 'I need you to make a short announcement to the audience.' So I stood in front of the closed curtain.

'Ladies and gentlemen, will you kindly take your seats as this evening's performance will begin again in five minutes. Can we remind customers that this is a non-smoking venue. And in view of this evening's inclement weather can we ask that no one touches anything metal for the rest of the evening. We hope you enjoy the show.'

Amazing to recount that we didn't lose our audience and got through the night without any lightning strikes. Health and Safety would have had a field day.

We had a lovely company on that show. Verity Anne Meldrum was Christopher Robin, Norma Dunbar was Kanga, David Glover was Eeyore and Michael Staniforth, whom I'd meet again in *Rentaghost*, was Tigger. We had great fun on that tour. I'm proud that I'm a good company leader. If I'm playing the lead I love to lead a company off stage as well as on. I love being in charge of people's welfare. In her autobiography *All of Me* the wonderful Barbara

Windsor says she told none other than Joan Collins, 'Every actress should have Biggins in the small print of their contracts as an essential.' I think I know what dear Barbara meant. I can make people's lives more comfortable because I enjoy making nests.

When you're on tour it can be hard, as you're away for weeks and months at a time from the people you love. I try to replace all the families, all the people we've left behind. The camaraderie of theatre is so strong. It's like no other industry in the world. When you work with someone for just three weeks, perhaps in rehearsal for a production that never comes off, you still feel the intensity of friendship. You may not see that person again for years and years. But there's something about showbusiness. When you do meet again, in some green room or some theatre tour, you start right back where you left off. It's as if you never went away.

Some tours can also enrich you in other ways. When the gorgeous Paula Wilcox and I were on the road alongside George Layton way back in *Touch of Spring* (one of the first plays Cameron Mackintosh did, before he gave the world the mega-musical), we made it a gastronomic tour. We would drive for miles each day to find great restaurants. We called it our great eating tour of England. We had so much fun and it's amazing, bearing in mind how close I feel to Paula and George today, that this was some 30 years ago.

Of course, all those years ago the other thing that was very different to today was the quality of the accommodation. Sometimes we got lucky and found half-decent hotels. But most of the time we were in the long-lost world of theatrical digs. It was a world of extraordinary landladies who offered rooms to all the touring companies. With these redoubtable ladies you never quite knew what you might get. You certainly never got bored.

My favourite story of the era – often told and probably apocryphal – is of the two actors who boarded together and shared a glass of dry sherry each night after the show. After a couple of nights they take a look at the bottle. Did they really drink that much the night before? A couple of nights later their suspicions are aroused again. Their precious sherry is disappearing far too fast. 'The landlady must be drinking some,' they agree. So they decide to take their revenge. They decant the sherry, hide the new bottle and pee in the old one.

'That'll teach her,' they laugh.

They laugh even more when they see that the subterfuge doesn't stop her. Every night the level on the new bottle has fallen just a little bit more. So when they leave at the end of the week they decide to confront her. 'I'm afraid we have something to ask you. Have you been drinking our sherry while we've been at the theatre?' they say.

'Oh no, dearies, I haven't drunk any. But I did mean to tell you that I've been putting it in your trifle every night,' she says.

While I never suffered quite such an indignity I do remember plenty of other horrors, including the time my digs were next door to a huge poster in an Essex churchyard that screamed out: 'Our God's Alive. Sorry About Yours.' I had a few sleepless nights thinking about that one.

Then there was the time when Maev Alexander and I joined a company called the Portable Theatre. The clues were all there in the title. Everything was done on a shoestring. Our set, props and equipment were all moved around in a van and we set up in whichever hall we were booked for and then packed up again afterwards. Which was when the fun began. Each night the company members had to go to the bar. We then stood around, like Roman slaves, while the locals looked us all up and down and decided which they wanted to look after for the night. Maev had a low point when she was selected by a pair of lesbians who chased her round their house all night. My low point was a bit different.

It came on the night I was the last to be chosen. Oh, the embarrassment. It was sports day at school all over again. 'Well, I'll have to take him, then,' said my charm-free host with a distinct lack of enthusiasm. I followed him sheepishly to his home. What was I letting myself in for?

We had a drink, then I admitted I was exhausted. 'I really must get some sleep. So where is my bed, exactly?'

'Right there,' he said. And he pointed to a patch of worn carpet in front of the fire.

Unfortunately, even if I did get a bed it wasn't always Savoy standard. One time I slipped right off the mattress and on to the floor because of the nylon sheets in a guesthouse in Brighton. Now it's cotton sheets only for me. I'd sleep in linen, if they weren't so expensive. Whatever tour I've been on, the big dream has always been the same: a transfer to the West End. I love travel. But London felt like home. And in 1975 I was about to move right to the heart of things.

Veronica and her husband Gerald owned the Phoenix Theatre on Charing Cross Road. It's a theatre that's somehow easy to overlook – though it had just the kind of pedigree I loved. It opened in 1930 with Noel Coward playing alongside Gertrude Lawrence and Laurence Olivier in the premier of *Private Lives*. Noel and Gertie were back again later that decade with *Tonight at 8.30* and apparently they referred to the place as 'our theatre'. I wanted to make it mine.

I had the chance because what very few people knew was that above the theatre were 25 small studio flats, all available to rent for just £14 a week. I had to have one. I'd moved on from Ifield Road and tried living with a fellow actor and his girlfriend in a flat in Oxford Circus. But it was a tense, tricky little household, and I soon realised that love triangles really aren't my thing.

I begged Veronica to let me know if any of her rooms ever became available – and I moved in the moment one did. It was just wonderful to be so close to the heart of London – and for an actor it was amazing to live, quite literally, above the shop. I loved my Phoenix rooms – well, room. I had a sofa bed and put throws over the tiny kitchen area to hide the fact that my whole world was in one single space. Overall I was convinced that I had created theatreland's most glamorous room. It seemed that word had got around.

We had a wonderful old prostitute in the building, living in the flat above me. She was in her fifties and had a gammy leg, but she was a game old bird. Off she went to work every day and she always wanted to see the inside of my flat. 'They say it's beautiful. Let me look,' she'd say.

'Come in, then, and have a drink,' I said one night.

She could hardly speak when she looked around. 'Oh, oh, oh, this is gorgeous. You see, my flat's all bed.' She said. Occupational hazard, I suppose.

Opposite I had another wonderful character, the mad woman across the hall who worked on the markets. Her tiny flat was chock-a-block with rubbish. She stacked up anything and everything she could sell – my dad would have loved her. One of my new pals, the actress Georgina Simpson, heiress to the Simpson's of Piccadilly clothing fortune and the woman who would marry Anthony Andrews, certainly fell under my neighbour's spell. She was round one evening and didn't have anything to wear for a party. So we went across the hall, knocked on the door to see if my neighbour had any dresses. Georgina got one for £3 – and she looked a million dollars.

Georgina soon turned into the sister I never had. We met through Jonathan and Vivien in Fulham. They had been invited to a 'society' party at some country pile and I was determined to come too. So determined that I offered to do the driving. Even though my dad had offered me plenty of flash, refurbished cars over the years I always stuck with something a lot less glamorous. A white van. I'd needed it when I was propping and had to help move the sets around on various tours. So I still drove it. And it certainly set us apart from the other guests out in the country. We pulled into a vast driveway, past Rolls-Royces, Bentleys and Maseratis. 'They'll think we're the hired help,' I screeched.

The three of us were laughing so much as we parked that I nearly hit one of the fancy cars. And that of course made us laugh even more. As soon as we got inside I nipped to the loo to try to calm down. But I couldn't. And because I couldn't stop laughing I peed all the way down my left leg – leaving a huge wet stain on my light-brown suit.

'Got to hide it, got to hide it.' But how?

I'm dancing around, as if movement will make a difference. 'Dry, dammit, dry.'

'Sorry, I'll be just a moment.'

Damn. Someone was knocking on the door. I imagined a long queue forming outside. Disaster. Then salvation. There was a beautifully patterned silk scarf hanging behind the loo door. I picked it up, did a bit more mopping and headed out into the vast hallway using the scarf as cover. But who should I see first but the lady of the house, Georgina's formidable mother, Heddy Simpson. I soon realised she was a woman who doesn't mince her words and doesn't hide her feelings. She was also a woman who owned a beautifully patterned silk scarf.

I'm not sure I'll ever forget how Heddy looked me up and down that evening. And my humiliation wasn't quite complete. As I tried to scarper a waiter bumped into me and spilled a tray of champagne down my right leg. It was a near-perfect match for the stain on my left leg. 'So sod it.' I left the scarf on a hall table and headed off to find Jonathan and Vivien.

It was quite a party. The rich are different – as I've been constantly reminded, all around the world, ever since. 'Time to go swimming!' The cry went up sometime around midnight. I was handed a pair of trunks, which I had to stretch almost to breaking point to fit my frame. I put my clothes in a neat little pile behind a tree in the garden. I might have just peed on the lavatory floor and tried to steal a scarf from the lady of the house. But I was still too well brought up to fling my clothes around.

We all splashed around wildly for a while – Christine Keeler, eat your heart out – and then everyone got dressed again. Everyone except me. Try as I might, I couldn't find my tree, or my clothes. So I spent far more time than I wanted (and probably more time than anyone else wanted) walking around half-naked that night. But by then I was feeling pretty comfortable at the party. I had been introduced to Georgina, the daughter of the house. We clicked straight away. I had made a friend for life.

Back at the Phoenix, the theatre itself was booming. Veronica had signed up a season of huge American stars for a series of very high-profile plays. Not surprisingly, the box-office managers were making the most of the stars' potential. Their names – from Rock Hudson to Charlton Heston – were all up in big letters outside the theatre, just below my bedroom window. I was ill with jealousy.

'Could you put my name there instead, just for a joke?' I asked Veronica one day. She set it up. So for a few blissful hours 'Christopher Biggins' got top billing, in big capitals. Rock, Charlton and the others were all relegated to lower-case letters below.

By now I had upgraded myself from my studio room – I was renting the flat next door as well. So for £28 a week I had 'rooms' in Covent Garden, right in the heart of theatreland. It was practically a 'salon' and I lived there for five very happy years.

When I did decide to leave I had one lovely moment with dear Lily, the lady who 'did' for me every week. Lily was always a gem – and a chancer. She was supposed to do two or three hours, but if I popped out just after she arrived and needed to dash back for something I had forgotten I almost always found she was long gone herself. But still, she was always ready for a laugh and a gossip and I would miss her. 'Lily, I need to tell you that I'm leaving at the end of the month. I'm moving out.'

She started to cry. 'I don't know what I'll do without you,' she said.

'Oh, you'll be fine, I'm sure,' I said, flattering myself that it was my winning personality that she would miss.

'No, I can't do without you. I don't know how I'll pay the electricity bill,' she said through her tears.

Now I got it. 'How much do you owe, Lily?'

'A hundred and eighty-four pounds and seventy pence.'

I wrote a cheque for £184.70.

'And I just don't know how I'll pay my gas bill.'

'How much is that, Lily?'

'Seventy-two pounds and fifty pence.'

I wrote a second cheque.

'Christopher, I will miss you. Would it be possible to have a memento of you?'

'What would you like?' I asked, looking at all my signed playbills, photographs and theatrical memorabilia on the walls.

'Can I have your Kenwood mixer?' she asked. That's when I finally learned to say no.

Of course, Lily wasn't the only person I was going to miss at the Phoenix – the building was stuffed with racy neighbours and great pals. The *Daily Mail*'s legendary theatre critic Jack Tinker was another resident – I had helped him get the flat there after telling him about the building at some first night or other.

He was one of my finest friends. I don't think I've ever laughed as much as I did back then. He was so small, so bright, so quick. And his reviews were brilliant.

The two of us were forever in and out of each other's flat, having coffee, gossiping and getting into scrapes and confessing all if we had been naughty boys the night before. Jack's lover Adrian Morris had a house in Brighton where Jack's three great daughters lived, and they were all like an extended family to me. As if I didn't already have enough wonderful people around me as it was.

But there was some tension – from some of my colleagues in the industry. People said I shouldn't spend time with Jack, not because he was older and not because he had a lover but because he was a critic. It was a bit like Bristol, when some people thought it odd that I spent so much time with Joan, the wife of our principal. But, just like Bristol, I carried on regardless. People are people. Who cares what jobs people do?

And I didn't want to lose Jack's friendship because, as I said, we shared so many laughs. The time we went to see a production in Stratford-upon-Avon was a key example. We had booked into a local hotel and arrived to find that all they had was a tiny room with a big double bed. 'Ah, so that's your game, Jack. You get young, impressionable actors out of London on false pretences and then play innocent about sharing a bed,' I joked. We laughed at that. We laughed even more after the play when it was finally time for bed. Jack was first into the bathroom, and while he was cleaning his teeth I got every piece of furniture in the room – including lamps, occasional tables, chairs and a chest of drawers – and lined them up down the middle of the bed as a sort of buffer zone.

We laughed so much we cried. We could hardly have made more noise. Then we had to move the furniture all back. God knows what the people in the next room thought was going on.

8

The Real Me

By the time I met Jack Tinker I was wonderfully comfortable with who I was. I don't have some angst-ridden tale of sexual awakening, nor do I have any terrible stories of prejudice or discrimination. But that's not to say it's all been easy. I look back on a world where attitudes to sexuality have changed dramatically. There have been times when things got much better, and times when they got much, much worse.

I grew up in a different age. Being gay wasn't thought of, let alone discussed. There were no role models, no good examples and no road map to follow. Yes, I mucked around just a little bit with a couple of other boys at school. I think on a hugely exciting school trip to Paris there were some rustles with none other than our head boy one night – I always did set my sights high. But even that wasn't really about sex, it was about boys being boys, I thought. Like I say, I always had this feeling of being different. And the other boys, the sporty boys and, yes, the head boys, all recognised it as well. But it wasn't discussed. The word 'gay' hadn't really been used in this context, still less as a term of abuse.

At Salisbury Rep I still didn't really understand what was going on in my head, or all around me. Though I can't exactly say I didn't have plenty of clues. I barged in one door backstage carrying an armful of props and found two men having sex in front of me. And being brought up as I had been, I simply apologised for not knocking, put the props down and said I would come back later.

I certainly wasn't troubled. I didn't agonise over my sexuality. I simply never gave it any thought. I saw how easily Raymond and Geoffrey fitted into the Rep's social scene in Salisbury and by the time I got to Bristol I had plenty of other friends who were gay. No one batted an eyelid about them, so I didn't worry about it myself.

Of course, one reason why I coasted through life so calmly was that I hadn't actually suffered in love myself. I'd been married and I had seen my short marriage end. But, like a Jane Austin heroine, I hadn't met the right man to make me really feel things. Well, I hadn't until Penelope Keith introduced me to him.

Penny and I had met back in my *London Assurance* days, well before her big television roles in *The Good Life* and *To The Manor Born*. She was so special and so sophisticated and we had a great chemistry – from the start we would talk ten times a day and meet up four or five times a week. She's a wonderful cook and had a lovely home in Putney where I spent a huge amount of time. It was there that she introduced me to another theatrical pal of hers: a fascinating, talented box-office manager called Robert Burns. Every successful theatre needs a brilliant box-office manager. So every producer in London wanted Robert to work for them. He could make money out of nothing. He would move seats and whole rows of bookings to squeeze in extra paying punters and keep his productions in the black.

I admired Robert's skills and I loved how passionate he was about his work. And I loved the man as well. He was a real cockney East End boy with a huge, warm and wonderful family. We laughed so much. I was 25 and in love, fully in love, for the first time in my life. We were together for a year. A year that gave me so much confidence and joy. But after we had gone our separate ways he decided he wanted to move on in his career as well. He wanted to produce. But, for all the fun and frivolity, theatre is a cutthroat business – as Robert knew only too well. Sadly, things didn't work out for him on the other side of the box-office counter. He lost a lot of money. Then he disappeared. He vanished off the face of the earth. He was such a special man, adored and loved by so many people.

But now an awful lot of years have passed. To this day none of us knows where Robert is or whether he is alive or dead. For someone like me, a man who values friendships above all else, that's one of the hardest admissions I have to make.

After Robert and I said goodbye I was never lonely. Many dear friends have lit up my life for a while – some for months and years, some for just one night.

In the theatre you're always going to have plenty of opportunities to meet dear friends such as these. Simply because they were the only places open late enough to serve us, back in the 1970s we would all troop down to some very gay bars in Soho after a performance. But the whole bar scene never really worked for me. I was never an obvious leading man on stage, nor was I an obvious person to pick up some stranger in a bar. I never liked the games people played, the attitudes, the poses, the 'don't even think of approaching me' confidence that clearly hides some sort of insecurity. Staying away from bars probably helped me when I was doing so much work on children's television. In the 1970s and early 1980s, some parts of the press still hinted at some awful link between homosexuality and paedophilia. So at least I didn't need to worry about being photographed coming out of the wrong door in the wrong part of town.

Anyway, I have always met dear friends in far lighter, nicer places. Waiters in wonderful restaurants. People who smile as they serve the drinks or meals. Many is the time that they lit up my life.

I enjoyed it all, on a very uncomplicated level. I've enjoyed sex all my life and I've never seen why we need to be so prudish about it – though I know this probably has more to do with selling those tabloid newspapers than people's real attitudes. And in the 1970s and early 1980s it wasn't as if gay people were the only ones having fun. Everyone was having a party in my world. Single, straight, gay, married. None of it seemed to matter and, if you'll excuse the pun, everyone was having a ball. How quickly everything changed.

The Real Me

I remember the first time I saw the word 'Aids' in a newspaper, sometime around 1980. Then you saw it almost every day. It always chilled me. Somehow I knew very early that everything was about to change. The spectre of that disease hung over everyone – and the theatrical world was hit harder than most. No one knew what the illness really was in the early days. The theories, and the fears, ran out of control. Tabloids took the line that all homosexuals were killers. No one saw us as victims. But I saw so many people waste away and die. Those first deaths were terrible and terrifying in equal measure. With no treatments and so little medical knowledge, strong men did simply fade into themselves. I lost so many fine friends, we all did. We sat at so many bedsides, went to so many funerals. And you never knew who might be next.

I look back on my life and I've seen homosexuality go from being invisible to being fully accepted, to being cast into the dark ages, and now, back to respectability again. When I became King of the Jungle and ran over that rope bridge towards the cameras, it wouldn't have occurred to me for a second that I shouldn't kiss Neil. To the whole crew's credit, it didn't occur to them either. It was only months later when I was chatting to a fan in the street that they said I had made a little bit of television – and perhaps social – history. It had been ITV's first live prime-time kiss between two gay men. I'm as proud of that as I am of winning the show. If it has made life easier for even one other young gay man, I'm thrilled. I will tell the story of Neil and I later in the book. But knowing that he would be waiting for me outside the jungle made *I'm A Celebrity* bearable.

It took me many years to learn how to make relationships work – and maybe you never quite crack it. I've had phases of being possessive and jealous. I fought that. I've struggled with rejection. It's tough if someone leaves you. But that's life. You have to move on, to get on with it. That's been true in every aspect of my life. Move on, get on with it. I'm like that when jobs pass me by. I force myself to be the same with lovers.

I know I'm not necessarily an easy person to live with. I'm selfish, though I'm always trying to be better. But I've always liked being in a relationship. I like having a partner, someone who's there for the highs and the lows and will talk about all the minutiae of the day. That's what Neil has been to me for 14 wonderful years. Two years ago we signed our civil partnership in Hackney Town Hall before heading off to a party at Joe Allen, where, as dear Barbara Windsor pointed out, we celebrated with everyone from Joan Collins to my cleaning lady. Don't ever let it be said that I've forgotten my roots.

Neil and I don't describe our commitment as a marriage. I'm not political about these things and I actually like the word 'partnership'. That sums it all up to me – the highs and lows and the mutual support of a proper, grown-up relationship. What I have with Neil is so important. It will need some pretty impressive developments in medical science for us to beat the 63 years my parents have already clocked up as a married couple. But if I am to go the distance with anyone it will be with Neil.

Anyway, long before I met Neil one of my performances was making waves in the gay community – and I was making enemies. In the early 1970s Gillian had found me that first job in LWT's comedy series *Doctor at Large*. My memory of all this isn't what it should be. But I think I played a mildly effeminate intern in that. A few years later I was asked back for *Doctor at Sea*. This time my character could hardly be forgotten. I played an outrageous, flamboyant, bitchy and bouffant-haired old queen. I thought it was absolutely fabulous. But I was pretty much alone.

The attacks began immediately. I came in for a lot of stick from the gay community for perpetuating outdated stereotypes. People wrote critical letters to the papers about it and I had some heated 'discussions' with friend and stranger alike on the issue. 'Why are you doing this?' people asked. 'Why are you feeding people's prejudices about homosexuals?'

My answer was always simple. Outrageous queens did exist – a quick look around the BBC canteen proved that. So why shouldn't they get reflected on screen? Why should I hide the kind of people who made life more fun? I didn't win all of these arguments. But they were the least of my worries. In career terms I was being warned that playing that role in *Doctor at Sea* could have had me typecast – not just as a gay man but also as a light-entertainment figure. I had won some decent cameo roles in mainstream dramas such as *Upstairs Downstairs* and *The Duchess of Duke Street* in the early 1970s (*Upstairs Downstairs* was great fun – my car-dealing father loved that I was cast as a dodgy car salesman in an episode about the advent of the motor car). But I knew that my frothy performance in the *Doctor at Sea* series could have stopped me getting considered for bigger, meatier roles elsewhere.

For a while my time with the RSC helped me through. Because I'd acted in the RSC, and trodden the boards alongside the likes of Judi, Donald and Dame Peggy Ashcroft, people took a little bit more notice of me. I had a hefty supply of professional credibility back in the mid-1970s. But I knew it wouldn't last for ever. And heaven knows where it all is now.

Anyway, I wasn't perhaps as bothered by the light-entertainment tag as I could have been. What's wrong with popular, frothy programmes anyway? I'd seen first-hand how hard it is to make good television comedy when I'd been cast in my first of two episodes of *Some Mothers Do 'Ave 'Em* back in 1973. The first was the one where Frank Spencer was trying to become a pilot – a very scary prospect for all concerned. I was a student at the flight school and a witness to most of his navigational errors. In the second episode, a few years later, I was a student in a canteen and after all the usual disasters I ended up covered in baked beans and gravy. It was great fun – and a step up the food chain from my first TV role with that chicken leg. Between those two episodes I was to have another master class in television sitcoms.

Gillian set up a meeting for me with Sid Lotterby, the director and producer of a new BBC show to be called *Porridge*. With that show almost everything about my career would change.

I won the part of Lukewarm, a cleverly drawn character who was gay, but not too gay. I toned down my *Doctor at Sea* act, though I didn't want Lukewarm's sexuality to disappear altogether. I thought it was really important that they kept in all the references to his love life on the other side of the prison walls. That was a pretty big deal in 1974. Don't ask why, but it was my idea to make Lukewarm knit. I had a feeling this might help get the message about him across. Perhaps I did that to take my mind off the way my character was described in the script. 'A rotund young man,' it said. 'Young' I liked. 'Rotund' I could have done without.

Being in *Porridge* was an incredible experience – to this day it makes me smile to think of it. And playing such a fun part, with such a classic Dick Clement and Ian La Frenais script, was only one great piece of the *Porridge* adventure. Working with Ronnie Barker and the dear Richard Beckinsale was the other true joy. What a lovely man Richard would have grown to be, had the fates allowed.

Ronnie, meanwhile, was a revelation. He was a huge star and could have been a nightmare to work with. He wasn't. And while most comics want everything to be about *them*, Ronnie was the true exception. Of course, his wonderful Fletcher dominated every minute of the show. But he was a truly generous man, always happy to give away part of a scene and let others soak up the applause for a while. He gave me and my character a lot more space than most other comics would have done. That's class.

We filmed *Porridge* in the BBC's East Acton studios and, despite how high-profile and important the show was, everyone had a ball. It was one of the easiest and most relaxed shooting schedules I remember. My favourite episode was the one where Ronnie wrote the same letter for all the lags to send to their wives and girlfriends – and for Lukewarm to send to his young man. The ruse is discovered when the partners all travel on the same bus to visit on the same day.

After the first series Ronnie gave all the regulars an engraved silver tankard as a thank-you gift. It read: 'Slade Prison: 1974' above our characters' names. Ronnie had given me an initial, so I was Lukewarm P. I think I can safely say that no one has ever drunk out of that mug without checking the contents with care.

When the show aired, I think we all knew it was going to be good. But at the time you can never quite know how much impact it might make. We could hardly have made more. *Porridge* was prime-time television. More than 16 million watched us every Thursday night; nearly 18 million watched the Christmas special. Our scripts became catchphrases. I might only have had a recurring role, but I was still recognised in the street. This truly felt like the big time.

What's interesting about being in a hit show is that you never know if you're simply riding a zeitgeist or if your show will stand the test of time. Three decades later and it's clear that *Porridge* has done that. Fletcher is one of the most popular characters in comedy history – and deservedly so. And financially speaking I've certainly enjoyed the benefit of this timeless popularity. I got £90 an episode when I was on the series in the 1970s. If they repeat the show now, I get something like £1,000. What a bizarre industry this is. How I wish they would repeat it more often.

Just before I'd got the job on *Porridge* I'd been moaning about the lack of really imaginative new characters. They don't write them like they used to, I would say. But it turned out that they did.

The Real Me

One hot June night in the early 1970s I went to the Royal Court Theatre on Sloane Square in London. To the Royal Court's very hot, and very small, studio theatre upstairs, to be exact. It was opening night of a bizarrely named show – with an equally bizarre plot. Ladies and gentlemen (and everybody in between), I give you *The Rocky Horror Show*. It was the most extraordinary, exhilarating evening. What an amazing show – and to see it in such a tiny, intimate theatre was mind-blowing. Tim Curry was magnificent. The whole performance was overwhelming and because I knew a lot of the production staff I was able to party away with them afterwards.

I wanted to be in that production more than anything – but its short run soon ended, so I never had the chance. A year later, towards the end of 1974, I heard they were going to make the show into a film. Twentieth Century Fox, if you please, and with big names like Susan Sarandon and Meatloaf on board. Dammit, Janet, I was determined to be in it too.

I got my wish. We had a two-month shoot (in Berkshire, not Hollywood) for which I earned the princely sum of £100 a week. I bought a sofa bed with my payments. Who says there's no glamour in the film business? But, as usual, the money wasn't the point. I think some of those involved spent part of the shoot stoned – and what a cast of characters we were. I met Gaye Brown and Annabel Leventon on *The Rocky Horror Picture Show* and they are still wonderful friends to this day. Then there was tiny Sadie Corre, whom I agreed to pick up and drive to work each morning. Was that a mistake? She talked so fast and was relentlessly chirpy. Lovely girl, but enough of the tiny details of life chez Sadie. Especially at dawn, when I'm never at my best.

The rest of us encompassed every shape and size you could imagine. One new pal was Fran Fullenwider, who did lots of shows in mainland Europe, where men apparently love big women. Poor Fran had a bad night at dinner with me back then. I was flat-sitting for some friends who lived on the fourth floor of a flash Mayfair block where the only downside was the lack of a lift. Poor Fran looked like she had run a marathon when she finally arrived. But this wasn't the end of it. She had to leave early and after saying our goodbyes the rest of us carried on partying upstairs.

Three hours later I headed down to nip to the corner shop for some tonics and there was Fran, sitting all alone on the scuffed carpet of the communal hallway. The door to the street was locked and the poor girl simply couldn't face going back up four flights of stairs to tell us she was trapped. Fran's no longer with us. But if she was I'd never let her out of my sight again without checking she had a mobile phone.

Going to the *Rocky Horror* premiere was a huge thrill. It wasn't Polanski, but I was still convinced it could be the start of something big. It seemed I was wrong. This was the year that the only film anyone seemed to want to see was *Jaws*. The critics hated us. We were slammed and we flopped. The so-called experts didn't understand this mad cross-dressing, pan-sexual plot line, and as the film was soon pulled from the cinemas the audiences didn't get much chance to enjoy it either. Try as you do not to take critics personally, it was deflating, to say the least. I'd loved that film. I was certain it deserved better.

But then something magical happened – just as in my life something magical very often does. We had a limited release in America and it seemed that little patches of the country fell in love with us. We were as camp as hell and we soon had a cult following. People began dressing up for midnight screenings. Word of mouth made us a hit. It's funny now but looking at the film it's obvious it would be a classic. But just like *Porridge*, like *I Claudius* and like several other shows I've been in, it's touch-and-go if others will see it that way. I was thrilled that *Rocky Horror* made some kind of history.

In 2006, so many years later, I was back on the live show as the narrator. We went on tour – over a year or so I dipped in and out and did gigs everywhere from Truro to York. It was an absolute blast – on weekends in particular the audiences were wild. So many people dressed up. So many knew every word. And because I'd been in the film I seemed to get extra attention from the real fans. Most nights I had a three-minute ovation just for walking on to the stage. How many people get that? Sometimes it seemed amazing that I was being paid for all this. Thank God, the producers didn't know I was so happy I would almost (but only almost) have done it all for free.

But I do have one admission to make. One night on that tour I did something I'd not done since *London Assurance* back with Dame Judi and the RSC. I fell asleep during the show. As the narrator I had a lovely comfortable armchair to sit in at the side of the stage. Too comfortable. One night I nodded off and missed all my cues. The cast apparently thought I was joking. Eagle-eyed people in the audience thought I was dead. Sadly, my performance in *The Rocky Horror Picture Show* didn't really trouble the judges of that year's Academy Awards. But shortly afterwards I did still get a Hollywood moment of sorts. Lauren Bacall was in town, slated to do a film version of the play *Applause Applause*, in which she was performing in the West End. My agent got the call. Would I like to be a partygoer in a scene with the great lady?

I think that would be a 'yes'.

I was thrilled to get close to blue-chip, cut-glass, rat-pack glamour. All I could think about was Bogie and Bacall and the golden age of Hollywood. This could be the start of something huge.

When my big day came I was on set at 9am for my 10am call. At 10am we heard on the grapevine that Ms Bacall had just got up. At 11am I was in full make-up. At 12 noon we heard Ms Bacall was on her way. At 1pm we were told she was in a foul mood. At 2pm we finally met her. Everyone was terrified, literally terrified of putting a foot wrong and facing the wrath of this wild woman. I was first to be introduced. And guess what? She was utterly charming.

My part was hardly extensive. I had one line: 'Margo, you were divine.'

Fortunately I delivered it to everyone's satisfaction. Then the fun began.

'Do you want to see something very sexy, Christopher?' the great lady breathed, that famously raspy voice everything I had hoped it would be.

'I'd love to!'

So she whipped back her dressing gown to display a huge bruise on her thigh.

We spent the next half-hour laughing about her ups and downs on stage. I told her about my opening night in *Toad of Toad Hall* in Worthing, where there was a hole in the middle of the stage from which Ratty would arrive in the first scene. It was covered with a blanket and, of course, none of us other actors was due to go anywhere near it. I forgot, walked right on to the blanket and disappeared from view. 'Fortunately I was so relaxed I didn't break a single bone,' I told my new Hollywood best friend. And we had a high old time sharing tales of other scrapes.

Afterwards, I kept thinking of all those hangers-on who had said she was in a foul mood, would eat our heads off and required totally obsequious behaviour from everyone on set. What rot. And in all my years I've found that it almost always is rot. People around the great stars conjure up these terrible atmospheres to try to make everything seem more exciting. But what a disservice to the stars. Maybe I've walked some gilded path. But in all my years I've hardly ever seen any nastiness.

Hugh Grant looked at me as if I was dirt once, or so I felt – or perhaps he just didn't hear me when I said hello to him and mentioned a few mutual friends while we were standing next to each other at some event in LA. But no one I have worked with has treated anyone badly. Even the famous perfectionists, people like Michael Crawford – I worked with him on those two riotous episodes of *Some Mothers Do 'Ave 'Em* in the 1970s – are tougher on themselves than on anyone around them. And when the going does get tough I just think back to my training. Oliver Gordon's words from Salisbury Rep normally do the trick. 'Don't muck about. Go on stage left, say your lines, then piss off stage right.' That normally sees me through.

Another instruction from Oliver was never to break your co-star's concentration. But couldn't that sometimes be great fun? I couldn't resist in my next role, a short season in Julian Slade's musical version of *Vanity Fair* in Guildford. I had a big number with *Grab Me A Gondolier* star Joan Heal – and I gave her a lift to work every day in my van. I seem to remember I bought a sofa from her as well, and a few years later I sold it to another old pal, the casting director Marilyn Johnson. Who says theatre is a closed shop?

Anyway, June Richie from London's original *Gone with the Wind* a quarter of a century ago was my Becky. It was her concentration I was determined to break. On our final day we did our matinee and then got ready for the evening performance. Just before the curtain fell on the two of us the broken Becky had to look me in the eye and accept my proposal. It was a sad, emotional and moving close to the play. Or it would have been if I hadn't decided to have the word 'Fuck' written under my left eye and 'Off' under my right. June was trying so hard to stop laughing that she couldn't say her final line. And without the final line the crew couldn't lower the curtain. We're lucky we got out of Guildford alive.

When I did need to escape from real life I always went to Shrublands Health Farm in Suffolk. Marilyn Johnson introduced me to it, and while it was in a beautiful setting it was all very serious. We had three days of hot water, honey and lemon. And every second on the television there seemed to be adverts for lovely sausages sizzling in pans and crying out to be eaten. One day on a walk around the grounds I saw half of an old banana lying in a flowerbed. How I stopped myself from picking it up and eating it I'll never know.

Back in the main building, Marilyn and I did have some distractions. I was sitting reading the papers in the conservatory one morning when another guest walked in wearing the regulation white fluffy dressing gown. 'Good morning,' I said cheerily as she sat down opposite me. She smiled back and I carried on reading. Then I looked up. Did she know her gown had fallen open at her waist and I could see everything? And I mean everything. I went back to my paper. And when I looked up I realised I had been wrong. There was more to see. My companion's gown had opened above the waist as well. Now I could almost see her breasts. Another attempt to focus on the crossword. Another look up. Hello. There they are. Two breasts and, basically, a naked woman.

That afternoon I mentioned it to Lady Julia de Saumarez, who ran Shrublands. It turned out the lady was a prostitute from Ipswich who came over for regular rest breaks but couldn't seem to stop touting for business. So was anyone at the health farm quite what they seemed? Marilyn met a man one weekend and stayed up until 4am playing backgammon with him – and I don't think that's a euphemism. The next day one of the other guests approached us. 'I saw the police came to collect your friend this morning,' she said. The backgammon man had been a criminal on the run. He'd thought a health farm was the perfect place to lie low.

Still laughing about our strange new friends, Marilyn and I began the usual torture sessions. I lay naked in a bath while a lady with a hosepipe shot warm water at every inch (almost every inch) of my body. Then I had to stand, still naked, in a corridor when she did the same with ice-cold water. It tones you up, we were told. The inches certainly fell off me.

9

Double Takes

I'm six foot one and, despite the best efforts of the Shrublands team, I've never exactly been thin. And fortunately thin wasn't always required in the early 1970s. My fuller figure would ensure I played the role of Emperor Nero – twice. The first occasion was in a commercial. I was called in to audition for Bob Brooks, a famously talented advertising director. My call was for a bank holiday Monday and my brief was mysterious.

'You will need to entertain the director for five minutes,' I was told.

'Doing what?'

'That's up to you. Just entertain him.' That was all I needed to hear – because no one entertains like Biggins. Stephanie Cole was the first person I called. Then I rang around 20 other old pals. We hatched our plot.

Bob was sitting behind a desk in a tiny rehearsal room

when my five-minute slot came up. I shuffled into the room with a dirty old coat buttoned right up to the neck. Without looking at my host I picked up a broom and began sweeping the floor. Then, after a few sweeps, I pulled off my coat and I was there, in black tie at 10am on a bank holiday morning. From inside the litter bin I picked out a big red book. 'Bob Brooks, this is your life,' I boomed.

Then I called them in. All my pals, all taking on ever more ridiculous roles and all wearing ever more ridiculous costumes – including some of my old kaftans. Stephanie played one of Bob's old school teachers complete with embarrassing stories of his youth. 'And these are your three triplet sisters who were separated from you at birth and who you have never seen before,' I announced towards the end of our skit when things were really getting out of hand.

It could have fallen totally flat and been a disaster. It wasn't. Bob roared with laughter and there were tears running down his cheeks as we all applauded at the end and opened a couple of bottles of cheap pomagne. My 20-plus pals then left the room.

'Hello, I'm Christopher,' I said, sober as a judge and finally sitting down opposite him at the stroke of five minutes.

'You've got the job,' Bob said. Just four wonderful words. It had all been worthwhile.

And after doing that first small commercial for Bob he called me back about his next production. This was the big one. It was for Heineken, part of the classic 'Heineken refreshes the parts other beers can't reach' series.

The advert was also one of the biggest commercials ever filmed – it was an MGM-style production and I think we really may have had a cast of thousands as this was long before special effects could magic these things up on a computer screen. I was Nero, sitting commandingly on my dais at the Colosseum while two young gladiators fought for my pleasure down in the arena. Then they froze, one with the blade at the other's throat, waiting for my decree. If I give the thumbs up the loser lives. Thumbs down and he dies.

But the joke of the advert is that my thumb is all languid and limp. The crowds grow restless while I fail to summon up a signal. So, amid much fanfare, a cool glass of lager is brought in by some over-the-top serving girl. I sip some lager. My thumb starts to twitch. Another sip. More twitches, more lager – then I give the definitive thumbs up. The gladiator is saved. But in the final frame I change my mind, stand up and give a big thumbs down.

By the time filming began I had heard the rumour that Peter Ustinov had turned the role down – despite being offered a staggering £250,000 fee. They had got me for £2,500. But they had promised me repeat fees – and I was convinced that these would make me rich. The advert was so good, so funny. It would never be off the screens, right?

Wrong. Complaints came in after our first broadcast. 'It is blasphemy,' said the first of them. 'How dare you try to sell beer by joking about the death of Christians?' The papers picked up the story and the commercial was pulled within a week – proof that religious censorship isn't exactly a new phenomenon. My hopes of sudden fame and fortune disappeared overnight. But blow me if I wasn't about to play Nero all over again – and this time I even got to fiddle.

The BBC had commissioned an extraordinary new series, *I Claudius*, adapted by Jack Pulman from Robert Graves's book. Like so many of my favourite jobs it was something of a family affair. Jack's wife, Barbara Young, played my mother and we had several old faces from Salisbury, Bristol and other places alongside us as well.

I thought the script was marvellous. I love good writing. I also love good company. And on *I Claudius* it was the best of the best. Our stellar cast included the likes of John Hurt, Sian Phillips, Brian Blessed, Patrick Stewart – the list could go on.

We filmed at the BBC's studios in the Television Centre – not as glamorous as I'd hoped but at least we got to star-spot in the canteen.

But none of us got an easy ride. We were still making the final episodes of the series when the first set started to be broadcast. Our early reviews were quite dreadful.

'It's cheap and nasty. It's like *Coronation Street* with togas,' complained one critic.

But that's the point! I wanted to tell him. We didn't want to do worthy but dull. We wanted to make this wild part of history come alive for the viewers. We wanted to show that life and humanity doesn't ever really change. We're all still flawed, all still making mistakes, all still human beings.

Other reviewers attacked the show on different fronts. They didn't like how it was shot, how it was edited or presented. The critical consensus was that everything was a vast creative misjudgement.

But then a funny thing happened on the way to the forum, so to speak. Our audience figures defied the critical mauling. People started writing to the papers saying how much they liked the show. And the critics changed their minds. More surprisingly still, they admitted they had been wrong. That had to be a first.

The new conclusion was that *I Claudius* was great television. The show went out on BBC1 on Thursday nights and we were watched by millions. We had gone from being hated to being loved in a matter of weeks. And everyone was talking about us. There were only the three main channels then, so if you were a hit on prime-time BBC you were a hit, full stop.

Little wonder that we were all on such a high as we reached our final scenes of series one. All of the big stars, John, Sian, Brian, Patrick and the others, were back to film a dream sequence – and I admit I was nervous about the run-through that Barbara and I had to perform in front of them all. Just before the director called, 'Action,' I turned to Barbara. 'It's like ice-skating. Any minute now they're going to judge us and hold up our scores on cards,' I whispered.

But I needn't have worried. We all wrapped up the shoot and everyone was mixing and mingling and getting on like a house on fire. The good chemistry was all part of the joy of *I Claudius*. I think it showed through and it's a shame so few people today have seen it. People tell me it's been a big seller on DVD, but the vast cast and sky-high repeat fees mean it's hardly ever shown on television. Once more I had enjoyed myself immensely – I had also shared the glory of being in an epic, Bafta-winning show. But once more the financial rewards weren't coming my way.

Now, not everyone would relish going from playing Emperor Nero to Widow Twankey. And I have to admit that I agreed with them. I was offered my first panto about a million years ago – well, 34 to be exact. Jamie Phillips made the call, a marvellous man who, with his partner, the director Dougie Squires of *The Young Generation* fame, was by now a dear pal. They wanted me to go up to Darlington's Civic Theatre, where I would be under the wing of the manager Peter Todd, one of the most wonderful men I've worked with. Peter was able to take a failing theatre, build it up, find it a local audience and make it thrive. That's what he had done in Darlington, where panto was big business and had big budgets to match.

I was asked to join their next production because, after *Porridge* in particular, I was a 'name' who could draw audiences into the theatre. Working with a trio like Jamie, Dougie and Peter would have been extraordinary. But I was insulted and horrified by the request. So I turned it down flat.

'Darling, I am a serious actor,' I said. 'I have done *I Claudius*. I have been on the stage at the RSC with dames of the British Empire. Panto indeed.' And there was more. All the pantomimes I had seen as a boy had been stuffed with old men – with has-beens. I was 26. Jamie and Peter could hardly have offended me more by wanting me to join their company. I told my agent, in no uncertain terms, that I was not, repeat not, doing panto.

I did panto. I did panto in 1974 and I did it every season for the next 33 straight years, missing out only in 2007, when I was in the jungle with Janice. In 2008, I couldn't get back fast enough. So what changed my mind? First, there was the simple fact that Jamie and Peter wore me down by keeping on asking me. They must have known somehow that I would look good in a dress. The other reason was financial. They kept on offering me more money and I'd long since developed very expensive tastes. When the figure got to £1,000 a week, an extraordinary figure in 1974, I knew I had to say yes. And thank God I did.

My first panto was *Mother Goose*, alongside Stephanie Lawrence and Frank Williams from *Dad's Army*. The top-price ticket might have been just £1.90 but the production values put Las Vegas to shame. That's why I fell for it. We had a sensational season at the Civic Theatre. The costumes and sets were so over the top that they made you laugh. And the audience reaction was just incredible. Forget polite applause in the classics. Soaking up the ovations in panto was like being a pop star. I was high as a kite on the buzz of it. Why on earth had no one ever told me about panto before?

'Will you come back again next season, Christopher?'

'One hundred per cent yes.'

And so I did. That year we did *Dick Whittington* alongside Eve Adam and my love affair with the genre grew. I was also introduced to one of Britain's most underrated theatrical dynasties – and a set of friends I am to proud to have in my back pocket to this day. The first of them was Cherida Langford, whose very little sister is of course Bonnie – who was a terrifyingly talented, terrifyingly precocious but terrifically nice little girl. She is one of our most underrated talents and a dear friend. But in the Langford family she wasn't alone. Cherida's daughter Scarlett Strallen is my god-daughter, and then I'm adopted godfather to Summer Strallen. Years later I would be the Baron in *Chitty Chitty Bang Bang* – Scarlett was Truly Scrumptious – and it felt like a real family affair. Years after that I was applauding like a man possessed at the London Palladium on the night Summer took over as Maria in *The Sound of Music*. Summer, you were great, just the way I knew you'd be.

I did three years of pantos in Darlington. *Dick Whittington* was followed by *Jack and the Beanstalk* and I ended each season desperately looking forward to the next. As a postscript, I met the brother of one of my early panto stars in London one summer. He had been married and might even have had children. But something told me to invite him back to my flat for a drink. Suffice it to say that he was a dear friend and he lit up my life for the best part of a year.

One other thing happened when I was doing those first few pantos in Darlington. I got a frantic phone call from Jack Tinker. 'It's opened!' he screeched. 'It' being a new Covent Garden restaurant called Joe Allen – a legendary theatrical haunt for Broadway stars in New York that we had all been desperately hoping to see open over here.

'What's it like?'

'It's perfect. You're going to love it. I'll take you, the moment you get back to London,' Jack said. He was as good as his word. And from then on we were never out of the place.

'Our bank managers will think we're being blackmailed by an ex-lover called Joe Allen,' I told Jack. Every cheque I wrote seemed to be to that name.

The room is an old fruit warehouse – and it's wonderful

that it's still so often full of old fruits to this day. Old fruits all gazing at London's most handsome waiting staff. Jack and I felt that the only bad thing was that the menu hadn't quite been adapted well enough for London. At the start there were still grits on it – my claim to restaurant fame is that I persuaded them to be taken off. Grits indeed. In Covent Garden.

Jack and I also had fun with the rest of the menu. We would have tapioca puddings sent around the room to other diners, in the way old rich men sent drinks to beautiful girls. One wild night we had literally dozens of puddings being passed around, often to people who were still on their starters. The cheque we wrote that night was particularly large, I seem to remember. But since when did I worry about spending money?

Joe Allen had wonderful staff – many of whom lit up my life, for a while, along the way. Tim Clarke was one who lit things up the brightest. He was one of the maitre d's and our really important relationship turned into a strong friendship.

What a lot of people don't know is that Joe Allen himself does exist, though he spent most of his time looking after the restaurants in the States. In London the new restaurant was run by Joe's right-hand man, Richard Polo. For the manager of such a marvellous, theatrical restaurant, Richard is a surprisingly quiet man. But when he does talk he is very funny, very dry and very good company. In rare quiet moments he would join Jack and I at our table. I said once that I had never quite got into opera. So he asked me to join him there one night to see if I got the bug. He enjoyed introducing people to new areas of life, though this didn't always go to plan. A good example was when he decided I should join him on a ski trip to St Anton.

'See you at lunch. Good luck!' he called out as he headed up to the top of the mountain on day one. I was off to ski school, where my instructor was about to learn that I wasn't a model pupil.

'Follow me,' he yelled at the group in a sexy foreign accent.

'No, no, no!' I yelled. 'I can't start because I don't know how to stop. None of us does. We're not following anyone, anywhere. You need to teach us here.' A mini-rebellion began. And by the time I met Richard at lunchtime I'd handed back my skis, cashed in all my lift passes and was preparing for a different challenge. I wanted to master the art of après-ski. Shopping, saunas, steaming hot drinks. Turns out I'm world-class at all of that. All these years on and Richard is still a good pal. His wife, Tricia, is the creative genius behind the Designers Guild empire and made the vast curtains in my double-height living room at home. Her brother and his wife, Simon and Alison, have also become great pals and I'm godfather to their two boys, Sebastian and George. So many good people – all because I fell in love with dinner in Covent Garden.

In the first few glory years of Joe Allen the bar would be full of everyone in theatreland, all desperate for a table. They'll kill me for writing this, but here are a few secrets. The rows of tables are all numbered. The 50s are furthest away from the door as you arrive and 52 is one of the best in the house. You can see everyone arrive from there. I saw it as my home from home.

Table 40, meanwhile, is in chilly social Siberia. Tucked away in a corner I chose to ignore. Until one particular day.

'Oh, Chris, would you mind sitting on 40 today?' I was asked at the desk.

I was appalled. 'Well, yes, I would mind actually. Why?'

'There is a reason but we can't say. Would you mind please just trusting us?'

So I agreed. Though walking through the restaurant to my social-death corner was mortifying. Forget the rope bridge on *I'm A Celebrity*. Walking across that was a breeze compared to my humiliating trudge across Joe Allen's that day. I ordered soup – perfect food for a social outcast. And as I waited for it to arrive I was fuming even more. What I couldn't understand was that table 52 – *my* table 52 – remained empty. It sat there, inviting, alluring, teasing. 'Why can't I sit there? Why?' I was screaming in my head like a sulky teenager. Then I found out.

In walked Elizabeth Taylor.

Everything in the restaurant seemed to freeze. You think time can't stand still? It can when Ms Taylor is in the room.

I found out later that the manager had wanted me at table 40 because they wanted the closest people to Miss Taylor to be the kind of guests who wouldn't spend the whole meal gawping. Bad call. Gawp I did. Some men, in the presence of those extraordinary lavender eyes, would have dribbled soup down their chin. I was one of those men. My friend Jeremy Swan and I had half risen from our seats as the great lady had arrived. We felt the least we could do was to welcome her to our little corner of the restaurant. When she and her companion left (there was no way on earth I was leaving before her and missing a single second of the show) we half rose again.

'Gentlemen, it's been a pleasure,' she said.

Pure class. And those eyes. Oh, those eyes.

'A decaff cappuccino, please.' Apparently, that was my catchphrase at Joe Allen. Back then it wasn't as common or as easy a drink to make as it is today. And at one year's staff Christmas party I had agreed to supply a bunch of pals to turn the tables on the staff by waiting at the tables for a change. The wonderful Patricia Hodge was one of the many who answered my call, as was my then agent, Jonathan Altaras. And how we all worked. We were all dripping with sweat by the time the desserts were served – even the famously cool-as-ice Patricia.

'Can I get anyone a coffee?' I asked one table of four at the end of service.

'Yes – a decaff cappuccino,' yelled 80 people in perfect unison.

I love that place.

Must all good things come to an end? They haven't at Joe Allen, but they have certainly changed. The restaurant world has been in a state of flux for some time now, probably since Jeremy King, Joe Allen's beloved maitre d', and Christopher Corbin, the extraordinarily tall manager at Langan's Brasserie, joined forces to start building their marvellous new restaurant empire. The boys took over the Caprice when its old chef left but they had some very tricky times.

Business was slow and the bills were adding up. So enter, stage left, Mr Biggins. They asked me to organise some Sunday-night cabaret. What an absolute hoot. I was in my element. We had a piano and I brought in drag acts from all sorts of dodgy East End pubs. It was a riot from start to finish. I can't claim that my Sunday nights were why the Caprice did ultimately offer the hottest tables in town. But it did certainly heat up.

The boys are now at the Wolseley, the former bank turned Wolseley car showroom near the Ritz on Piccadilly. Breakfast, morning coffee, lunch, afternoon tea, dinner, late dinner. I've enjoyed them all there. Their newer place, St Alban in Regent Street, is just as good. As someone who adores New York, I have to say that London is still so far ahead in the glamour restaurant stakes. It's equally far ahead in the glamorous restaurateur stakes. Jeremy, Chris, Richard Polo, Richard Caring and all the others. I love them all. And I particularly love that they always give me a table.

After three seasons doing panto in Darlington, Peter Todd moved down to Brighton – and I moved down with him. We did three seasons at the Theatre Royal, starting with *Aladdin* with dear Dora Bryan. As a boy I had seen Dora dominate the stage in *Hello Dolly*, and now it seemed so amazing that all these years later I wasn't just sharing a stage with her, but also had top billing over her. It was actually slightly embarrassing, though very, very wonderful. How extraordinarily the world can turn.

My Brighton years ended with *Dick Whittington* with Sheila Burnet and the underrated cabaret performers Kit and the Widow. I'm glad to say love was still in the air in theatreland that year. Kit met the model Katie Rabett and I was thrilled to see them marry shortly afterwards. They're a lovely couple and fabulous friends of mine.

I'd been happy on the south coast because I like doing several years in the same place. Every year you seem to get better reactions. The audiences seem to like to see familiar faces in the casts. Coming back adds to the sense of occasion. The local papers and radio stations like it and you can earn a little extra cash doing some openings and personal appearances around the towns. When you don't have much other work lined up for the year ahead, that kind of thing is a useful bonus.

Just along the coast I had a good and bad experience in Eastbourne. I had agreed to do *Nosferatu* – with just one week to rehearse, learn the lines and get ready for the opening. I had one particularly complicated big number but as we used taped music rather than an orchestra I thought I had a way to make life easier. I wrote out my lyrics on huge cue cards and put them in the orchestra pit so I could read them in an emergency.

Then the audience arrived. Every old lady in Eastbourne seemed to be in the house. All of them had big coats. And all the coats in the front row were draped carefully over the edge of the pit, obscuring all my vital cue cards. The moment I saw what was happening from the wings I started to laugh so much that I forgot my first-night nerves – and I did the show without getting a single line wrong. But would my pal Peter Straker, playing the vampire, be as lucky? He had a big number in a bed scene with one of his victims – and he had put pages of sheet music all over the sheets.

Luckily for him, even Eastbourne's redoubtable old dears couldn't scupper that plan. He was word-perfect as well.

Cambridge is another city where I put down some strong panto roots. I did five years there in the late 1980s and early 1990s and all this time on people still ask me when I might be taking a show back there. My answer is always the same: 'As soon as someone gets the right budget and makes me a good enough offer.' The Cambridge Arts Theatre is a beautiful place to perform – and the city is a wonderful place to live for a few months. It was also where I learned a big new part of my craft.

'Do you want to do several seasons with us?' producer and pal Ian Ross asked me when I first got the booking there. He too knew the value of having familiar names back year after year and wanted a way to tie me down. 'You can have a completely free hand. You can cast, write and direct as well as star.'

How could I say no?

We started with *Jack and the Beanstalk* and I was on cloud nine to be in control. I'm at my happiest when I'm in charge of a whole production. And that has to be good for everyone concerned. If the man at the top is on good form the whole company does well. I was on good form in Cambridge. I had the marvellous Michael Kirk as my co-writer – and he was my clear first choice for each year's new villain. His Abanazah in *Aladdin* was particularly good, though my Widow Twankey wasn't too shabby either.

But now we're back to all the swings and roundabouts of my life. The good times in Cambridge became a memory when I moved on and locked myself into a new two-year panto contract to perform with Cannon and

Ball. It was at the height of their fame, but it's hard to realise now just how popular they were. They were box-office gold. Audiences went crazy for them. On stage they were hilarious and could do no wrong. But off stage it was all a little bit different.

After seasons in Birmingham, I joined the boys at the Mayflower in Southampton, a lovely theatre where I'm opening again in *Cinderella* in December 2008. Book now to avoid disappointment. I'm hoping for fewer crises this time. With Cannon and Ball I was Nurse Tickle in *Babes in the Wood*. I had a short ra-ra skirt for one scene, and when I bounced on to the stage wearing it I always got one of the loudest laughs of the night. Maybe that was the problem. One night, halfway through the first act, I was in the quick-change room and found that the skirt had been lengthened so it fell well below the knee. I couldn't believe it. But there was nothing I could do. I only had seconds to change before heading back on stage. My entrance had no impact at all. It got precious few laughs and my whole first scene went flat.

Now I very rarely get angry. I very rarely lose my temper. But, when I do, be very afraid. I got angry after that performance. I tore into the two stars so ferociously that little Bobby Ball ran from the theatre to get away. 'Why are you spoiling things for the audience? Why don't you want them to have something to laugh at? Why does it all have to be about you?' I'd shouted.

Years later Bobby wrote to me saying it had been a misunderstanding. He said the skirt hadn't been changed because they wanted to stop me from overshadowing them. It was because they hadn't thought it appropriate that the kids in the audience should see my knees. If that was their opinion, then they were wrong. Not only were my costumes perfectly acceptable for kids, many of them had actually been designed by them. 'Design a dress for Biggins in panto' or some such phrase had been a *Blue Peter* challenge earlier in the year. At this point I'd had a close and happy relationship with *Blue Peter* for some time. They'd suggested the costume competition when the theatre first said I was going to be Nurse Tickle. Thousands upon thousands of entries came in – I still have them in a book at home and they're extraordinary. So there was no question that kids – or their parents – wouldn't approve of my ra-ra skirt. It was panto, for God's sake. That's what we do.

Funnily enough, the boys were very nice socially. The skirt aside, we always got on well backstage, just as I have got on well with almost everyone else I have worked with. It was on stage that they seemed different – and that's a pattern you see repeated time and again with comedians. It's incredibly hard to find generous comics. The stress of making people laugh does terrible things to people – that's why so many comedians get divorced, turn to drink or die young. That's why a lot of them do all three.

10

Panto Dames

For far too long I felt I was always fighting against the snobbery about panto – and I couldn't get too angry about it because I suppose I had felt it myself when I'd first been approached for the gig. The gentle mockery has come and gone in waves. There were years when I heard people in box offices talk about 'has-beens' in the casts. 'But these are the same has-beens you need to win your biggest audiences of the year. And win them we do,' I wanted to scream. In fact, I probably did scream it on several occasions. So, to whoever it was whose ear I bent, I apologise.

I got irate because box-office staff of all people should know the industry a bit better. In the lean years – lean decades even – panto money saw me through many bad times. For some theatres panto money keeps their lights on when all their other worthy productions play to half-empty houses. So don't knock it or mock it. Admit that you need it.

Also, I know it sounds a bit of a cliché, but panto really is a breeding ground for new audiences. We bring in first-timers as kids. We let them get comfortable with the inside of a theatre and we show them true magic. We only need to get a few of them hooked to secure our futures. I'm sure Ian McKellen got new bums on seats when he first did panto at the Old Vic in London in 2004. I didn't really like that production. But Sir Ian did make a most sensational Widow Twankey.

And don't knock panto performers either. Panto is the hardest work I do all year. It is relentless. My dear pal Paul O'Grady had something like 19 costume changes when he did *Snow White* at the Victoria Palace in London in 2005. He says he used to thank God for good old hook-and-loop fasteners every night and I know just how he feels. You need flu jabs and you need to be fit and fast to survive. Forget matinées on Wednesdays and Saturdays. With panto we do two shows a day, six days a week. I sleep in my dressing gown with my make-up on between them. Then I wake up, try to eat something, touch up my face and it's show time all over again. I'm savagely anti-social. Even if I'm near home I like to stay in a hotel so I can know the towels on the bathroom floor will all be picked up and replaced for me and for a few brief weeks I won't have to worry about running my house.

If you're going to make it in panto, you need to have quick wits as well. At best we have two weeks of rehearsals. Sometimes it's just a week of technicals, then you open. And the big shows are mini-musicals. If the money is there we can have a cast of 20, a full band if not an orchestra. We have dancers, lavish sets and, yes, a seemingly endless series of costume changes. And, oh yes, we have some of the most challenging audiences in the business.

'There's a bit of a lull here. The kids all talk through this bit,' one producer said to me during a run-through years ago.

I was immediately at my imperious best. 'My dear, no one talks through my songs,' I declared. And no one did.

It's harder to achieve this effect now, as kids' attention spans get ever shorter. As performers we either give in to all this and go on to autopilot or we fight back. I fight back. I think laterally, come up with ideas, devices, movements, visual jokes, anything at all to keep the kids' eyes on stage and on me. Talk through my songs indeed. But while the challenge of panto is to win over a new audience, the reward is to see it in their eyes when you succeed.

It's worth it when you do. Richard Briers wrote me a lovely note four years ago after a show in Richmond which his family had loved. Other letters have meant just as much. Here's one I've treasured for years.

'I would like to make a strong complaint about your pantomime and would be grateful for a refund for 14 tickets in the upper balcony. We came in a gang of 14 and among us was my elderly mother who unfortunately gets a big confused occasionally. She is a lady who had a protected upbringing but has had great experience of the world having been a General Practitioner in Airedale, Castleford, for 40 years before her retirement. She has experienced many strange things in her life as you may now realise, since Yorkshire people are a little odd. However, I do not think she ever expected that she would experience the strange sensation of some chocolate fudge being fired up her skirt from a catapult by a woman wearing a hat containing a dozen eggs and a chicken. She has never been the same since.'

Fortunately my correspondent, a Dr R Sloan, added a postscript. 'Seriously, we enjoyed the pantomime very much indeed and wish you all success.'

What I also love is to see the faces in the front rows to gauge whether or not they've got it. Catchphrases always help with this. How I love them.

'Now, you'll probably have noticed I'm a little on the plump side,' my Mother Goose said in one of the early Darlington years. 'I've always got a carrier bag full of sweeties ready in case I feel a bit peckish. But I've got to stop eating them all the time, so if you see me reach for the bag can you all shout out, "Naughty, naughty" to stop me? Will you do that, boys and girls? Will you?'

Will they ever.

The kids deafened us throughout all the years I used that line. And they never missed a thing. If all I did was move my hand to my side, even in a moment when I wasn't the centre of attention (and I hated not being centre of attention), at least one set of kids would scream out their warning.

But for all that hullabaloo I sometimes think I like it even more when the kids go completely silent. When they're captivated and transported by the story or the spectacle. I respond to the kids who are feeling it. Back in Darlington in the early years, one little boy was certainly doing that. His hair was perfectly combed and he was all smartly dressed in his Sunday best – a blue sweater with a shirt and tie. He was only about seven and he seemed adorable – something about him told me he was proud to be looking all grown up, but still nervous about the whole occasion. I responded to that.

The only odd thing was that, every time I looked over, his mum seemed to be talking to him. And, as I say, no one talks through my numbers. I redoubled my efforts to draw everyone's eyes to me. I got my reward when we got to the song sheet. The little lad from the front row was first to rush up on to the stage, pushed around a bit by some of the older, bigger kids but determined not to get left behind. I picked him to talk to and was blown away. He was so confident, so thrilled to be there and he helped me win so many extra laughs. At one point I looked down at his mum to check she was enjoying it – and saw her dissolve into tears. Odd.

At the end of that number I would dash into the wings for my final, and fastest, costume change of the night. I had a whole new outfit for the finale. But my usual helpers were, frankly, useless. They were all crying too. What the hell was going on? 'Tell you later, Chris. Do us proud.' And I was pushed back on stage.

My little friend was beaming with pride in the front row as I did the curtain calls. His mum, meanwhile, was still wiping away tears.

'He's blind, Christopher,' the director told me when the curtain finally fell.

I'm not sure, really, why that story means so much to me. I never saw that little lad or his mum ever again, though his mum did write me a lovely thank-you note for taking him up on the stage. I so hope he never lost the magic of that night. It would be wonderful if he's working in the theatre in some way. It would prove that fairytales don't always end.

I got my next big job offer in 1975 and I was determined to resist it – just as I had been determined to resist the call to do panto. So much for my so-called professional judgement.

Jeremy Swan made the call. He was in charge of a new children's show about a group of ghosts trying to become millionaires. To be honest, it did sound like a bit of a hoot. But I didn't want to know. 'I'm a serious ac-tor,' I declared, yet again. Sure, I had enjoyed my various guest appearances on *Blue Peter* and the show even gave me a special silver *Blue Peter* badge for a lifetime of services rendered. It may well be the closest thing I'll ever get to a knighthood from the Queen, especially bearing in mind my excruciating 'Puck, Philip' incident, which I will also get to later.

Anyway, back in 1975 I turned *Rentaghost* down. Then, just like panto, I was asked a few more times and eventually caved in. Thank God. All my years on *Rentaghost* were extraordinarily happy times – which I think shines through on the screen. Jeremy, a mad Irishman and one of the funniest men I know, helped create that perfect atmosphere. In the past I'd done a few *Jackanory Playhouse* shows with him and Willie Rushton and had a feeling it would be good to be back in company. I was oh so right. In my *Rentaghost* days, we had Michael Staniforth, already a big West End star, playing the lead. Another great pal was Anne Emery, one of the maddest and most talented women you will ever meet. It was Anne who taught Wayne Sleep how to tap dance and I saw her recently giving a tour-de-force performance as the grandmother in *Billy Elliot* in London.

Back to *Rentaghost*. The show wasn't just camp. It was way beyond camp. It was actually surreal, which is quite an achievement for what people constantly denigrate as 'just' kids' TV. The show was also stuffed with a roster of wonderful performers and over-the-top performances. I was Adam Painting, the department-store owner who was always being plagued by the ghosts' failed ventures.

All the episodes were bizarre and kitsch and hilarious, but our first totally surreal Christmas special still stands out in my mind. I come down a flight of steps singing 'Santa Claus is Coming to Town' as the whole set around me vanishes in a whirl of glitter, lights and totally fake snow. It was really an MGM-style fantasy sequence, though it was all done on a budget of, well, almost nothing. BBC penny-pinching at its best – but we made something wonderful out of it, just the way professional entertainers always do. If you've got enough talented people around you, and if everyone thinks laterally and goes the extra mile, the cheapest sets can still look fantastic. And the show will be great. The *Rentaghost* era turned out to be a hugely important part of my life. Kids loved the show – and today those kids are 30- or, more likely, 40-something people who haven't quite forgotten it. I'm sure it could stand a revival and, yes, I'm available.

What else do I love about kids' TV? The things that go wrong that only the adults spot. On another *Jackanory Playhouse*, we were once filming a scene where six beautiful princesses sleepwalk into a fantasy world where they dance with six handsome princes. I'm one of the princes, believe it or not, and one of my favourite ladies, Edward Fox's wife, Joanna David, was one of the princesses. Now Joanna likes a laugh as much as me. Embarrassingly enough, it proved to be her downfall.

'Now you have to do this in a single shot because we can't go into overtime,' came the call from the directors. In those union days overtime was the producer's biggest fear. This sequence was particularly important – we had to get it right first time.

The main camera was at the centre of the set and the 12 of us were to dance fast and furiously around it. Just before we got the call for 'Action' I told a joke. The good thing was that everyone laughed and as we were supposed to be having fun it made it all look good when the camera did roll. The bad news for poor Joanna was that she laughed so much that she peed herself. The worse news for everyone was that the mini centrifugal force we set up in our circular dance meant that the effects of her little lapse spread far and wide.

Then there was the *Rentaghost* episode with Sue Nicholls when I unaccountably farted at the end of the scene. We both fell about laughing and Sue, understandably thinking we would have a break and then do a retake, signalled past the cameras for someone to get her a cup of tea. What she didn't know was what a slave-driver Jeremy was. Retake? Just because someone farted and someone else made a 'T' sign to her colleagues behind the cameras? No way. 'Let the audience see what amateurs you are,' was Jeremy's verdict. So we just carried on with the next scene. It's something else I've not seen (or, more accurately in my case, heard) in a blooper show. Or at least not yet.

Shows like *Rentaghost* bring one big benefit to a social butterfly like myself. You do a lot of filming in a very short time. Then you get plenty of time to do other jobs, spend all your money and have fun. I did all three.

On the work front I'm proud to say that I was in one of Cameron Mackintosh's last straight plays, *Touch of Spring*, and in one of his first hit musicals, *Side by Side by Sondheim*. His is another friendship that I treasure. He is someone else I think was born laughing.

The Sondheim musical review was the brainchild of dear old Ned Sherrin. Ned was the ultimate theatrical raconteur. He was one of the funniest men I had ever known – and I've known a hell of a lot of them. I always hoped he would do me the honour of reading the eulogy at my funeral. How awful, in October 2007, to have to go to his. He was loved, and he is missed. Maybe that's the best eulogy any of us can wish for.

Anyway, back in 1977 Ned was my idol. He loved Sondheim's musicals and created *Side by Side* himself with Julia McKenzie, Millicent Martin and David Kernan at his side. The show opened in the most unlikely of places – a theatre at Guy's Hospital near London Bridge. The story behind the venue makes me laugh to this day. Apparently, a Shakespeare-loving, theatre-mad doctor is behind it all. When he died, leaving a large bequest to the hospital, his eccentric explorer of a wife was asked what should be done with his money.

'Build a new theatre in his memory,' she said, before setting off on her travels.

So the trustees found the land, got the builders in, created the auditorium and when she got back from her latest journey they invited the doctor's widow to the gala opening.

She walked through the doors and stopped in horror.

'What's wrong?' they asked.

'I meant an operating theatre,' she replied.

I do hope that story is true. But, either way, the doctor's – and perhaps the hospital's – bad luck is our good fortune as actors. It's a bijou but lovely performance space. And that night in 1977 it staged some pure musical magic. I was buzzing with excitement after the curtain calls and got a pile of 10p pieces to ring Cameron, in New York, from the phone box in the hospital's main entrance. 'Cameron, you have to buy this show.'

So he did. Sight unseen.

He raised the money to take the production to the West End and, after a hugely successful run, he wanted to take it on tour. Unfortunately, the members of the original cast were committed to other shows, so it had to be recast. Everyone told Cameron that he had to cancel the transfer as no one else could play the key roles. It was ridiculous. Doom-sayers got even more negative when I was mooted to replace dear Ned. 'Biggins can't play that kind of role,' went the rumour.

'Biggins will be brilliant,' said Ned. And Cameron listened, so I got the job. It was a marvellously flexible contract. The likes of Michael Aspel and I took turns to be narrator in various theatres around the country.

What fun that so many years later I was able to renew my connection to a more modern version of a Sondheim classic.

'Biggins, Biggins, Biggins.' In 2008, the crowds outside the Empire Leicester Square were screaming my name as

Neil and I arrived for the premier of *Sweeney Todd*. I probably sound like a classic luvvie, but there really were tears in my eyes at that reaction. And once inside the cinema I loved the film, I loved the ridiculously underrated Helena Bonham Carter and I loved Johnny Depp. There was a suitably big party afterwards – for some 2,000 people, I believe. Neil and I fortunately got let into the VIP area and in the corner I spotted director Tim Burton talking to Johnny.

I decided to go for it – if Tim is ever casting another Sondheim film I want to make sure I'm the first person he calls.

'I just wanted to say congratulations, Mr Burton. It was a brilliant film,' I gushed shamelessly.

'No, congratulations to you, Christopher, for being King of the Jungle,' he replied, to my huge surprise and pleasure. To think that Tim Burton watches *I'm A Celebrity*! Less surprising was the fact that Johnny Depp clearly didn't have a clue who I was.

'This is Christopher Biggins and he has just won a really big reality-television show,' explained Tim.

'Christopher, how fascinating,' said Johnny, not entirely convincingly.

I decided it was my cue to melt back into the crowds. But I await a call from Tim. Once again, I am available.

11

The Reverend Ossie Whitworth

Now, I've never really seen myself as a wicked, sex-crazed vicar. But others did. In the Queen's Silver Jubilee year of 1977, I got my greatest, meatiest television role so far. I was cast as the monstrous Reverend Ossie Whitworth in *Poldark*. It was probably the most delicious part I could have imagined.

The show was based on the books by Winston Graham, a pal whose own life was as fascinating as his fictions – though not always in the way he might have wanted. He had written a novel called *The Walking Stick*, he told me. And the moment it got published his wife came down with a mystery illness and had to use a stick for the rest of her life. But what an inspirational woman Jean was. Her disability never got in her way. It never stopped her living, or having fun. Big groups of us from the cast went for days out on the beach in Cornwall with them and once I joined them on holiday in Menorca. To this day I can picture Jean swimming around in a rubber ring and yelling, 'Get me a gin and tonic, darling,' as I watched from the shore.

One other time that week we were all laughing because a lady sunbathing near us was reading one of Winston's other novels. So when she went into the sea for a swim he dashed over and signed it. Did she see him? Did she ever notice the signature? Did she dismiss it as a joke? Who knows, but it was lovely to conjure up a mystery for her. Maybe she can solve it by reading this.

All the exterior scenes for *Poldark* were filmed in Cornwall and cast and crew were all put up in hotels there for around six months at a time. Six months of pure bliss. As usual, I'd fallen on my feet and found myself surrounded by wonderful talents. Angharad Rees and my friend Robin Ellis from Salisbury Rep were the two leads and dear Jane Wymark was my wife. Trudie Styler, who had been at drama school a year below me in Bristol, was Emma Tregirls. Now, years earlier I had been sitting on the floor at one of my old friend the actress Miranda Bell's parties next to a serious and seriously handsome teacher from the north called Gordon Sumner. He talked a lot about music, but who knew that many years later he would get divorced, meet and marry Trudie – and become richer and more famous than all of us.

Anyway, back to *Poldark*. Our lovely bonding time in Cornwall was about to come to an end. There was a lot more work ahead.

For the interiors we rehearsed in London all week, then went up to Pebble Mill in Birmingham to record them. One of my favourite scenes was where the doctor had to tell me I was too heavy to have sex with my pregnant wife. 'Too heavy?' I had to say, appalled, in a tight close-up. It wasn't acting. I wasn't thrilled to have my weight drawn to the nation's attention. But this was far from the most embarrassing of my love scenes. The worst one – though not for me – was when I had to make love to my on-screen wife's sister's feet. Yes, to her feet. *Poldark* was as complicated as that. And that's why it was so hysterical.

Dear Julie Dawn Cole had tried to make everything as wonderful as possible for this tricky scene. All week in London she had spent every moment she wasn't on set down at Dr Scholl's to keep her feet in tip-top condition. They were pummelled and pumiced into the feet of an angel, she swore. On the day we filmed the scene she bathed and scented them before being carried on to the set and placed on the bed for her big moment.

'And, action.'

In a typically tight close-up I loomed up to Julie's feet and out snaked my tongue to do its thing on her toes.

My tongue's big moment was ultimately cut from the show. The producer told us that after much consideration they had decided that the public weren't quite ready for a vicar with a foot fetish. All that effort from poor Julie to have the most fragrant feet in the land was all for nothing. Secretly, I had to admit I quite liked being cut – it made me feel a bit racy, as if Mary Whitehouse herself had deemed me a threat to the morals of the nation. And on this subject I did have a little bit of form. One other scene of mine that ended up banned in America was from *I Claudius*. I had gone to see my mother, played by Barbara Young, to complain that my wife had said she wouldn't have sex with me. 'There are other things you can do,' she said, deliciously suggestively as her hands pulled mine south on her body. We broadcast the scene in Britain, but not in the States. They're happy to show someone getting out a machine gun and killing dozens of passers-by. But suggest a little consensual incest and the networks go crazy.

When *Poldark* was broadcast, the world seemed to go mad. It was a huge hit for the BBC and we all had such good times doing publicity for it. I was voted 'Most Hated Man on Television' by the *Daily Mail*. Which of course I absolutely loved.

One day when I was in the BBC's marvellous rehearsal studios in the wilds of East Acton, I found out that everyone who was anyone was watching. The three main studios in west London were where almost all of the Corporation's main shows were put together. I got into a lift one time to find myself standing next to none other than Eric and Ernie.

'Oh, hi there. How are you?' I asked them, relaxed and friendly as you like. I didn't feel as if I needed an introduction because I felt like I knew them. In Britain we all did. They had been in all our sitting rooms all our lives, after all.

To their huge credit they were charm itself in response. Apparently, they loved my sex-mad vicar in *Poldark*, so they said they thought they knew me as well (which is a little worrying, now I think about it). That lift journey was the start of a lovely friendship. A little while later they both asked me to come on a *Morecambe and Wise* special, which was about the biggest honour in showbusiness. But then Eric died and it never happened. We all lost a great man that day.

Did *Poldark* cast too long a shadow? Perhaps the Reverend Ossie Whitworth was too hard an act to follow. Either way I got a little lost as the 1970s came to their recession- and strike-hit close. Yes, I won several one-off and cameo roles. Crime and comedy dramas were doing well and I had bit parts in *Shoestring*, *Minder* and all the big shows in those worlds. I did a mini-series called *Crime and Punishment*. I still did my wonderfully well-paid pantos each year. I toured with some great theatrical companies. And I spent a lot of money and travelled the world meeting some quite extraordinary new friends – of which a lot more later.

But in the shop-window world of prime-time television I was in danger of fading away.

'Something's going to come up,' I told myself, the way I always have. And in 1981 something did. My career was about to take another bizarre turn. I was on my way to Hollywood.

12

Hollywood – and Back

I was cast in a big-budget American television film called *Masada*. It was serious stuff, telling the story of Mount Masada in Israel. Legend has it that high up on that plateau the Jews had a secure little piece of paradise. They kept their animals, grew wheat and other crops and lived self-sufficient, totally impregnable lives. The Romans, though, wanted some of the action. Our show followed the final assault by the Romans, who apparently built vast ramps up the hillside to the encampment. When they broke in, they found that everyone in the settlement was dead. It was a huge mass suicide and it all added up to a marvellous drama. So much for me being typecast in light entertainment and panto.

The production was told almost entirely from the Jewish point of view, with these good guys all played by American actors. The Romans were the baddies. So they were all played by us Brits. Nothing ever changes there.

It was celebrity city with big-name actors all around. Peter Strauss was there to show us the ultimate in method acting – apparently he had lived in seclusion for months before arriving on set to get fully into the tortured character he had to play. As an aside, however, I must add that he hadn't got Hollywood out of his system entirely. When he found out that another actor's Winnebago was one foot – one foot! – closer to the set than his, it was as if the Third World War had begun. I think this was my first taste of true Hollywood diva-like bad behaviour. I absolutely adored it.

Heading up the list of baddie Brits was Peter O'Toole, a wonderful face from my Bristol days, but if anything a man who had become somewhat aloof since then. He also proved to be a lot less fun.

My role was as a sort of aide-de-camp to Senator Pomponius Falco, played by David Warner. The first set of filming took place on Mount Masada itself in Israel – we had been flown there first class and I was in my element. Even on that first flight I lived the dream. I had fillet steak and scrambled eggs at 35,000 feet and thought it was, quite literally, the height of chic. The good times carried on rolling when we got to the location. On our days off most of the actors lazed by the pool, getting drunk and throwing furniture into the desert. I probably did my fair share of that. But Clive Francis and I also wanted to get out and see some of the country. David Warner was kind and lent us his driver, so we had a chance. I loved it.

Back on set, Clive and I had an obvious way to repay David's favour – by trying to help him out on what turned out to be a very difficult shoot. David was strangely nervous about his role – and Peter O'Toole was for some reason being difficult with him, which just made everything worse. Clive and I tried to hold David's hand and keep up his confidence. But it wasn't easy. As an actor, once you lose confidence in your ability in a role, it's very hard to get it back. Directors, other actors and even audiences are like sharks – they can smell fear. I know that David triumphed through this bad patch. If you watch the show today I don't think you'll know how tense it all was at the time.

After the location work in Israel, the interiors were due to be shot in Hollywood. No surprise to hear that I was beside myself with excitement. But for a while my California dream was under threat. The unions weren't happy with these uppity Brits coming over and taking jobs from all the American actors busy bussing tables in restaurants. But sanity prevailed and our passports got the right stamps.

I was handed another first-class air ticket to LA – but just before the flight date I cashed it in. I wanted an even ritzier experience. I used my refunded ticket money to fly Concorde to New York. As this cost more than the LA fare I needed to squeeze on to a cheap and far from cheerful commuter flight across to the west coast. But I didn't regret the journey for a moment. Concorde was a truly wonderful plane. With Neil's help I managed to fly on it twice more before it disappeared from the skies. I still think it was a tragedy – and a mystery – that it got taken out of service. Yes, it was small and cramped and noisy inside. But the people. The glamour. The thrill of it. You just can't feel that special on any other plane.

When I finally made it to sunny LA, I found another way

to fiddle the system and make some extra cash. We were given money to cover the cost of whatever accommodation we chose. I chose the apartment above LA's Joe Allen, kindly lent to me for free by the man himself.

I adored California. I was having a ball and partied and networked like a man possessed. I loved the mood of LA and was convinced my future would be played out under those tall palm trees. So many doors opened for me when I was in Hollywood with the *Masada* crew. If only I'd known how fast they would close.

When the *Masada* shoot ended I spent three months tying up loose ends in Britain before returning to Hollywood in triumph, ready for acknowledgement as the leading actor of my generation. Oh dear. Three months in Hollywood is like three millennia. I had been forgotten faster than you can say 'valet parking' or 'facelift'.

Kids' TV saved me when I came back from America with my tail between my legs. In 1982, when I was a rapidly filling-out 33-year-old, the producer Tony McLaren approached me about a new show he was planning. It was to be called *On Safari*.

'We think it's perfect for you, Christopher. Are you interested?'

'I'm so sorry but I'm not.'

Another catastrophic career misjudgement was on the cards. But once again I was blessed. Because the more often I turned the show down the more Tony and his team increased the money.

When it reached £1,000 an episode, I knew I had to say yes, if only to save my agent's sanity. It was incredible.

After several fallow years when I was spending most of my time socialising and spending money, I was suddenly catapulted into the big league. Unlikely as it seemed, I was apparently the highest-paid children's television presenter in the country. You could buy a house for £30,000 back then, I'm told. So when people asked me about the show I told them I was doing it purely and simply for the money.

Like hell I was. Just like panto, just like *Rentaghost*, just like everything else I ever turned down, *On Safari* turned out to be a blast. I loved it – not least because I was lucky enough to be given such a big part in the pre-production meetings. We all sat around talking through the format, the challenges, the structure of the show. Then we had a session trying to think of decent catchphrases. 'Safari So Goody' was mine – if only I could have earned royalties every time someone used it.

The show we came up with was full of challenges, eliminations, endurance ordeals and an awful lot of swampy, gungy mess. No wonder I took to *I'm A Celebrity* so easily when the time came. Best of all about my new show was the chance to get all my favourite old pals on board as guest stars. We had a famous guest each week. So I could repay an awful lot of favours and spend time with all my favourite people. Liza Goddard was one of the first pals that I called. A few years earlier she and I had done a very forgettable show where, I think, I played an advertising agency boss, and I got on famously with both Liza and David Cobham, her husband. What I loved about Liza was that she never stopped laughing. But I was so mean to her. I would do terrible things to wind her up. I would dry up on set and make it look as if it was her fault. And I would be so convincing that she would end up apologising to the crew for messing up the scene. Off set she never stops laughing. So as pals we were pretty well suited from the start.

In other *On Safari* shows I brought in everyone: Bonnie Langford, Wayne Sleep, Suzi Quatro, Ruth Madoc, Christopher Timothy – the list goes on and on.

Even better news came when the ratings were announced. We were incredibly popular, so one season turned to another, then another. We had long runs, we did Christmas specials, we lasted right until 1984.

Throughout most of it I also had one other great pal at my side: Gillian Taylforth. Right at the start the producers had asked who I thought they should approach to be my Girl Friday for the show. Gillian is one of the funniest women I have ever met, dry and quick, and I adore her. She was an obvious choice and loved the programme as much as I did. Best of all, she didn't even mind our awful closing lines.

'Say goodbye, Gillian.'

'Goodbye, Gillian,' she chimed up as the theme tune played. I don't know how we got away with it for so long.

Kenny Everett was another great *On Safari* guest – though, through no fault of his own, some of our other meetings ended in disaster. I went to his last Capital Radio broadcast, where they were serving canapes and little snacks around the room. I thought the smoked salmon looked and smelled a little bit suspect. But look at my waistline. I'm hardly a fussy eater. So I tucked in anyway. What was the worst that could happen? One poor lady out for a big night at the theatre was about to find out.

I began to feel ill later that afternoon. A bit sweaty, a bit sick. But I had a dozen or so people coming round to the flat at the Phoenix Theatre that night before we all headed off to see a new production of *Oklahoma* just down the road at the Palace Theatre. The lead took a deep breath and sang out his first note – and I threw up all over the hair of the poor, poor lady in the row in front of me. It was explosive and awful. I staggered out of the stalls and threw up again all over the carpet in the lobby. As I stumbled towards the street the last thing I saw was the poor lady who had been in front of me rushing to the ladies' loo. She was so well dressed. She had probably spent all afternoon at the hairdressers for the big night. Whoever you were, I do apologise. And if it is any consolation at all, you weren't the only one to suffer in this fashion.

When it comes to socialising, booze has been my only real downfall. I think I'm a pretty happy drunk. I don't pick fights, I don't get maudlin, I don't start singing unless people really insist. But back in my party years I did have one key failing. I threw up. Really quite often.

One of the first dear pals to experience this first-hand was the wonderful former hotelier Sally Bullock – who I learn, as I write this book, has sadly died. But I shall tell these few stories because I know they would make her smile. When we first met she was managing the gorgeous Pelham Hotel in South Kensington and threw a lot of lavish parties for guests and friends. I loved to be there. The first time I threw up in Sally's presence was after one of these parties at the Pelham. I did at least make it to the lavatory in time. Though I fear I made such a mess it was out of service for about a week afterwards.

Anyway, dear Sally ensured I was put in a room in the

hotel to sleep it all off. And it's just as well as I simply didn't remember a thing about it. The following morning I woke up with no idea where I was. Or even who I was. I wasn't at home and as I was alone I didn't seem to have got lucky with any kind stranger. It's a hotel, I decided, after looking at the layout of the room. But where? And who was I, again? I picked up the phone by the bed. 'Good morning, Mr Biggins,' said a charming lady. 'Can we bring you some tea, coffee or perhaps some breakfast?'

It all came flooding back. As did a sense of over-whelming nausea.

'No, thank you. But I do need a toothbrush,' was all I could think of to say before hanging up and rushing to the en suite. They brought me the toothbrush within five minutes. Hotels don't get much better than that.

Scrapes with Sally became a feature of my life at that time. And they weren't all my fault – at least not at the start. A classic example came when we went to watch some polo at Windsor Great Park. At the end of the event, Sally decided she had drunk too much to drive, so she headed home with friends, leaving me in charge of her Porsche. Oh dear, oh dear.

I headed to a house party given by some very wealthy friends nearby and when I parked I somehow managed to sever the cable that took the brake fluid to the brakes. When I left the party – still sober – I accelerated towards the main road and realised I couldn't stop. It was my typically trivial *Sophie's Choice* moment: crash into the line of Rolls-Royces, Bentleys and Porsches or crash into a tree. I chose the tree.

How to tell Sally? I rang her, mortified. And she didn't

just forgive me, she helped get the AA over to transport me, and the wrecked car, back to London. The only thing she didn't do was wave or smile when my very, very nice man and I pulled up outside the Pelham. She was standing talking to her boss and really didn't want a tow-truck spoiling the ambience of her chic hotel. We were dispatched to a side street so I could hand her back the keys in private.

But back to my now legendary ability to throw up in all the wrong places.

Many years ago I was having Sunday lunch with casting director Marilyn Johnson and a group of other equally great pals. All was going well until someone suggested a few glasses of some thick yellow liqueur. Then a few more. 'Let's go dancing,' someone said.

We all headed off. I was squeezed into the tiny front seat of the tiny Fiat Uno driven by my pal Catherine Hale. I could blame the car's poor suspension as well as the drink for what happened next. But either way I was feeling distinctly queasy by the time we pulled up outside the very ritzy Intercontinental Hotel in Mayfair. And the very moment the charming and uniformed porter opened my car door I let go. I threw up all over his shoes. He stepped back in shock and I threw up again. This time it reached his knees.

Mortified, I slammed the door to try to hide. Catherine slammed on the accelerator and we shot off into the night. To this day I still think of that poor man. What could he have thought of the monster who drove up, threw up and then disappeared?

Maybe Leo Dolan could answer the question. I was at Leo and Sheila's house one New Year's Eve. I'd had too much to drink and was on my way to the loo when I saw their big bed lying empty and inviting through an open door. 'If I just lie down for a few moments I'll feel much better,' I told myself. So I did. I nodded off and when I woke I knew, in an instant, that I was about to be sick and wouldn't make it to the loo. So I did what I had to do. I threw up in Leo's slippers.

Worse still, my host popped upstairs to check up on me as I tried, desperately, to clean up my mess.

Fast forward a few years and I'm on my hands and knees trying to clean another carpet in another dear friend's house. Or, to be exact and far worse, in a dear friend's mother's house. Oh, the shame. This time it was Cameron Mackintosh at his mum's holiday place in Menorca. He is a good, but mad, cook. That night he had concocted a first course laced with vintage champagne, a second course stewed in brandy and a pudding that seemed to include an awful lot of sherry. By the time we got to the coffee stage – with liqueurs, of course – we were all paralytic. When the guests had left I did my throwing-up thing. The carpet that took the brunt wasn't just old, cherished and beautiful. It was a traditional Spanish rug covered in tassels and knots. Trying to clean that up sobered me up faster than any amount of coffee. All my life I have been so lucky to have made so many wonderful friends. The way I've behaved, I know I'm luckier still to have retained so many of them.

After I asked Kenny Everett to guest with me on *On Safari* in the early 1980s, he returned the favour by inviting me to join him in a spin-off show about the Snots. Remember

Above left: 'He won't make old bones,' said Grannie Biggins when I was born. I proved her wrong ...

Above right: My mum and dad, Pam and Bill, on their wedding day. The honeymoon was interrupted by Dad's call-up.

Below left: With my mother and grandfather.

Below right: Biggins beach babes. With my mum and dad, at the seaside. Whatever our circumstances, the three of us always made the most of what we had.

Above left: With Grannie Biggins and my dad. It was from Grannie Biggins that I learned how to be a straight-talker.

Above right: Proving that I had outgrown the 'weak constitution' with which I was born.

Below: St Probus School for Boys – it was at the school's theatre that I first fell in love with performing on the stage. My pal John Brown is pictured on the left of the left-hand picture.

A

Certificate of Merit

awarded to

Christopher Biggins

for representing

South Wiltshire

at the

Wiltshire Drama Association

Verse Speaking—1965

Chairman ....   Drama Adviser ....

Above: An early triumph!

Below left: My small but perfectly formed role as Jenks in the RSC's production of *London Assurance*.

Below right: With Bea Aston, the woman who became my wife. We are still great friends.

Above: My role in *She Stoops to Conquer* was my first proper taste of acting – and after that I was completely addicted.

Inset, above: The wonderful Bristol Old Vic Theatre School.

Inset, below: With Jeremy Irons and Julie Hallam before we all departed for our honeymoon!

I had great fun in TV dramas such as *Upstairs Downstairs*.

Above: The first production I ever directed – *The Orchestra* by Jean Anouilh.

Below: Oh Puck! Playing the lovable sprite in *A Midsummer Night's Dream* at the Regent's Park Open Air Theatre – a wonderful venue, but one that is packed with hazards for actors!

Above: My very first panto, *Mother Goose* in Darlington. Once I had been initiated as a pantomime dame, there was no turning back.

Below: Extraordinarily happy times working on *Rentaghost*.

With the tremendous Barbara Windsor in *Guys and Dolls* – she was Miss
Adelaide and I was Nathan Detroit.   *(© Andrew Mardell)*

There's nothing quite like live television! Prime-time success on *Surprise Surprise* – Cilla and I regularly pulled in 15 million viewers. Sadly, she died just before this book went to press. *(© Rex Features)*

Some of my dearest showbiz pals.

Above: Liza Goddard plays Anne Boleyn to my King Henry VIII.

Below left: With the incredibly talented Bonnie Langford.

Below right: Neil and I having fun with Cilla.

Above: With legend of stage and screen, Julie Andrews.

Below: I couldn't believe it when Michael Aspel pulled out his red book on me!
I had such fun on *This Is Your Life*.

Those famous Margaret Thatcher photographs. What on earth were we talking about? Dennis? Cecil Parkinson?

Above: Showing Her Majesty around backstage – this was the 'Puck's shoe' occasion.

Below: Happy times with Neil. The photograph on the right shows us on the day of our civil partnership ceremony

Above: I finally got my chance to play Baron Bomburst in *Chitty Chitty Bang Bang* at the London Palladium. Louise Gold was my Baroness.   *(© Tristram Kenton)*

Below: And the champagne flowed freely. Dinner at Sue St John's with, amongst others, Jackie Collins, Michael and Shakira Caine and Johnny Gold.

Above: One of the not-so-nice moments on *I'm a Celebrity, Get Me Out of Here!*, partaking in the Bite to Bite Bushtucker Trial. Revolting though it was, I still won dinner for all of us at the camp.

Below: 'Biggins!' was the cry as the winner was announced – and I was somewhat overwhelmed.

(©Rex Features)

King of the Jungle. Going on *I'm A Celebrity Get Me Out of Here!* was quite unlike anything I've ever done before, but I'm tremendously proud to have taken part in it. On to the next challenge!

them? They were one of Kenny's most marvellous creations. The ultimate dysfunctional family, who had first been seen in *The Kenny Everett Video Show*. Thames Television decided they should star in their own spin-off series. Kenny said there was no one better than me to play the wildly gay brother. It was hysterical. So near the knuckle and with a lot more leather and S&M than your average ITV audience had ever seen before. But it turned out that they wouldn't see it this time either.

Halfway through filming, the head of Thames came into our rehearsal room with a grim face. 'I'm so sorry but we will have to pull it,' he said. 'It's too much and we just can't transmit it.' I'd love to see some of those scenes now. All these years on they might look pretty tame. But then again, this was a Kenny Everett production, so you never know.

One afterthought on the much-missed Kenny. I used to joke with him that I should get at least some of the credit for his Cupid Stunt character's 'All of a sudden all my clothes fell off' sketches. My own Cupid Stunt moment came years earlier when I was driving my van back home to Salisbury. I realised too late that they had changed all the one-way systems, so I toppled the van trying to make a dangerously late turn. I was left suspended, by my seatbelt, amid all the rubbish from the floor which was now piled up around my head. I turned off the engine – I'd seen a lot of American films where cars explode the moment they take even a minor bump – and tried to work out how to free myself. As I did so, something started to drip down my back. It turned out to be acid from the battery. Which was very bizarrely set just behind the driver's seat.

My dear father saved me, as usual, by heading over with

a truck to right the van and drive me home. Then, as I told my mother about the accident, the acid finally finished eating away at my trousers. They disintegrated completely and left me standing half-naked in the living room. All it needed was Maisie and it would have been Monday bath night all over again. But at least it was all in the best possible taste.

No prizes for guessing that it was Kenny who introduced me to Freddie Mercury. What a mad, wild and surprising man. I was terrified of him at first. He was a huge rock star with a reputation to match. And he did know how to party. When he, Kenny and I got together I was the shy, quiet one in the corner, which is saying something in itself. And through Freddie I met a whole new set of people from the music world.

Kenny also introduced me to someone else I could both admire and fear: Margaret Thatcher. He had asked me along to the infamous 'Let's bomb Russia' Conservative Party rally when he had the crowd eating out of his giant foam hands. Despite the furore it all caused, the key supporters at the event got personal letters of thanks from Margaret and were then invited to Downing Street for a thank-you reception.

What a place. What a privilege to be there. It's the ultimate Tardis. It keeps on getting bigger and bigger. You go through that wonderful door, up the stairs past the pictures of all the previous prime ministers and into a vast room on the first floor. There are paintings galore up there. 'I collect paintings. I absolutely love all of these,' I told the great lady when she and Denis passed my way.

'Aren't they fantastic?' she said. 'They're all on loan

from galleries and museums around the country and they change them every three months.'

'Do you have more in the flat upstairs?'

'Oh, absolutely not. We've got nothing on the walls there. Just a lot of old rubbish.' And that, I swear, was pretty much that.

But somehow the official photos of the event suggest a different story. Four shots were taken of my conversation with the PM – I've put them in this book because they always make me smile. In the first we are both laughing uproariously. In the second she is holding her fingers around six inches apart and I am looking on fascinated. In the third I have my fingers a good foot apart, we're both laughing uproariously and looking inordinately impressed. If only I could remember what we were talking about. Ronald Reagan? Cecil Parkinson? Denis? Who knows?

Postscript to Margaret. I was driving down Marylebone High Street in 1990 when I heard on the news that she was being ousted from Number Ten. I actually cried. I had to pull over while I listened to the full story. Yes, perhaps she had outstayed her welcome. But what a way to bring the curtain down. I'm not the most political of people. But I believe in self-reliance and getting on with the job in hand. Margaret had seemed to personify all that. And she had star quality, which of course I loved.

13

East End Boy

'Peter, look at this.'

I'd just finished filming as yet another vicar in a short-lived show called *Brendon Chase* and was sitting reading the Sunday papers with my real-life vicar, Peter Delaney. The property section had an article about some new houses being built near Victoria Park, out in Hackney, east London. Peter and I had both talked about each buying ourselves a nice little house. But then we remembered that he was as poor as the proverbial church mouse while I could spend money as fast I could earn it. Faster, in fact. Making matters worse, I'd just found out that neither *Brendon Chase* nor *On Safari* was getting another series and apart from panto I didn't have much else on the horizon.

'Let's go and take a look after church,' Peter said, ignoring our precarious finances.

We were just in time. All but two of the 14 houses had

already been built and sold. So should we try to get the last of them?

'Oh my God, you've got to come and live here.' I was standing outside looking at the development when a woman opposite dashed across the street. 'I'm Pam,' she said, grabbing my hand. 'You're Christopher Biggins. I recognise you from the telly. You have to come and live here. We're a great street and everyone's wonderful. You'll love it.'

And in a way that was what swung it for me. I wanted a neighbour like Pam.

But on a more practical level I also wanted some of the home's other key features. It had its own garage – even then, in 1984, I thought that this would be important in London. It also had a huge, double-height and galleried living room with a great big wall for my ever-growing collection of paintings. I desperately wanted that house – even more so when I was told it was an architectural gem – designed by Piers Gough, no less. So I spoke to the estate agent. The houses were both on the market for what seemed a staggeringly expensive £57,500. I remembered the way Dad did business.

'Tell the builder we'll give them £100,000 for them both,' I said.

'I'm afraid there's no way they'll agree to that.'

'Just tell them.'

Two hours later the agent called back to say that we had a deal.

Peter and I had to beg, borrow and all but steal to raise the £5,000 deposit we each needed. But what fun those early years were. My new best friend Pam opposite. My old best friend Peter next door.

It has been a happy home from the very start. And while Pam is no longer with us and Peter has since sold up and moved on, I now have Neil here to ensure it stays the true centre of my life. I have never felt the need to move to some fancy address in west London or some huge pile in the country. And that's just as well as I've never had the cash. Hackney might not exactly have any Hollywood glamour. But it suited me. And anyway I didn't have time to house-hunt all over again. Life was about to get busier than ever. My lifelong belief that something always comes up was about to come true yet again. This time in spectacular fashion.

I was playing *Babes in the Wood* in Birmingham when Alan Boyd came to see me. He was a big-league London Weekend Television producer and I admit I was flattered by his attention. So many people were still laughing at me for staying loyal to my panto all those years. But it was always my primary shop window and most regular pay packet. It still is, funnily enough. 'Look, I'm doing a series with Cilla Black,' Alan told me amid the wigs and wild costumes of my stuffy little dressing room.

Cilla was in an interesting position in the early 1980s. She had been a huge star, of course. But after 'Anyone Who Had A Heart' and 'Step Inside Love' and all the other number ones, she had disappeared to raise her family – and all credit to her for that. She had stormed back into the public consciousness with a barnstorming performance as a guest on *Wogan* in 1983, proving that we can all have second chances.

After *Wogan*, everyone had been desperately trying to

find her the right comeback vehicle. Boyd's proposal was a huge, studio-based, audience-participation show to be called *Surprise Surprise*. He wanted me to be Cilla's co-host. 'What do you think?' he asked when he had finished explaining the new show's concept.

What did I think?

I was staggered. Practically floored. Yes, I had earned a lot of money in panto and on children's television. Yes, I had been on major BBC dramas, long-running shows and major commercials. But this ITV production was clearly going to be huge. *Surprise Surprise* was set to be a massive, prime-time Saturday-night production. And, while even I forget it sometimes, the show's full title was actually *Surprise Surprise, with Cilla Black and Christopher Biggins*. Beat that.

We were an instant hit with upwards of 15 million viewers. The show was hugely popular, wonderful antics. We did six live shows in one series, and there is nothing quite like live television. On one of them we needed a boat to go under Tower Bridge, which was due to be raised for the occasion. But for some reason it didn't open, so our boat couldn't sail and we moved on.

As usual, Cilla and I said our goodnights and then Cilla got her cue to do her final song, the way each show closed. As she sang Alan rushed up to me. 'Biggins, we're seven minutes under. You need to get Cilla back and keep it going.'

I thought this was the most exciting thing that had ever happened to me. Cilla is standing there, taking in the applause, and then I come on. She looks at me in horror. I will never forget her look as I approached. All the viewers would have seen was her usual lovely smile. But I could see the questions in her eyes. What's going on? What's gone wrong? What do we do?

What we did was talk – and fortunately neither of us is exactly backwards at that. Cilla and I talked and joked on for those long last minutes. Then we collapsed in our usual fit of giggles. I don't think we've ever stopped giggling, which is why I love her.

A lot of the sketches and skits we did on *Surprise Surprise* are forgotten now. What people remember are the reunions – the 'surprise' element that ran through each show. What Cilla and I soon discovered was that lots of these reunited people didn't want to see each other again. Many of our families and so-called 'loved ones' had split up for very good reasons. It took some careful editing to keep the tone light and not give that away each week.

I did three seasons on the show and was on top of that world. The learning curve hadn't just been about big-budget, prime-time television. It was also about fame. Being in 15 million living rooms every week changes everything – if only I had known it wouldn't last – and it wouldn't return until the jungle all those years later.

Being recognised everywhere is marvellous, not least because for a long time everything is free. People don't let you pay for things, even when you have the money in your hand. That goes for small items like coffees in cafes and right up to hotel stays and travel. No wonder I got carried away.

On the show everything was just as lavish – and I was swept along in Cilla's wake. She had her own driver, so I had my own driver. She had to have a new dress every week. So I had to have a new suit. I had them run up by Tommy Nutter and Dougie Hayward, who'd both been tailors to the Beatles. I had a seemingly endless series of shirts made by Turnbull & Asser. The pair of us were treated like true, old-fashioned movie stars. Nothing was too much trouble. No request was denied. No expense wasn't worth spending if it would make Cilla or me happy.

I was, of course, in absolute heaven right through those first fabulous years of the show. But as our fourth season approached Alan talked me through some changes they wanted to make for the new series. 'Biggins, you're so good with people. We want to make more of that. We want you to be out in the audience with a microphone and a camera crew,' he began.

I knew, throughout our conversation, that Alan was right. I'm good with audiences – I'm proud of that. I get the skill from panto but I've honed it in a thousand other productions over the years. When I did the spoof *Three Musketeers* on tour one year, each night I walked into the stalls dressed as a caretaker while the audience took their seats. I was up and down ladders, changing light bulbs and having a chinwag with people before climbing on to the stage and starting the play. I loved it and the crowds seemed to love it.

So, yes, on *Surprise Surprise* I could have thrived in that roving role. But I took the suggestion quite badly. I didn't understand why the request had come, or what the implications might be.

Insecurity might be the curse of the jobbing actor but until then it had hardly ever hit me. I felt it when I considered the new-look *Surprise Surprise* – not least because, as the original title of the show had been so long, my name no longer seemed to get many mentions when the show was written about in the press. If I was out with a crew in the audiences, what would be happening back in the studio? Who else might be drafted in to be with my Cilla? I didn't want to be like one of Esther Rantzen's supporting players, appearing to be happy to stand in the great lady's shadow.

And, however much the producers tried to put my mind at rest, I felt as if I was being demoted. I felt as if Cilla's husband and manager, Bobby Willis, wanted *Surprise Surprise* to be her show now, which of course he did.

So I said no. It was probably one of the worst decisions I've made in my whole career. I could probably have become a multimillionaire if I'd swallowed my pride and stayed with that show for the next four or five years of its run.

But at least I never for one moment lost my friendship with Cilla or Bobby. They both understood how I was feeling. Nothing was personal. She's a good egg and a great pal. Cilla and I share a zest for entertainment. Bobby is still sorely missed.

But the end result was that I walked out of the country's biggest and best-paid light-entertainment television show. And to do what, exactly? Good question. When I look back on my life, I know I've never suffered as much as some. I've been blessed with good fortune, in my family, my friends, my career. But I'll admit that after *Surprise Surprise* I hit a few lows. I still had panto. I still had a wonderful social life. I still had a belief that one thing would always lead to another. But what if I was wrong? Time passed and my bank balance was starting to look very shaky. My agent's phone wasn't exactly ringing off the hook. Where was I going to go next?

China was the unlikely answer. Peter Delaney and I were going off on a very rare holiday. We booked on to a tour, starting with two days in Hong Kong and then a big trek around mainland China – Beijing, Xi'an for the Terracotta Warriors, Shanghai and all the other places. I in particular had an extraordinary time in the Forbidden City in Beijing – and not just for the sights. I sprained my ankle and someone in the group suggested I try acupuncture. As if that kind of mumbo-jumbo is going to work, I thought. But when in China I thought I might as well do as the Chinese do, so I called up a little lady with her bag of needles.

I swear she didn't even come close to me. She pretty much propelled the needles at me from three feet away like some kind of mad martial-arts heroine. And the pain disappeared immediately. I've used acupuncture ever since.

Back on the road I needed to be fit. The Great Wall is huge and high, at least it was where we climbed it. How the dear old Queen managed on her visit I'll never know. But so much for fitness. My next focus on this trip turned out to be food.

Everywhere we went in China there seemed to be people showing us animals in wicker baskets. 'What a cute puppy,' I said the first time I looked into one.

'You want?' the owner's body language seemed to be saying to me.

'But I can't take him home,' I said to the guide.

'It's not a pet. He'll cook it for you,' he told me with a smile.

It was the same with the bags containing cats or even the mongoose we were offered the following night. My appetite disappeared in a flash. All I ate for the next ten days was white rice – and I've had an aversion to it ever since, which was a bit of a problem in the jungle as it was pretty much all we were ever given. But in China I wasn't even safe with the rice. I got a terrible stomach upset one afternoon. An explosive one.

'Is there a toilet here?' I asked in panic at one tour stop.

'Yes, over there,' said our guide, pointing helpfully to, well, nothing. The toilet was a hole in the ground, which we were pretty much used to at that point. The difference here was that this hole in the ground didn't have anything at all to sit or lean on. Nor did it have any walls at all.

But when a sick man's gotta go, he's gotta go.

The incident was mortifyingly embarrassing – especially as Peter and the rest of the group were right there looking and (unfortunately for them) listening. Thank God, those were the days before camera-phones. That wouldn't be a clip I'd like to see on YouTube.

Weak with hunger, shrinking by the day, embarrassed by my dicky tummy. None of this stopped me from taking charge when our group got bad news. The 13 of us were told that our trip to Xi'an and the Terracotta Army was off. The flight we had been booked on to had been cancelled and no other flight was available. That was it.

Enter, stage left, Biggins the drama queen. Earlier in the trip the guide had let slip that the tour company had put a VIP tag against my name on the booking sheet. I decided to play that card. 'That's simply not good enough. I'm a VIP. All of us here would agree that the Terracotta Army is the one key attraction that we have paid to see above all the others. There must be another way to get us there. You must find us that way.' It was like a revolt in *Tenko*. Dear Stephanie Cole would have been so proud.

Anyway, all our little Chinese guides buzzed around in a state of shock. And then they found the solution. We were packed into vans with blacked-out windows and whizzed over to a military airport. An army plane, with benches rather than seats, was on standby for us. Safety announcement? We didn't even have seat belts. In-flight meal? We had a lady behind a curtain at the back of the plane who was heating up a kettle on a naked flame. It's fair to say we weren't the most relaxed set of passengers as we zipped low over the paddy fields.

But, oh, was it worth it! To see the warriors in situ, all different, all ancient, all seeming to come towards you, is mesmerising. At the end of our trip we checked into the Peace Hotel in Shanghai – the place where Noel Coward wrote *Private Lives*. The wall lights are Lalique glass and a 1920s jazz band plays in the basement cocktail bar, where I swear we saw bats fly around. It was like being on a black-and-white movie set. It was the last word in bygone glamour, sophistication and class. And what did I do? I'd lost a couple of stone, so I ordered the one thing I had been craving for the past ten days. A hamburger. Shame on me.

When the holiday was over, theatre saved my sanity, if not my finances. Theatre on tour across the country, theatre outdoors in London and theatre under the hot sun of the Caribbean. I did more plays in the years after *Surprise Surprise* than I care to remember. I performed in front of the Queen and alongside some of the country's very biggest stars. I started directing. And while I earned far less than I spent I loved every last moment of it.

The good times began in *Lady Windermere's Fan* with the first fabulous Liza in my life, Liza Goddard. We were a great company. Also in the cast was the grand old lady of comedy, Fenella Fielding. Fenella is the most divinely eccentric woman you could ever meet, all the more so because she simply couldn't see it herself. Everyone knew she wore a wig, but woe betide anyone who acknowledged it. If she was in a period drama where she had to actually wear a wig she would insist on having it on top of her own wig, as she did in *Lady Windermere*. And you didn't even think of trying to get into her dressing room when she wasn't ready to be seen. I found this out to my cost when I went to speak to her one day. 'Who is it?' that deliciously husky *Carry On* voice crept out from under the door.

'It's Biggins.'

'Wait a moment. Come.'

She had a huge napkin thing over her head. She was doing her make-up underneath it. I spent 20 bizarre minutes gossiping with a woman who was covered in a cloth. Later, I found out that Fenella wasn't only putting make-up on her face. She had shaded in her costumes with make-up so she would look slimmer from the back of the stalls. Bill Kenwright, who had spent a fortune on the costumes, had a far larger than expected dry-cleaning bill that season.

Later that year, our producers had other big cleaning bills to pay after even more eccentric behaviour by an equally marvellous old dear. I was in panto at the Theatre Royal in Brighton, playing alongside Irene Handl. Irene was deliciously off the wall. She had a little dog with her and would often bring it on stage during a performance without explanation and with no warning at all. Worse, as she got going with her scene, she would often tire of the dog and hand it to someone else. That someone always seemed to be me. And as if holding a dog wasn't enough to put you off your stride, this was surely the most incontinent dog in the world. I normally left the stage with big wet patches spreading down my costume.

But dear Irene neither noticed nor cared.

'Sit down, Christopher darling,' she would say when I popped into her dressing room for a gossip. But I couldn't. I knew from bitter experience that the only chair in her room would always be soaked with dog pee.

Pantos have always kept me working every winter. But what of the summers? In the first few post-*Surprise Surprise* years, I was having too much fun to worry about work. Cilla's then agent, John Ashby, had introduced me to a marvellous couple at a party. There was the fashion queen Jeanne Mandry, with whom I fell in love that first moment. We exchanged numbers and I think we spoke on the phone two or three times the next day. We spoke on the phone two or three times the following day as well. And I think we've done so every day since. Not bad as our friendship enters its third decade.

At Jeanne's side that first night was her marvellous partner, Arnold Crook, who runs the Theatre Royal Haymarket and, gloriously enough, gets to sign his cheques 'A. Crook'. They rented a house in the hills in the South of France and I spent a very happy summer with them there. One year, while Jeanne whizzed us round the narrow lanes in her Bentley, I was feeling like a matchmaker again. 'You make the best couple I know,' I shouted out. 'Why don't you just get married and have done with it?'

'Married? Married?' Jeanne exclaimed. 'Arnold's not nearly rich enough.'

And you know what? Some 20 years later they're still not married, but they're still as much in love as ever.

If I wasn't in the South of France in the summer I did fortunately have a career option at home. Years earlier the very talented David Conville had offered me the chance to start acting and directing at the glorious outdoor theatre in London's Regent's Park.

David had taken charge of the seasons there back in the 1960s. And when I was first in London he had seen my lunchtime production of Jean Anouilh's *The Orchestra* – a production which I think is worthy of a mention in its own right, not least because I'm hoping to film it one day if anyone will put up the cash. This was the first show I had ever directed and it had been a challenge from the start. The first issue was the venue. We staged it in the Maximus disco in Leicester Square. The London Palladium it was not.

Next there was the financing. We had almost no cash, so I asked around and raised the production money from a huge circle of friends. Many of the old faces from Salisbury and Bristol helped fund the show, including Jeremy Irons, Anthony and Georgina Andrews, Cameron Mackintosh, Veronica Flint-Shipman, Queen's manager Jim Beach, John Caird and Ruth Tester Brown. Even my dear mum and dad chipped in – they were probably glad to give money upfront rather than simply see half their furniture end up on stage like the old days. The whole production was a team effort. Old pals Michael and Felicity Scholes drew up our poster and Jonathan Cecil, Annabel Leventon, Gillian Morgan and Marcia Warren were all among my cast.

My good fortune was that directing came naturally to me. I like to think it's because I started in theatre at the ground floor. I know what happens at every level of the organisation. I know what can and can't be done. And I love bringing out the best in people.

My dear friend Thelma Barlow had been in the first production of *The Orchestra* I'd seen, back in Bristol. It is an absolutely lovely play. The ladies – and one man playing the piano – are in a palm court orchestra and between the music they talk, gossip and bitch. John Asquith, who at that time lived above me in the Phoenix Theatre, taught the cast how to mime on their instruments and everyone loved it. David Conville saw one of the sell-out performances, and in the late 1970s, when I was very much at a loose end, he said to me, 'Come and direct for me. You'll have a fantastic company and a much better stage than that bizarre old disco.'

But while he was right about the company he wasn't telling the whole truth about the stage. The Open Air Theatre in Regent's Park is one of the great joys of an English summer, but from the company's point of view it can take some getting used to. I maintain that if you can play Regent's Park you can play anything, anywhere in the world.

It has the most wonderful gem of a location, tucked away within the inner circle of that beautiful royal park. But it also offers every hazard known to an actor. Flocks of birds fly overhead, or land in front of you. Ducks waddle across the stage. At matinees tourists sometimes seem to miss the fact that the ordinary rules of theatre still apply. So they will send children on to the stage for photos in the middle of the action.

As an actor there you have to learn plenty of other survival techniques. My top tip is, whatever your director says, never agree to sit or lie down if you can possibly help it. The British weather means you'll spend most of your season moist, at best. And if your costume is heavy when it's dry it will weigh an extra ton or so once it's soaked up a lot of ground water.

Fast moves are also a problem – when you are as heavy as me a slip can send you skating across the stage and right down in the mud. However hot the summer, there always seems to be mud in Regent's Park. A bit like being in the jungle, as it would turn out. And how I loved the challenge of working there.

In my first season I was asked to direct *The Dark Lady of the Sonnets* by George Bernard Shaw. It's a playlet about Shakespeare meeting Elizabeth I that worked beautifully outdoors. The following year David directed me in *A Midsummer Night's Dream* – a fixture on each year's production list. I was cast as Puck, which was a pretty brave decision, because I'm not exactly a small man. But I was bloody good at it, though I say so myself.

Fortunately I was helped by some great colleagues. The

marvellous Kate O'Mara was my Titania, wearing a costume that enhanced her already magnificent tits with Madonna-style metal cones. I faced some other hazards. That year we had gone for imaginary fairies rather than the real thing. So instead of talking to fellow actors I spoke to some very cleverly done little lights. They appeared on the top of car radio aerials that popped up from the ground when required. Trust me, it actually looked a lot better than it sounds.

In my first scene I arrived on stage with a bang. Literally a bang. I appeared in front of one of the false trees in the middle of the stage amid a flash of pyrotechnics and a deep whiff of cordite. It was a fun moment. But one night I find I'm getting laughs where I never got them before. So I surreptitiously check my wig. It feels in place. But after a few more words there are more laughs. I check my codpiece. All seems in place there too. But more laughs. Then the call comes out from the fifth row, I think.

'Look behind you, Puck!'

'This is Shakespeare, not bloody panto,' I want to reply. But I turn around all the same. And it seems that the flash has set the grass alight. Having suffered in the damp all season, I'm about to suffer even more now the grass has got tinder-dry. Anyway, the show has to go on. So I tell three very modern jokes while the stage hands put out the fire. I carried on because the one thing you never do at Regent's Park is leave the stage before you get the call. The call – a disembodied voice saying, 'Will the actors kindly leave the stage' – comes when the rain gets too heavy to continue. But the definition of 'too heavy' has always varied widely. Audiences will sit through typhoons. But on stage rain can play havoc with a performance in more ways than just sending you sliding into the mud.

In a scene in that year's *Midsummer*, I was prostrate at Kate O'Mara's feet when the rain started to fall. It began slowly. A single drop hit one of her surgically enhanced bosoms. *Ping.* I tried to ignore it. Then a drip hit her right tit. *Pong.* Then two drops. *Ping, ping.* And then the drops began to land on each tit in turn. *Ping ... pong, ping ... pong.* The audience couldn't have heard it. But I couldn't hear anything else. So my shoulders started to shake as I started to laugh. Fortunately for me, Kate was having to do all the talking. She made her big speech. *Ping ... pong ... ping ... pong* went the rain on her chest. But soon I knew my lines would come. Could I spit them out through the laughs?

'Will the actors kindly leave the stage.'

Never have I been so pleased to hear that voice.

That summer Kenny Everett had some fun with the rain as well. We were doing a one-off charity concert night when the heavens opened. So he did what he thought was natural. He took his clothes off, there on stage, right down to his underpants.

A year later Bernard Bresslaw was due in our hardy little company to play the lead in a stage version of Mark Twain's *A Connecticut Yankee in King Arthur's Court*. But, so sadly, he died just before rehearsals got under way. I took over and it was one of the hardest jobs I have had. Bernard was so loved and so missed. But it was lovely old Regent's Park. The show had to go on.

None of us did those shows for the money – you earn next to nothing out there in the night air. I did them for the magic. And because I have met so many wonderful friends in those casts. Artistic director Ian Talbot became one, actress Janie Dee another. And a great one is the desperately glamorous Anna Nicholas. What I love about her is her underlying air of naughtiness – she reminds me of dear Judi that way. From the first castings and rehearsals I remember Anna wearing so many bracelets, necklaces and rings. She literally dazzled us. She was hoofing away in one rehearsal, about to go into her song alongside a troupe of dancing boys, when she fell over.

'If you will wear so much jewellery you're bound to have trouble staying upright,' I called out to her. We've been best friends ever since.

14

Oh, Puck – It's Liza

'Oh, Biggins, we're in deep trouble here.'

Peggy Mount's incomparable voice didn't really lend itself to a subtle whisper. But she was trying her best the season we turned up for first rehearsals with a new director who didn't know that theatre in the park is a skill all its own. 'You'll have to sort it out, Biggins,' Peggy commanded.

She's not someone you argue with. Besides, I was itching to take charge.

Our fledgling director had been putting us in corners of the stage, corners that were going to be too muddy for fast moves and from where, we felt, parts of the audience could neither see nor hear us. He even had us talking with our backs to the audience at one point – not a great idea when the planes lining up for Heathrow can drown out even Peggy's booming voice. Anyway, on the great lady's bidding, I spoke to Ian Talbot and ended up co-directing that year's performance of *Bartholomew Fair*.

When I was in *Midsummer* again later that year we had our royal visit. The Queen was due to help celebrate the 50th anniversary of the New Shakespeare Company, which had run the theatre since 1932. But would she enjoy it? It is well known in the business that the Queen loathes theatre. *The Royal Variety Performance* is the cruellest form of torture for the poor lady. So I was guessing that she had absolutely no wish to sit through an entire three or four acts of Shakespeare, let alone in a park.

As we talked about the visit, David suggested, 'Why don't we do *The Dark Lady*?'

This one-acter runs for little more than 90 minutes, and the plot was timely. The performance came a matter of weeks after a character named Michael Fagan had broken into the Palace and sat talking at the foot of the Queen's bed while she waited for help to arrive. The play was about Shakespeare suddenly coming across the Queen, so I felt it had some extra, light-hearted resonance. When we put it on I think Her Majesty may well have enjoyed it more than she had feared. Whether she enjoyed the next part of the evening is open to question.

The night was a big gala event and after the show the Queen was due to do a mini-tour backstage. Her people had arranged for her to see the likes of the scene dock, the costume department and the lighting rig. Whoever had been in charge also thought she should see one of the actors in their dressing room. That actor was me.

'Take down some of your dirty cards,' David told me as he looked around my postage-stamp-sized dressing room just before the visit. All around my mirror I had pinned various first-night cards, some of which had some (surely enhanced) pictures of naked men, while others had written instructions to 'Break a fucking leg' and suchlike.

'I won't take anything down,' I retorted. Even the Queen must have seen naked men before. And I didn't expect that Philip would be put off by a bit of blue language. So the cards were still there when the royal party arrived.

'And this is Christopher Biggins, Ma'am, who plays Philostrate and Puck,' came David's introduction.

'How lovely,' said the Queen, totally true to form.

'Yes, it's marvellous to have two roles,' I began, uncertain whether to pause or carry on talking. I carried on talking. 'I have two sets of costumes as well. This is Puck's costume and this is Philostrate's.'

'I've just seen Titiana's costume,' said the Queen, sounding as excited as a schoolgirl. And yes, it was 'Titi-ana' she said, not 'Titania'. But I knew, I just knew, that I couldn't laugh. So I tried to distract myself as well as Her Majesty. I launched into an endless description of the way we put on our make-up, the way we did our hair, the way we looked after our costumes. I'm talking 19 to the dozen so I can forget the tits when suddenly the poor Queen interrupts.

'What are those?' she asks, pointing up at the shoes I wear as Puck.

'These are Puck's shoes, Ma'am.' I have no idea why this was so fascinating to her, but it was.

'Look, Philip,' she exclaimed, turning to where her husband was jammed in the doorway. 'Puck's shoe'.

And then I really did lose it.

How do you top meeting the Queen? I did it by meeting Liza Minnelli. And, contrary to expectations, we didn't meet at a glitzy party or a wild celebrity gathering (all that would come later). No, Liza and I met in church.

It was All Hallows near the Tower of London. She was there to support a new production by Peter Delaney. So, of course, was I. We had a riot, from the moment we got out of the church and into the sunshine. I loved her spirit, her courage, her passion and her talent. Over the years I would see her on stage in Las Vegas, New York, London, you name it. I have to say that she is the greatest stage performer I have ever seen. At her peak no one else can hold a candle to her. The problem, of course, was that with every peak could come a trough. I found that out pretty early as well.

One of the first times I saw Liza perform was in New York. I arrived in style. I had been invited on Virgin Atlantic's inaugural flight to the city. It was one of my most amazing trips ever. As far as I can recall, no one sat down for any of the flight. I drank so much champagne my hangover began mid-Atlantic. I was so drunk I tried to leave the plane at that point so I could go home.

Once I got to New York the madness continued. It always does with Liza. She was appearing in Kander and Ebb's *The Rink* with the equally legendary Chita Rivera. Liza was on a low, I soon realised. But she put on an incredible performance and certainly wasn't in any mood to stop partying. I was backstage afterwards, trying to rush her along so we could all go out for dinner.

'Biggins, I've a present for you.' It was a Cabbage Patch doll, which was all the rage back then.

'Oh, how lovely,' I said.

Oh, how weird, I was thinking.

When we lurched off to the restaurant, me on one side, Peter on the other and Liza in the middle, we walked by Chita. 'What's that?' she asked, pointing to my floppy little doll.

'Liza gave it to me,' I said proudly.

'Well, my brother just gave it to Liza,' she informed me.

It was a long night. Just before 9am the following morning, not having been to bed, we went with Liza while she got the owner of a junk shop to open early so she could look for bargains.

In Las Vegas a little later, she was as ready for new experiences as ever. That, I think, is why we got on so well. We're both the most social people you could find. Together we were insatiable. In Vegas we were chatting in her hotel suite and I was reading out extracts from a *Vanity Fair* article by Dominick Dunne, the man who chronicles the lives of the rich, famous and infamous. The feature that had caught my attention was about the McGuire Sisters. One of them, Phyllis, had been in love with the mobster Sam Giancana and was now living in Vegas.

'Let's see if we can visit her,' said Liza as if it was the most natural thing in the world.

I rang the magazine and managed to get a number for Dominick Dunne. Amazing what you can do with Liza behind you. Dominick then said he would try to pass the message on. 'No promises. But I'll tell Phyllis to call you back if she wants to meet,' he said.

Phyllis did indeed. 'Come round for a little lunch, after church on Sunday,' she said.

Well, on the big day I eventually got Liza up and ready. Is anyone ever as late as Liza for appointments? A chauffeur had been sent to pick us up. A handsome chauffeur who had a very visible gun in his pocket – a real one, not a Mae West 'pleased to see me' one, more's the pity.

And so, long after lunch had probably been served, we were whisked down the strip and out across a bit of desert to the McGuire estate. The vast security gates swung open, we swept up the drive and were greeted at the door by a butler, a maid and what looked like another security guard.

Phyllis ignored how late we were and greeted us with grace. She was wearing the most fantastic Chanel suit and the diamond ring on her finger was big enough for Torvill and Dean to have skated *Bolero* across. Less certainly wasn't more with dear Phyllis. Nor, it has to be said, with her interior decorator. Apparently, after she and Giancana visited Paris, she wanted a replica Eiffel Tower built in their home. And it's Vegas, baby, so build it they did. The span was so high you could walk underneath it on stilts. So high, in fact, that they had to take out the dining room's old ceiling and rebuild it.

'Thank God, I wore trousers,' Liza said as we walked over the vast mirrored floor to greet the other guests. And from then on the surprises kept on coming. From the urinal in the men's loo – what a clever idea – to the beauty room with a sink, hairdryer and massage table for each of the three sisters. And the closets? 'This one is for day wear, this one is for evening wear, this one is for Chanel, this one is for shoes, this one for handbags,' our hostess trilled as we had our tour. And when I say 'closet' I mean a room the size of the entire ground floor of my London house. There was a tenpin bowling alley and not so much a 'panic room' as a 'panic apartment' in the basement where the sisters could hide out in a crisis.

Best of all, Phyllis wasn't bragging. She was so matter-of-fact as she walked us around her world. This was simply the way she lived. I absolutely adored it. Our tour continued, and as we headed outside she said, 'This is the lake for the black swans.' Which indeed it was.

'This is the lake for the white swans.' Indeed it was.

'This is the lake for the black and white swans.' And indeed they all were.

It was fabulous. And there was no need to ask why a white swan didn't stray into a black area or vice versa. It wasn't even the small army of staff Phyllis had. It was the sheer force of her personality. She wanted the lakes the way she wanted them. No swan would have dared disrupt her. At the end of the vast garden was a sort of restaurant with a grill and a bar with optics and that's how that Rat Pack lived in Las Vegas. Frank, Dean, Sammy, all of them. Perform all night, sleep all day. This lavish compound suited their climate and suited their lives. I was thrilled to have seen it first-hand, before it fades away for good.

Racing ahead a bit, it's clear that Liza has had her problems and made her fair share of mistakes. The worst of which was David Gest. When she met him she dropped out of all our lives. Me, Peter, her PA, her musical director, everyone who cared for her and loved her and helped her. We lost her almost overnight. Her numbers changed. Messages weren't answered. It was so sad, and knowing her as I did I knew it was so dangerous.

Just as worrying was Liza's decision to forget the old and rush headlong towards the new as her wedding approached.

Two old pals of mine, Lee Dean and Toni 'Petal' Nelson, were at the Ivy one night and found themselves sitting right next to Liza. 'Thrilled' is not the word. 'I think, Miss Minnelli, that we have a mutual friend,' Petal said.

'Who's that?'

'Biggins!'

Apparently, Liza turned to David with a huge smile on her face. 'Biggins! That's the man I was trying to tell you about! What's his first name again?'

After just a few more words, Liza gave Petal two invites to her upcoming wedding. Now Lee and Petal are wonderful company and scrub up very well. But neither Liza nor David had met them more than half an hour before inviting them to what should have been the most important, personal day of their lives. If that's not a warning sign, I'm not a panto dame.

No invitation ever came to me. Nor did one come to Peter, the man who had buried Liza's mother and had been a family friend across the generations. When I read the tacky lists of who had been at the ceremony – had Liza known any of them for more than half an hour? – I nearly cried at the tragedy and the waste.

She has seen past David now, thank God. But I don't think she's the girl I used to know. Seeing the performance she gave at Bruce Forsyth's 80th-birthday party almost made me cry. I'll carry on trying to see her because, of so very many dear friends in my life, she is one of the very few who have slipped through the net. I relish and cherish all my friendships. I never discard people and I'm lucky to have very rarely been discarded myself. In time I hope Liza and I regain our old momentum.

In the late 1980s the best job I did was the UK tour of Frank Loesser's fabulous *Guys and Dolls*. I was cast alongside the mighty Barbara Windsor, who, unusually, was at a low ebb. Although the great comedies and the *Carry On* films loomed large in her recent past, new film and television work had dried up. She was touring in theatre and doing great work, but still this business seemed to dismiss her. 'Oh, it's only Barbara Windsor' was the general attitude of producers and directors alike. Just as the phrase 'Oh, it's only Christopher Biggins' was haunting me. So in 1988 it was little wonder that we became such close friends so quickly. We both recognised who and where we were.

We also knew how lucky we were to be cast in a tour of the wonderful *Guys and Dolls*. I was Nathan Detroit, Babs was Miss Adelaide, and we got marvellous reviews. Barbara proved to be such a generous performer, just like Liza Goddard. And, like Liza, she was happy to let me do all the organising and the nest-building when we were on tour together. I found our hotels, did our deals and tried to smooth our path.

But in Scotland it all went just a little bit awry. A dear pal of mine, William Mowat Thompson, had a marvellous house in Edinburgh where we could escape the bad hotels and dodgy lodgings for a while. But there was only one spare room. 'Don't worry, Barbara, because we've found a flat for you just around the corner,' I told her.

'No, I don't need it, darling. A friend of my hairdresser

has a place, so I'm staying there.' But as we left the King's Theatre in Glasgow for our Edinburgh engagement Babs wasn't quite at ease. I was with Vincent McGrath, another dear friend who was lighting up my life at the time. 'When we meet the guy, will you follow me to where we're going? Just in case,' Babs asked us.

So after her luggage had been piled into this stranger's car we began our watching brief. We drove away from the city centre. And we drove. And we drove. About 45 minutes later we were on some dreadful council estate in the absolute middle of nowhere. I'd never seen Barbara's eyes so wide. She was horrified.

'Now, you've got my number? You absolutely must ring if you need anything. I can leap in a cab and be here in no time at all,' I said as loudly as I could, to warn Babs's host that at least someone knew where she was and who she was with.

'I'll be fine, darling. Don't you worry about me,' Babs said, not too convincingly.

After I had gone it turned out that the lift wasn't working, and it was about a thousand steps up to the flat (not that dear Barbara would ever exaggerate). And I know she wasn't exaggerating about the final detail: the fact that the flat itself was a shrine to – you guessed it – Barbara Windsor. That night she rang her husband, he rang me and I set off to rescue her. We got her into a box room in William's house, which wasn't up to her usual standard but was most certainly better than where she had been. It was the last time she ever organised her own lodgings.

One of the many things I love about Barbara is her belief that everything always comes right in the end. It did that night and she's the living proof that it does in life as well. Her lovely husband Scott is adorable and totally right for her. And her career in *EastEnders* has finally shown the world what I always knew. 'It's only Barbara Windsor' indeed. At last everyone now knows that that's enough.

Back in London after the *Guys and Dolls* tour, I had been at yet another London dinner party where the introductions didn't quite go to plan. Penny Keith had introduced me to the trichologist Philip Kingsley, whose shampoos really are the only ones I'll use. I then introduced him to Dinsdale Lansden, the hugely successful actor.

'Dinsdale, this is Philip, the famous trichologist,' I said.

'Oh, marvellous. I used to ride a bike when I was a child,' said Dinsdale, to everyone's total confusion.

It took quite a while, and a bizarre conversation where everyone was at cross purposes with everyone else, to work out what he was on about. 'He's a "trichologist"? I thought you said he was a "trick cyclist",' Dinsdale explained. So a trick cyclist was what Philip would always be to us.

Back then I fell in love with Philip's wife, Joan, as well. She loved theatre and organised some wonderful concerts. The three of us clicked. We had years and years of wonderful holidays together. They had a marvellous apartment in New York, as well as other homes on both sides of the Atlantic, and they were generous with all of them. Over so many glorious years of friendship we spent Christmases together and built up so many memories.

One early highlight, at their apartment just across from Central Park, was the night Tennessee Williams came to dinner.

Now he was my idol. *A Streetcar Named Desire* and *Cat on a Hot Tin Roof* are classic texts with marvellous roles. Which actor hasn't wanted to play Blanche Dubois? And I do include all the men in this question. The thought of meeting Blanche's creator made me shiver. I wanted an evening of *bons mots*, words of wisdom, poetry, ideas, a celebration of language and literature. This I didn't get.

The outrageous Dodson Rader had set up the supposedly literary dinner. He was a very political writer, a great friend of the Kennedy clan and as off the wall as his name sounds. The evening promised to be a corker. Joan had made one of her usual wonderful meals for our big night. We had all boned up on literature. And then Tennessee himself arrived. That was when it all started to go downhill.

Tennessee was so drunk he was incoherent. He was paralytic and didn't string two words together all night. Worse still, he hadn't arrived alone. His sober, calculating companion turned out to be a male escort. When the boy kept excusing himself from the table to go to the loo we all assumed he must be taking drugs. He wasn't. He was rifling through all the bags, coats and drawers around the apartment, stealing money. The pair took off just after midnight, leaving us all in shock – and much the poorer.

Fortunately, the boy got his comeuppance. Tennessee had installed him at the Plaza Hotel, but somehow snuck out and left town without paying the bill. The rent boy, so we heard, wasn't allowed to leave without handing over all his cash to cover it.

15

My Golden Girls

By the late 1980s and early 1990s, I had pretty much disappeared from the television screens. I still did panto every year, and I was on tour in countless marvellous musicals and plays. But what I mainly did was have a good time. I was still more focused on meeting an extraordinary cast of characters than I was on climbing up any theatrical career ladder. In 1992 I met two of the best: Joan Collins and my ultimate golden girl, Bea Arthur.

Joan and I met in New York. I love that city – and very many of the people I know there. In more than 20 years of visits I've never once stayed in a hotel. I've always had dear friends who have offered me their hospitality. One dear American pal is the theatre-loving and dryly hilarious Weston Thomas. She always persuades me to have a manicure when we meet up in the city. She's a fabulous, sophisticated lady with a marvellous daughter. And, like me after a visit, she has great nails.

I may well have been looking at my nails in the lobby of the Carlyle Hotel when an extraordinarily handsome man came up to me. He was mesmerising. Just drop-dead gorgeous – and, better still, he seemed to know who I was. 'We've met before,' he said, after shaking my manicured hand.

Perhaps for the only time in my life I was (almost) speechless. I couldn't imagine how I, of all people, could have forgotten someone as good-looking as this.

'Come and join us,' he said, with a relaxed, open friendliness. And by 'us' he meant he and his girlfriend, Joan Collins. She was looking fabulous and I was so excited it wasn't true. Joan Collins! With me! I talked non-stop I was so thrilled to meet her – and fortunately I was able to say all the right things. Joan had been working in the US for a while and was desperate for gossip about the industry back in London. Who better than me for a gossip?

It turned out that we were all at the Carlyle for the same reason – to see the new cabaret act there. Joan and I ended up sitting next to each other and very naughtily we carried on gossiping right through the performance. I remember thinking that Joan was an absolute riot. As gloriously dry and as wonderfully sharp as I had hoped. What an absolutely marvellous evening, I thought all the way back to my friend's apartment. But would it be repeated?

A few days after I had got back to London I got a call from Stella Wilson, Joan's PA. 'Joan loved meeting you in New York and would love you to go to a charity event with her,' Stella began.

I was beside myself with excitement. Perhaps there is always a lonely child in all of us, an insecure figure who craves affirmation that people like us. My inner child was certainly in a good mood that day. Joan liked the man I had become. Her PA was telling me so. My bubble only burst when Stella got to the end of the conversation.

'It's £100 a ticket,' she said of the event in question. Well, hell. For an evening with Joan I'd have happily paid double.

Being close friends with Joan and her partner Robin opened up a whole new world for me. He was an art dealer who knew everyone in London and pretty much everyone in the rest of the world as well. And Joan, of course, was Joan. They were a couple made in social heaven. The pair moved in the most exalted of circles. Or, should I say, they glided in those circles. Everything seemed effortless, though the actor in me always knew how hard Joan had worked to get everything that she had.

We had wonderful times in the South of France in the beautiful house Robin had found for his lady. He had decorated it as well, with impeccable taste. And they were my hosts in the hills of Los Angeles as well. My classic Hollywood moment came at the iconic Mr Chow's restaurant in Beverly Hills. When we arrived Tony Curtis was at the bar. Then, suddenly, across the room came Spartacus himself – the incredible, unmistakable Kirk Douglas. I'm just a boy from Oldham, by way of Salisbury Rep, I kept thinking. The cheek of it that I should end up here. The joy of it. The sheer wonder of life.

As usual, from one new friendship sprang another. Sue St John lived above Joan Collins in Belgravia and through Sue I met Michael and Shakira Caine. We would all spend lots of weekends at their house in the country – Michael does an amazing roast.

'What's going on? What are you girls laughing about now?'

Michael always ended up on the mezzanine level of the house watching sport on television in the afternoons while 'the girls' sat below gossiping. No prizes for guessing that I was one of the girls driving him mad with loud giggles.

From Michael Caine to Michael Winner – Joan and I were in the film of Stephen Berkoff's *Decadence* with Winner and I adored him. What a character. What a zest for life.

Someone else I met through Joan was dear Tita Cahn, whose husband Sammy Cahn had written all those Frank Sinatra and Doris Day songs. I accompanied Joan to the shiva for Sammy and as I didn't know that many people I was trying to be quiet, and staying at the edge of the room. It was then that I saw Tita struggling, of all things, to get a stereo to work. I tried to help and, amazingly, succeeded. And, as a result of that tiny event, I made a dear pal that day.

Two others who had been at the shiva were Barbara and Marvin Davis, the billionaires who owned MGM. I was at Joan's house when Barbara called the next day. 'Hello, Christopher. We're having a 97th-birthday party for George Burns. We'd like you all to come,' she breathed.

So Joan, Robin and I all did just that. It was the night of a thousand stars, all squeezed on to just six tables of eight. And I was on the top table. I was sitting with Frank

Sinatra, Sidney Poitier, Carol Channing, Shakira Caine, our hostess Barbara Davis, Frank Sinatra and, of course, George Burns. Dan Aykroyd, with whom I chatted just before we took our places, could clearly read my mind. 'Pinch yourself, Biggins, you don't often get evenings like this,' he whispered with a wink.

Indeed you don't.

The only thing the evening lacked was a microphone for George Burns himself. His stories, all night, were pure Hollywood and comic gold. But only our table could hear them.

There was one other thing that only I could hear that night – though I soon repeated it to all my friends. It was what Frank Sinatra said to me. I was in awe of that man. Sure, I've met plenty of queens in my time. But he was a king. Pure, solid showbusiness royalty. Not only was I unsure what to say to him, I didn't know what to call him. Christopher Biggins doesn't do tongue-tied or shy or false modesty. But I came close that Hollywood night. The first time we spoke I think I called him 'sir' – the way Americans often do. Then I tried 'Mr Sinatra'. Then he interrupted.

'Christopher, call me Frank,' he said. Four words I wish my parents could have heard. They would never, ever have believed it.

'A few years ago I played Nathan Detroit in *Guys and Dolls*,' I said, thinking back to that wonderful tour with Barbara Windsor.

'Christopher, so did I,' he replied, as if I really needed to be told.

Then Frank asked me to be his bodyguard. The man infamous for mafia links, heavies and strong men wanted an old fruit like me to protect him. Though it was from no ordinary enemy. 'Christopher, will you come out and guard me from my wife while I have a cigarette?' he drawled.

From Frank Sinatra to Bea Arthur via Darlington. Years ago I had been doing panto up north with an ambitious, starstruck and supremely talented dancer called Jeff Thacker. He loved Cilla and he loved me because I knew her. From such superficial connections great friendships can be born.

One of the many things I admired about Jeff was his ambition. He was focused and hard-working – he soon left Darlington behind and had become a huge producer in America. His partner, the singer Robert Meadmore, is just as good a pal and just as talented a performer. But it was Jeff who opened a brilliant social door for me.

'Biggins, I've met this woman. It's Bea Arthur,' he told me by phone. I had roared with laughter over *The Golden Girls*. And the tall, gravelly Bea was my favourite actress in the group. 'She's over here renting Jerry Hall's flat and I want to throw her a dinner party. You have to come. Bring friends,' Jeff instructed.

I didn't need to be asked twice. So, on the night, myself, Una Stubbs, Julia McKenzie and my great friend Paul Macbeth were all present and correct nice and early, awaiting the arrival of the star. We got a shock.

When Bea finally arrived she was slightly inebriated. She had been indulging in a spot of vodka. She was quite cutting to me, and sharp with Julia and her own American friend, whose name I'm afraid I can't remember. Una was only saved because she was too smart to say much and remained out of the line of fire. It was a bit like Tennessee

Williams all over again, but nowhere near as bad. Though at least tonight we didn't get robbed, I thought afterwards. But it wasn't quite over.

'Is that Christopher Biggins?'

'Yes, it is.'

'This is Bea Arthur. I must apologise for my behaviour last night. But my friend says that you are quite adorable, so I would like to see you again.'

The second time around we hit it off. Bea was charming and we have been having fun and sharing good conversation ever since. Once, when we went out for dinner in LA, I was the designated driver charged with getting her home. I wasn't drinking because I was driving but we had a wild time and Bea ended up drinking a bit too much wine. The end result was a bit like that first night in London.

'Where do I go?' I asked as I pulled away from the restaurant.

'Whad-daya-mean?' she drawled.

'I don't know the way.'

'Neither do I.'

Tension mounted as I drove aimlessly round the Hollywood Hills hoping something would remind my companion of where she lived. In the meantime I decided to try some light conversation.

'What was it like making *Golden Girls*?' I asked.

'Betty White's a c**t,' she said, with a mischeivous smile on her face. I nearly crashed her car.

Somehow, in the midst of this wild, global socialising, I did manage to do some work as the 1990s got under way.

Too little, as it turned out, but every little helped. I did *Country Cousins* in a club in the West End – a step up from the Maximus disco, but only just. Then Marilyn Johnson and our old pal Bryn Lloyd put together a spoof show called *Mr Warren's Profession*. Linda Bellingham, Linda Marchal (soon to re-emerge as Linda La Plante), Jackie Anne Carr, Tudor Davies and I were all signed up. It was dinner theatre and at one point I was on a huge swing, sailing over the audience while singing 'Keep Young and Beautiful'.

One time I got a really fantastic reception. The whole place was a riot: everyone cheered, no one ate a thing. And why? Because my voice was so mesmerising? My characterisation so spot on? No, because my flies were open. When the swing swung back everyone could see everything. Just everything.

My short but sweet return to prime-time television was in *Cluedo*, where I was once again playing a vicar. Surely the oddest piece of typecasting ever. My dear pal Peter, the true vicar in my life, reckons I will have a head start on other applicants if I ever decide to take the hints and join the church properly. In *Cluedo*, I was the Reverend Green and played alongside the booming Tom Baker as Professor Plum. Our season also had Pam Ferris as a comely Mrs White and the glamorous Susan George as Mrs Peacock. We had fun, but not for long. We were contracted to do just half a dozen programmes, with a whole new cast called in for the following year. *Cluedo* certainly didn't make any of the performers rich. But because it was a prime-time ITV show the ratings were pretty good. My phone didn't ring off the hook afterwards, but hopefully it reminded a few people that I was still alive. If they were casting another dodgy vicar they could always count on me.

More seriously, I was well aware of the importance of getting back on TV as often as possible. The entertainment industry has the memory of a goldfish. You can blaze your way across theatre stages and win every Olivier Award going (unaccountably I have won none) but if you're not on the telly every now and then you struggle to pay the bills. In the 1990s one great way for actors to earn big money was to get into the soaps – as dear Babs would soon do in seemingly effortless style. But that wasn't the way I wanted to go. I wanted to be me. I wanted people to know Christopher Biggins, not to shout out some soap character's name when they saw me in the street. I also knew how hard my dear friend Helen Worth worked on *Coronation Street*. In the years ahead I would see how hard Babs worked in *EastEnders*. Never say never.

But I didn't feel ready for all that in the 1990s. I had a few nice cameo roles in shows like *Minder* and *Shoestring*. But then I started to relax even more. For a while I even considered giving up my life's one big anchor. For the first time in so many years I said no to my next panto.

It was 1993 and I was feeling exhausted. Can one man drink too much bubbly and go to too many parties? I was testing the theory to the limit.

The bookings for pantos tend to be done, and the contracts signed, in April. That April Billy Differ had called as usual to try to book me for a season at one of my favourite theatres up in Glasgow. Billy was such a dear friend and had booked me for so many shows – including that *Guys and Dolls* tour with Babs. He was just like Peter Todd, a great theatre manager with a real instinct for knowing what audiences wanted to see.

I don't think he could believe it when I turned him down.

'But you always do panto. You are pantomime,' he said.

'Billy, I need a break. It's time I branched out into something else. I'm sure that if I keep my diary free something even better is going to come up.'

But of course it didn't. April turned to May and May turned to June. My diary remained stubbornly empty. By July I was twiddling my thumbs and worrying about the bills. In August I rang Billy for a chat and a gossip and he seemed distracted and depressed. 'What's wrong?'

'The headline in today's paper is what's wrong,' he told me. It seemed that his lead for Dick Whittington was in the news. He had been arrested on child pornography charges and his career was over. Billy, meanwhile, was left with a gaping hole in his panto cast.

'Well, I'd better come up and take over,' I said.

'You don't mean it?'

'I absolutely do.'

'Then you're booked.' And I was saved.

The money, of course, was desperately needed. But the performances themselves gave me just the boost I was looking for. Panto in Glasgow is like panto nowhere else in Britain. The audiences are wild and wonderful. The atmosphere is raw and it's like being on stage for a pop concert every night. And that year's *Dick Whittington* was the best ever. I was the only non-Scot in the cast, which brought plenty of extra laughs at my expense. All of which I milked shamelessly. I also hammed up the famous sketch often attributed to Morecambe and Wise. Allan Stewart was Dick, his wife Jane played Alice Fitzwarren. 'I love you,' I tell Alice at one point.

'I love you too. But I love you like a brother.'

We get a chorus of 'ahhhs' from the audience. Which I again milk for all they are worth. Then Dick and Alice sit on a wall and sing a love song. I come up behind, pull Dick off and sing his part. Then he comes back, pulls me off and repeats the trick. And so it goes on, until at the end we're both on the wall, him on one side of Alice, me on the other – and we both push her off and sing to each other. The audience goes hysterical. Glasgow is my favourite city in Scotland, and pretty much my favourite in Britain for panto.

The best thing about that year's production was that it had cemented my already solid friendship with Billy. We had enjoyed some real laughs that season. And it had been nice to do each other a favour: I had filled the gap in his cast, and he had filled a gap in my bank balance. The season ended in the third week of January in 1994 and I headed back south feeling full of optimism about the year ahead. If only I had known that I was about to get a visit from the VAT man.

16

The VAT Man – and Neil

He came to my house in Hackney. My accountant was with us and I fussed around getting the tea, coffee and biscuits ready as they spread all sorts of files and papers around the room. Pages of figures all over my lovely books on theatre and Hollywood stars. Piles of receipts and returns covering up all my framed photographs and little ornaments.

Amazingly, at that first visit, everything was in order. Crisis postponed, if not entirely averted. My real financial nightmare would come later. 'OK, we're fine.' Getting three words like that from the VAT man had to be good news, I felt. But then there was something else. 'Mr Biggins, can I ask you a personal question?' he said as he packed his case and prepared to leave.

Blimey, was I going to get asked on a date?

'You sometimes have a lot of money and sometimes you don't. How do you survive?'

'On the kindness of strangers,' I said, misquoting Oscar Wilde. And I never said a truer word. My VAT man had got to the heart of the highs and lows of my financial life. As an actor it really is feast or famine most of the time. That's why so many actors have second or third jobs to fall back on when times are hard. We need to. Or at least they do. I break ranks with many of my peers in several unusual ways. One is that I have always loved being out of work – just as well, my critics might say. But it's true. When I didn't have a tour or a panto season or a television show to worry about I could get on with my life. More importantly, I could socialise. There are always parties to go to and people to meet. There are first nights to see, new restaurants to try. Champagne doesn't drink itself, as one dear friend often points out. And I have never worried about the future. I never sat and watched what jobs my contemporaries were getting and spat blood because I was jealous. I was too busy getting ready for a party.

In theory, the only problem was that when I was out of work I would carry on spending as if I was working. But for a long time even this didn't seem to matter either. For years I seemed to get one fantastic bank manager after another. If things got a bit dicey I could just take them out to lunch and they would agree to let me have even more lovely money. Why on earth, I used to ask myself, do so many people moan about their bank? Don't they know how easy it is to play them for a little extra?

I valiantly ignored them all. After all, less than 12 months earlier the VAT man had said everything was in order. Surely it couldn't all have gone pear-shaped so soon.

It had, of course. And one day I sat down in my living room to work out just how badly awry it was. I added everything up and slumped back in my chair. The figure was shocking. How could it all have got so out of hand? I needed £50,000 just to stay afloat. It's a lot of money now. It felt an awful lot worse 15 years ago. How the hell had I allowed things to slip so far? And, more importantly, what could I do about it?

I gave my new bank manager one more lunch invitation. I was rebuffed again. The man must be a computer. More seriously, it was clear that overdrafts and loans were no longer being thrown around like pantomime candy, at least not to me. Beg, borrow or steal. If I couldn't borrow and as I wouldn't steal, I knew I had to beg. 'The kindness of my friends.' I'd been laughing when I had made that comment to the VAT man the previous year. I wasn't laughing now.

There was one dear friend, whom I will not name, who I knew would be able to help me. But how could I ask? I was on my way down to see him, out in the country, as I tortured myself over the conversation. I can't do it, I decided at the last moment. But then I thought of the consequences if I didn't have the money. I had to go through with this.

When I arrived, we gossiped and we laughed, as we always did. But there was something different in the air. I think we both knew why I was there. We both knew what was coming. And he didn't make it easy for me. Rightly so.

'I need to borrow some money.' It was probably the hardest line I have delivered in my whole career. But it was the right thing to say. A cheque was written. An excruciatingly embarrassing situation did ultimately pass. And my worst fear wasn't realised: a friendship did not end. 'I will pay you back,' I said at the end of that awful afternoon.

And a few years later, when I was struggling again and was unable to clear the debt, I renewed that vow. 'I'll make it a gift,' my dear friend said. 'But with one proviso. You have to be a friend for the rest of our lives.'

'Of course we will always be friends. But I will pay you back. One day I will pay you back.' I meant that statement then, and I mean it now. I just wish I'd known that my financial crisis was very far from over.

I'm in a fat, Club-class British Airways seat on my way out to the Caribbean. I'm pushing my money worries aside and going on another big theatrical adventure. The cast of characters here includes the fabulous interior designer and old pal Richard Hanlon, and Johnny and Wendy Kidd, parents of Jodie, Jemma and Jack. The family had a vast, stunning garden at their old plantation house in Barbados, as you do, but they had been using another garden, at JCB millionaire Sir Anthony Bamford's Heron Bay, for an annual operatic evening.

It was a magical event, in a magical place. But the Kidds decided they should do a Shakespeare and opera season in their own home, Holders House. The Holders Season was to be born. But who should put it together?

Richard had seen the *Midsummer Night's Dream* I had directed at the Open Air Theatre in Regent's Park the previous season. It had been a good one. 'And it was all due to my Bottom,' I liked to say, the old jokes being the best.

'Would you like to go to Barbados to direct the show there? You can pick your own actors and...'

I had said yes pretty much the moment Richard got to the word 'Barbados'. Who cared what the rest of the pitch was all about?

'Barbados?'

'Yes.'

Simple as that.

I took Berwick Kaler in that first year; he was a dear friend and a spectacular pantomime dame who I had worked with in Regent's Park. This was the start of a truly wonderful new phase of my life. It was quite wonderful for all my colleagues as well. We all got put up in hotels on the seafront. Some got very lucky with the most marvellous suites. Others just got lucky with magnificent rooms.

I, of course, went one step further. In my first year I stayed with the Kidds themselves. And one evening we had drinks with a beachside neighbour, a lovely Italian countess called Carla Cavalli. I was finding out, once again, that the rich are so very different.

'Your house is absolutely beautiful,' I said. 'Do you live here full-time or do you have another house elsewhere?'

'Oh no, darling, it's a holiday home. I also have a house in New York, an apartment in New York, a place in...' and the list went on. And on. I think in total there were ten or maybe a dozen properties.

Tao Rossi, of the drinks company, was an equally gracious and generous host. In my second year I was offered her guesthouse – a three-bed, three-bath property with maids and other assorted servants. The fridges were stocked with a dozen bottles of wonderful champagne. And after a couple of days Carla accosted me to see why they hadn't been touched.

'Why do you not drink it? You drink it up and I fill it up again,' she promised. And she was as good as her word. And so a picture of Barbados emerges. One of luxury.

The key hotel is the Sandy Lane. Renowned visitors

from yesteryear include Maria Callas, Aristotle Onassis and the Kennedys. There's Platinum Mile and billionaires galore. I loved it. One day I walked along that unique, white sand beach with Joan's boyfriend Robin. We were walking along the beach towards, as I now know, Heron Bay. We stormed the castle – or at least we climbed over the wall and joined the Bamford family around their pool. Robin's connections and easy charm made that sort of thing so simple. I was blissfully happy in his wake.

I was introduced to the matriarch of the Bamford family, and oh how I love a good matriarch. Her name was Meggi and I fell in love with her that first day. She had split from her husband but she had remained the lady of the family. We often had tea together over so many years. She had an amazing doll collection and made ornately decorated boxes as gifts for her confidantes. I treasure mine. I also love the fact that with Meggi, as with so many people in my life, I don't just make one friend, I make a whole family of friends.

One time back in London Anthony and Carole Bamford arranged for eight of us to be flown to Paris for lunch in a private plane. I was so stupid, thinking that because we were only going for lunch I wouldn't need a passport. So for a while it looked as if the table for eight would need to have one place setting removed. I waved everyone else off in the chauffeur-driven cars and sat in the sad little hut on the wrong side of the immigration line at a tiny French airstrip. At best all I could hope for at lunchtime was a baguette. But fortunately Anthony could pull strings. He found someone who could produce a form that would allow me the freedom of France for the rest of the day. So a car came to whisk me to the Paris Ritz and join the others just after their starters had been served.

On another occasion we were put up at the Paris Ritz overnight. It is the most exquisite hotel in the world – and Carole had made it even more so. She had put special flower arrangements in all our rooms for a more personal greeting. So classy – unlike me. I took the flowers with me when I checked out the next day, and persuaded the others to do so as well. 'Common as muck,' my dear mother would have said had she seen me sneaking out of the Ritz with my booty. But at least, for once, I was economising. Surely even my increasingly grim-faced accountant would approve of that.

The only downside to that first glorious season in Barbados was that it hadn't paid very much money. And I didn't have any hugely well-paid jobs lined up for my return in 1994 either. More sobering still was the fact that the £50,000 I had begged for the previous year hadn't been enough to clear more than my most urgent debts.

In my quiet months I had to ask other friends for smaller amounts to tide me over each new crisis. It was so awful to ask. And in my heart I knew I was barely keeping my head above water. I knew I couldn't go on like that. At the back of my mind was my biggest worry: what if I lose my home? Would any bank trust me with a mortgage again if I got repossessed? I was in my mid-forties, working in the most precarious, youth-obsessed profession known to man. Could I go back to renting a room from friends – or, worse, from strangers? Of course I couldn't. I'd had all those glittering years. All the parties, all the nights at the Paris Ritz and in the

Hollywood Hills. I couldn't – wouldn't – go back to living out of a suitcase.

Or at least that was my plan. I would find more work. A commercial. A new prime-time series. Something in America. But the jobs passed me by and the fear ate away at me, insidious, insistent and awful. Months passed and it was there first thing in the morning and last thing at night. It woke me up at 4am and didn't leave my mind all day.

So when would the nightmare end?

My accountant had a solution. 'You need to declare voluntary bankruptcy,' he said after yet another grim meeting.

The process might be different today. But when I went through it everyone sat down to work out a figure for what I owed and then recalculated how much of it I could afford to repay and when. The final figure was still quite awful, but I worked like a dog so that I could clear it in a single year. Everything went towards that goal. I'd seen my dad go though the same VAT-inspired crisis and fight his way back when his garages collapsed in the 1970s. I was going to follow his lead. This wouldn't break me.

As a postscript, I think now that voluntary bankruptcy was the wrong thing for me to do, not least because it was all so crazily expensive to arrange. I had to pay £7,000 or £8,000 in fees to go bankrupt – how can that make sense? But whether the actual bankruptcy was the right thing for me or not, the perfect storm of a financial crisis was the making of me. It made me aware of money for the very first time. I was nearly 46. And I was only just growing up.

I had to say goodbye to my lovely bank, Coutts – having given them so many good customers over the years. The only other bank that would take me was Allied Irish Bank. And I will always be loyal to them for that. I was only allowed one credit card, and today that's still all that I have. And I pay it off the very moment the bill arrives at my door each month. Now when my agent, Lesley Duff, gets my money her slice is taken off, the VAT slice is taken off, the tax money is saved and what's left is mine. I have never been in debt since. I've never forgotten how close I came to losing it all.

The one good thing that came out of this terrible period was that I met the love of my life, Neil Sinclair. Or, I should say, I met him all over again. The way we got together reads like a film script, or a love story, in itself.

I first saw him some 24 years ago in his native Scotland. I was doing *Dick Whittington* at the Theatre Royal in Brighton for Jamie Phillips and, as usual, I was having a whale of a time. Jamie, meanwhile, had another panto running in Glasgow and was in a state of crisis. His lead had left the show early and they were desperately seeking a replacement star. My gig in Brighton finished the next day. Could I hotfoot it up north and take over? Glasgow is a city I love, so that was one reason I said yes. Another, of course, was the money. But the final one was the challenge. What Jamie wanted me to do was theatrical madness – and I was mad enough to go for it.

I took the curtain calls in Brighton on the Saturday night – and then threw myself into the fun of the end-of-run party as normal. The next day I got the train to Scotland with the *Jack and the Beanstalk* script on my lap and lots of coffee at my side. On Monday afternoon I was on stage for the matinée at the Pavillion Theatre. I only made one mistake. In one loose moment I turned to Jack and called him Dick.

The audience just loved it, though. They knew that I was a very last-minute replacement, so they were in a forgiving, supportive mood. There was such a buzz that week and I was so glad I had taken Jamie up on the challenge.

Towards the end of the week I decided to let my hair down a little. I went to a bar in town and met this lovely air steward called Neil. We had a short, sweet fling and I just thought he was the most wonderful man. He made me laugh and seemed to be able to read my mind. We were finishing each other's sentences within a few days. But then it had to end. I was with someone else and so after much soul-searching Neil and I said goodbye. Our Highland fling would have to be the end of it. But as I headed south I couldn't stop thinking about him. Could he actually be 'the one'? Had I been a fool to let him slip through my fingers? Fourteen years would pass before I found out.

I was on a plane back from Barbados after going out to discuss that first season there. I had been put in Club – thank you, British Airways. And one of the cabin crew, Liza Higgins, a close friend of Neil's, came up to chat to me. 'Mr Biggins, I think we have a mutual friend,' she said. 'His name is Neil Sinclair.'

In that one moment I remembered everything. 'Could you give him my number?' I asked, feeling like a teenager.

She passed it on and he called. And for no other reason than that it was the closest date we could make, we met up on 14 February, Valentine's Day, in 1994. We have been together ever since.

Neil was living in Hove but we knew we wanted to be together straight away. So he sold his house and bought into mine in Hackney. That helped me clear my final remaining debts from the voluntary bankruptcy. And it gave us the foundation for the life we have had ever since. Neil is funny, caring, a typical Cancer and a home-maker. He still flies, so we have plenty of space, and we're not glued together when we do go out. I remember that when we first went to showbusiness parties I used to worry about how he would get on. As if I needed to. One early, ridiculously over-the-top date was at a charity dinner party where Neil was placed on the top table next to an ambassador's wife. 'Will he cope?' I asked myself. Then I looked across the room. The two of them were talking so much they hardly drew breath. At the end of the night they exchanged phone numbers.

Neil was a total star. He fitted into my world from the start and he loves it. So nowadays I'm quite happy that we arrive at places together and then I often leap off and leave him for the rest of the night as I talk shop with other theatrical pals. What I love is that at the end of the night we leave together. And we relive the whole night from our different perspectives.

Best of all, Neil and I are both very good about laughing when things go wrong. Which, of course, they do. Just after we got together I was showing off about being offered a new Saab convertible to road-test for a *Daily Express* article.

'Won't it be a bit dull if we just drive around near here?' I said to Neil beforehand.

'Where else can we go?'

'Well, the Channel Tunnel has just opened. Let's try that. And I'll treat you to a night at the Ritz in Paris.'

So off we went to France. This time I did have my passport. But once more I didn't prove to be the sharpest tool in the box. For some reason I thought the tunnel went underground in Kent and popped back up slap bang in the middle of Paris. Neil and I were two men without a map and without a clue. But somehow, through the laughs, we made it to our destination. That's when we started laughing again. 'I can't drive this up to the Ritz. I just can't.'

As we got to the centre of the city I was overcome with embarrassment. Because, while our car might be brand new and expensive, it was also bright orange. And I mean bright, bright orange. It looked appalling. And understandably, the moment we parked at the Ritz it was whisked away by the staff to protect the sensibilities of the other guests. If I knew the French for 'That man in the horrid orange car was the one who stole his hostess's flower arrangement last summer', I'm sure I would have heard it that day.

But as it happened our Parisian adventure was only warming up.

Now, there's nothing I love more than getting a bargain. So I had been on the phone to Mohamed al Fayed's office the moment I had the idea of driving to Paris. Can we get a deal on our room? Unfortunately we couldn't. 'We don't do deals,' I was told. 'But we will make sure you are well looked after.' And the lady was absolutely right. Neil and I had a to-die-for suite. The Ritz is the essence of Paris and has tremendous style. And there was more to come.

When I had been talking to Mohamed al Fayed's office I had decided to be cheeky. (Thanks, Dad, for teaching me that if you don't ask you don't get.) I had been reading about Villa Windsor, the home in the Bois de Boulogne where the Duke and Duchess of Windsor had lived and which al Fayed had lovingly restored. 'Would it be possible to have a tour of the property?' I asked. Nothing ventured, nothing gained.

'You do know that it's a private house? It's not open to the public.'

'Yes, I know that. But I do know some other people who have seen what Mr al Fayed has done and they say it's magnificent. I would so love to have the chance to see the property myself. Would you please just ask Mr al Fayed?'

Clearly she had done so. And she must have found her boss on a very good day. As Neil and I left the hotel for dinner that evening the concierge approached us. 'Mr al Fayed's chauffeur will pick you up at 11am tomorrow,' he told us. We had been granted our royal tour.

Our driver was none other than Henri Paul. At the time we had no reason to pay him particular attention – and I can certainly say that I don't remember us driving too fast, or being nervous in any way in his charge. He was neatly dressed and conservative, just as he appeared to be in those awful CCTV pictures of Diana and Dodi's last moments. As he didn't seem to speak much English and our French is limited, we didn't talk very much. But he seemed professional and competent. Both the man and the mood must have been very different those few years later when Diana and Dodi were in our place in Henri Paul's car and the paparazzi were on their tail.

As an aside, I do have an opinion on Diana's last summer. I think the bright girl I had spent some lovely evenings with would have enjoyed her summer fling enormously. But I don't feel that marriage was ever on her mind, especially to someone as controversial as Dodi. Diana loved her boys too much to put them in the middle of that sort of situation. She knew, none better, that being royal was complicated enough already.

The Duchess of Windsor's former butler opened the doors to us at the villa – he had been retained, which is wonderful in itself. And what a property. The words 'lovingly restored' just can't do it justice. Apparently, the place wasn't in great condition when the royal family moved on. But now Mohamed al Fayed had spared no expense. He had also shown extraordinary good taste. For an arch-royalist like me it was a dream come true to be inside such a treasure trove. The al Fayed family have rooms somewhere, I believe. But the rooms the Duke and Duchess used are left just as they were. And I mean just as they were. Neil and I opened drawers to see her panties and stockings laid out, his underwear folded and stacked. There were suits, coats, dresses on hangers. It was eerie, as if their owners had just popped out for lunch. A true slice of living history. I ran my fingers over the desk where the Duke had written his abdication speech. How many people are lucky enough to have done that?

Back to the next set of Barbados shows. Taking control of those seasons was fabulous fun. Casting my plays was the highlight. Well, normally. As I got ready for the second year I rang Nichola McAuliffe to offer her a role in *The Taming of the Shrew*. And there was something funny about the way she agreed to take part. She was so flat, so matter-of-fact, that I was worried she might be ill. Then, seconds later, she rang me back. 'Biggins, I wasn't paying attention. Did you say Barbados?'

'Yes, Barbados. In the Caribbean.'

At that she screeched so loud I nearly lost my hearing. She had misheard me first time around. I think she thought the play was in Battersea.

So many other great names and good friends were able to join me on the jaunts. But I didn't always push my luck. In London I was leaving a restaurant one day when I passed Maggie Smith and Joan Plowright at their table. They called me over with fabulously imperious gestures. 'Now, Biggins, we want to go to Barbados and do your season there,' said Maggie.

'I'm sorry, I have to say no. You would both be far too diva-ish,' I said. I like to think I'm one of the few to refuse Maggie Smith and Lord Olivier's widow a job. Though I'd have got them plane tickets faster than you can say 'And the winner is' if I'd thought for one moment that they were serious.

In my third season in Barbados I directed *Tosca* – who says I'm not up for a challenge? Richard Polo's enthusiasm for opera had finally rubbed off on me, though I often felt that in Barbados it was never staged as well as it could be. This was my chance to see if I could do better. But who to cast? Richard Wagner's niece Rosemary Wagner-Scott was training to be an opera singer and I called her for an audition. She was breathtakingly good and it was lovely to give her such a good role to play.

These wonderful seasons ended in a spat over money. For three glorious years we had attracted some extraordinary talents. Our performers always had their flights paid and were put up in the island's gorgeous hotels. But should they be paid as well?

From the start I had made sure that we all were. It was pocket money, but I felt the principle was important. We worked very hard to rehearse and put on such strong performances in the short time we were on the island. But I think the question of fees began to grate.

'Why do we have to pay these actors to come out here?' I was asked in the third year.

'Well, because they have mortgages and bills and need to eat,' I suggested.

But by this point I think the seasons were going so well that the family thought they would run themselves. And they had just had an amazing offer from Pavarotti. He agreed to do the following year's season for free and clearly my band of travelling players could hardly compete with that. As it turned out, though, we might have been a better bet. By all accounts Pavarotti gave a magnificent performance. But, while he didn't charge for his services, the bill for the orchestra and his entourage was rumoured to have topped £1 million.

17

Men Behaving Badly

I showed Tommy Steele my dick shortly after going back on tour in the UK. And he went on to show it to pretty much everyone he could find. I was in the Frederick Lonsdale play *On Approval* which Lee Dean produced (who would get that invite to Liza Minnelli's wedding ahead of me), the mouthy *Liver Bird* Polly James, Tessa Wyatt and Robin Sachs (Leonard's son). The play is a comedy of manners about two couples going away for a weekend. Polly was a bit of a diva, but we coped. She had just done *Half a Sixpence* with Tommy Steele and was off on holiday with him towards the end of our run. She turned up at the theatre that night with a new camera for her holiday photos and was snapping away as the curtain rose.

'Oh my God, I'm on!' she whispered, thrusting the camera at me.

I couldn't help myself. I dropped my trousers and pants.

'Take some pictures of my dick,' I told Robin. He did, but then it was my cue and after the show Polly got her camera back and I forgot all about it.

Fast forward to Tommy and Polly's mini-break. After finishing the film she took the camera in to get the pictures developed – and of all places she chose one of those camera stores where developed pictures are hung up in the window for everyone to see. Tommy was dispatched to collect the prints – and returned hysterical with laughter. He proceeded to pass the offending pictures around a restaurant, saying it was the funniest thing he had ever seen. Polly, I feel obliged to say, was less than thrilled. Our friendship has survived because I think that we're in the right world. Theatre seems to breed eccentrics. I love larger-than-life characters – and the larger the better.

I've already talked about several of the great ladies in my life. Here are a few stories about the most outrageous of the men.

George Borwick was a divinely eccentric man, an old-school gentleman straight out of central casting. He was the heir to the Borwick's Baking Powder fortune (I kid you not) and we had one very larger-than-life friend in common: Kenneth Williams. Get me, George and Kenneth together and you were in for a very good time indeed. George had a home in South Africa and there were many happy afternoons when he returned to England with packs of photographs of naked South African men from around his pool to show off. Yet again this proved to me that the rich are different. When he got down to his last quarter of a million, George panicked. So he did what so many others have done over the centuries. He married for money.

The bride-to-be was a wealthy fellow South African lady he had known for years. I sat with Kenneth gossiping in a restaurant one night. 'Well, George has fallen on his feet as usual. He should finally be able to relax a little about his finances. And his wife seems nice enough. She must know the score. At least he won't have to do it,' I predicted.

'No! No! No!' trilled the incomparable Kenneth. 'He'll have to do it all the time. She loves the dick!' Never have so many fellow diners choked on their soup en masse before.

Sir Ralph Richardson was another eccentric hero of mine. My favourite story about him is set at the fabulously old-fashioned Savile Club on Brook Street in Mayfair. The *Poldark* author Winston Graham had made me a member and every time I went – thanking Mrs Christian for my elocution lessons – it was always full of classic old colonels. It wasn't really my scene and I loved it and laughed at it in equal measure. The club has a rigid set of rules. If you are on your own you are seated at a long table next to other members and left to sink or swim in conversation. Fortunately small talk is something I'm good at. I swam away happily. Ordering meals took some getting used to as well. The waitresses aren't allowed to interrupt the members to ask them for their orders – instead you have to write down what you want on a bit of paper and they have to peer across at it. How quintessentially English, and bonkers, is that?

Anyway, my favourite Ralph Richardson story is when he was so engrossed in conversation at the Savile Club that he didn't write down his order. At 1.45 the waitress felt she had to interrupt him. 'Excuse me, sir, I'm very sorry but the kitchen is about to close. Can I take your order?'

'Of course you can. I'd like a jam omelette, please.'

And off she went, only to return within moments. 'I'm sorry, sir, I've asked the chef and he wants to know who it's for.'

'Sir Ralph Richardson.'

Off she went again, and back she came. 'I'm sorry, sir. The chef says no.'

You hardly need Sir Ralph's punchline ('Who the hell do you need to be in this place to get served a jam omelette?') to love that story.

Finally, in a roll-call of mad old actors, how can I leave out John Gielgud? In my favourite story about him he was directing a cast of dreamy-looking military men in a new opera. The cast were lined up on stage waiting for his instruction. 'Right, I want you over there at the back,' he said to the first to present himself. 'Now I want you to the left. I want you next to him and I want you – oh my God, I want *you*,' he spluttered as the most handsome young man yet reached the front of the queue.

Ever since our risqué little Regent's Park chat I had worried that I might have offended Her Majesty. Fortunately, I found out a little later that, in fact, she has a surprisingly sharp sense of humour. We were reintroduced in the interval of a charity function at a gala performance of Andrew Lloyd Webber's *Bombay Dreams*. 'This is Christopher Biggins, who is going to be hosting the charity auction after the performance,' her omnipresent guide told her as she approached.

'How lovely,' was her typically noncommittal comment. Everything in me told me to smile and simply say I was pleased to see her. But one tiny part of me decided to be cheeky. That part of me won.

The Queen was wearing a most incredible set of pearls. They were glowing and gorgeous in the softly lit room. 'I don't suppose you've got anything we could auction?' I heard myself ask, looking very pointedly at them.

It seemed that the Queen took great umbrage. She moved on to the next group of people a little too fast for my liking. And then, breaking all convention, she turned around and came back to me.

'What are you auctioning?' she asked.

'Well, I've got some art, some memorabilia. I've got holidays and, yes, I've got jewellery.' My eyes fell again to those pearls.

'How lovely,' the Queen said one last time, putting her hand protectively over her necklace. She left me. But there was a twinkle in her eye that was so pronounced it was almost a wink.

There was never any doubting that Princess Diana had a sense of humour. I met her at several charity events over the years and was impressed at how well she remembered people's names. Of course, I also respected the charities she chose to represent. Names and causes so many others felt were too hot to handle. The first time I met her in a purely social situation came about because of Liza. She was headlining at the Albert Hall and rang me just before one performance.

'Biggins, I've got a friend in tonight, who I wanted you to come in and look after,' Liza said.

I said yes, without even asking who the friend might be.

It could have been Liza's pool boy, for all I cared. In fact, I'd have been very happy if it had been Liza's pool boy. But in the end it was Diana. She was bright and funny, tactile and warm. And, oh, how she loved her boys. When we met at the Albert Hall she had just been photographed on the royal yacht in Canada. It was that famous picture of her with her arms stretched wide as she reaches out to hug them. It's one of my favourite images of her. 'It's so rare to see anyone in the royal family being so demonstrative to each other,' I said.

'How could I not hug them?' she asked me. 'I hadn't been able to stop thinking about them all the time we'd been apart.'

In the months and years ahead, Diana and I had plenty of gossipy lunches, dinners and laughs together. And after a while our friendship made the news. An *Evening Standard* reporter was always writing humorous references about us. In one full-page article he and the picture people mocked up a shot of Diana wearing a big Miss World-style sash over her dress saying, 'Miss Biggins 1995'. I thought it was hilarious. So did Diana.

A letter arrived the following week. 'I hope life is treating you kindly and yes, a big smile was evident from a particular lady in W8 last Friday,' she wrote.

Diana's big mistake, her tragedy, was falling in love with Charles. I like and respect him a great deal as well. I believe in his charities, which have often been in fields as unfashionable as those chosen by his former wife. But no one told Diana she was applying for a job, not marrying her hero.

Men Behaving Badly

The only major member of the royal family I didn't get the chance to meet properly was the Queen Mother – though I once sat opposite her at a church service and am convinced I got a smile. But I did hear a lot about this grand old lady, through the much-missed Billy Talon. Billy had joined the royal household at just 16 – and never left. The Queen Mum was the Queen of England then. He told a wonderful story of how they had become so close.

It was at a Christmas party when the dance called the Paul Jones was about to start. The men and women lined up in circles around the room and when the music stopped you had to do the next dance with whoever was in front of you. For the poor, nervous Billy, that person was the Queen. 'Do you dance?' she asked, clearly sensing how uncertain he was.

'No, Ma'am.'

'Then walk with me.'

And he walked with her for the rest of her life.

I spent a lot of time with Billy at his tiny house on the Mall, a treasury of royal family photos and keepsakes. He was a joy as a man, someone who loved his life and loved his job. That, I am sure, is why we always got along.

Another of my favourite Billy Talon stories about his extraordinary employer concerned another terrified new recruit.

'Tomorrow you will take Her Majesty her breakfast,' he was told.

'But I can't.'

'You must.'

'Please don't ask me to. I can't do it.'

But the following morning the terrified youngster was

one of the four men outside the Queen's bedroom door. One was there to supervise. One to knock. One to open the door. Our young friend had to walk in with the tray.

'Only speak if you are spoken to,' was the breakfast rule. And as the boy had put the tray down and was leaving the room he thought he was in the clear. Then the Queen Mother spoke. 'You're new here,' she said.

'Yes I am, Ma'am.'

'Are you gay?'

'Yes I am, Ma'am.'

'Then you'll love it here,' she pronounced.

'Economise, Biggins. Economise.' I really did try hard in the quiet years after *Cluedo*.

But there always seemed to be one more party to attend. And, really, they were often too good to miss.

Some of the best were thrown by Teddy and Bee Van Zuylen. He's a big bear of a man and she's a beautiful, slim and charming lady. I bumped into them at Nice airport when they were setting off on their honeymoon. But fortunately, after gatecrashing Jeremy Irons's honeymoon all those years earlier, I had since learned to leave newlyweds alone. Perhaps as a reward for my newfound manners I was soon invited to Teddy's family home, Kasteel de Haar, just outside Amsterdam. It has a moat, spires, battlements – everything you could expect in a fantasy castle. It's open to the public for 11 months a year and is his for all of September.

If you are lucky enough to be invited there, chauffeurs pick you up from the airport, butlers take your luggage at the castle door and maids seem able to unpack and iron all your clothes by the time you get to your room. I should have taken a few duvet covers with me to save my dear cleaning lady a job. All the vast rooms have four-poster beds and every night someone runs you a vast bath at 6pm and tells you that at 7pm the water will be the perfect temperature.

That, surely, is how I was born to live.

After that perfect bath I remember dressing in black tie and playing Oh Hell, a poor man's bridge, after dinner. And amid company that can hardly be described as poor.

On another occasion Neil and I went to Paris on Eurostar to another of the couple's parties. Sitting opposite us on the train was a fellow guest, Tessa Kennedy, and we had a picnic of bread and wine along the way. In Paris we met one of Tessa's pals, the film star Leslie Caron, then headed to the Van Zuylens' house on an island in the Seine. It was like a Disney fairytale. Our car swept through a deliberately ordinary gate and into a heart-stoppingly beautiful courtyard. Practically a whole orchestra was playing inside on the staircase, and there was room after room of unbelievably glamorous people to meet. And meet them I did. Feel intimidated and fade into the background? I don't think so. I mingled to the manor born. And that was just the start.

When Teddy's 70th birthday came around, we all arranged a surprise party at Tessa's place in Runnymede near Windsor. We tried to recreate the vast dining table from Paris – though things were a little more cramped on this side of the Channel. We certainly didn't run to a waiter for every second guest, which was the ratio over there. 'I want to come as the baroness,' I joked when we laid down the dress code. 'That way I'd get the best bedroom in the house.'

Nice joke, Biggins, everyone was thinking. But I did want to come as the baroness. So I got a white panto outfit with acres of diamante and bucketloads of fake jewellery. We had some very grand, very serious French people at the party that night. The world's banking industry was particularly well represented. But, thank God, they knew how to laugh. And, thank God, Teddy saw the joke.

Late in the evening he admitted he had guessed that some sort of surprise party was on the cards. 'But when I was told to come out to Windsor I thought I was having dinner with the Queen,' he said.

'You are, dear, you are,' I told him.

When you are living the high life with such marvellous friends you really don't want to be arrested for shoplifting. In 1996 I was arrested for shoplifting.

I call it my Richard Madeley moment, because of course it was all just a terrible misunderstanding. It began when I was in bed with the flu. Neil was on a trip and I woke up ravenously hungry. We had absolutely nothing in the house so I staggered off to our nearest supermarket. I know I looked dreadful – I hadn't washed, shaved or even attempted to tame my hair. And I wasn't exactly inconspicuous. I had pulled on the nearest clothes I could find as I stumbled out of my sickbed – a bright-pink tracksuit with 'Joe Allen' printed down one leg, one of a number specially made for the restaurant's best customers. But it was hardly right for Hackney.

I bought absolutely masses of food, the way you do when you're not well. You never quite know what you might feel like eating, so you go for it all. I had enough comfort food to last a week. I even had a bit of healthy food tucked away in my trolley as well.

'Could you come this way, please, sir?' The lady stopped me at the exit. What on earth was going on? It sounded a bit more formal than an autograph request.

'Could I see the receipt for your shopping, sir?' And then she asked me to empty my pockets.

In them, to my absolute horror, was a packet of batteries. I'd put them there because they were so small they slipped out of my trolley – and, yes, I'd quite forgotten to pay for them. Surely this lady would understand. But no. The police were called and I was taken to the station. The only good thing was that the horror of the situation had taken my mind off my flu.

After a long wait I was told, 'Mr Biggins, you've just spent over £60 on groceries and you have nearly £200 in cash in your wallet. Why would you steal a set of batteries?'

'Exactly,' I said. 'That's why it's a mistake. I'd never steal a single thing, even if I didn't have the money to pay for something.' I could finally stop protesting. The police were on my side. I was released and headed back to my sickbed. It was all over.

Yeah, right. At what seemed like dawn the next morning my doorbell began to ring. It didn't stop. The *News of the World* was there, desperate for quotes, and on Sunday my supposed shoplifting shame was one of the lead stories of the week. The world had gone mad. But at least I got a few more laughs out of it. I went to Peter Delaney's for dinner that Sunday night. When I sat at the table and reached for my knife and fork I saw the joke. He had chained them down.

18

Fabulous at 50

A pack of divas were unleashed as my 50th birthday approached in 1998. They were planning a top-secret party, which of course I knew almost everything about.

The divas were Joan Collins, Carole Bamford, Jeanne Mandry, Sue St John, Dame Maureen Thomas, Billy Differ – oh, and last but not least, dear Neil. As I wasn't supposed to be aware of the plans, I couldn't ask Neil how it was all going. But I could well imagine it was fraught with ego problems and dramas. I thought it was all hilarious.

What I didn't know was that something else was going on. The surprise party was real, but it was really only a smokescreen. I found that out when I was on stage at the end of my panto matinee in Brighton. We didn't have an evening performance that day and I was looking forward to putting my feet up. I began my curtain speech as normal and halfway through I got a real roar from the crowd. I think I self-consciously congratulated myself on my comic timing. You're better at this than you thought, Biggins. They love you.

When the second roar began something told me there was more going on than my repartee. So I turned to see Michael Aspel and his famous red book. Someone was going to get the *This Is Your Life* treatment. But who? I looked around the stage in a genuine attempt to work it out. It's not false modesty to say I really didn't think it was me. But how pleased I am that it was. *This Is Your Life* is a fantastic programme. It's wonderful for friends and family, perhaps as much as for the person getting the honour. My parents were treated magnificently. They were driven up from Salisbury, put in a fantastic hotel and loved every minute of my show. Such a privilege to be able to let your parents into your professional and personal life like this. And oh, what fun to have all your old friends brought together for a marvellous party.

After coming off stage in Brighton – wearing a vast strawberry-blonde wig and an even more outrageous costume than normal – I got out of make-up and into my normal clothes. Then the producer took me outside. A white Rolls-Royce was waiting to take me to London. 'Is there anything you want, or need for the journey?' she asked.

'I'd love a nap, if that's OK.'

I woke up in a mild panic as we approached the studio in London.

'Will anyone have a toothbrush? What will I need to wear?' I asked the producer.

Neil, of course, had thought of everything and left everything I might need in my dressing room.

Cilla was the first guest to speak on the show, then Gillian Taylforth, Anthony and Georgina Andrews, my brother Sean and my parents, John Brown from my school days, Linda Bellingham. They all made me laugh. Cameron Mackintosh spoke via a video link (he's far too grand to do a tacky show like *This Is Your Life*). My old *Poldark* pals Angharad Rees and Julie Dawn Cole were there with that gang. Then there was Paula Wilcox, Bea Arthur, the actress Amy MacDonald, Nichola McAuliffe, David and Jackie Wood – old pals from my Salisbury days – Bonnie Langford, my tiny little niece Alice and nephew Jack, neither of them more than five, who were led on by their mother, Louise. We had a video greeting from Joan Collins and, wrapping up an incredible night as my final guest, Barbara Windsor.

Then of course were all the other people who hadn't had a chance to speak in the half-hour show. In the audience were so many other dear friends. I look at the photographs – you're given them in the big red book – and to this day it moves me to tears. As I turn the pages I see my agent, Jonathan Altaras, Barry Burnet, Philip and Joan Kingsley, Anna and Graham Smith, Tony McLaren and his wife Veronica Charlewood, Esther Chatham, Gerald and Veronica Flint-Shipman from my Phoenix Theatre days, Sally Bullock, Stella Wilson, Jeremy Swan, Peter Delaney, Michael Codron and Mark Rayment, Paul Macbeth, Sian Phillips, Paula Wilcox, Lynda Bellingham, Peter Todd, Edmund and April O'Sullivan, Grace and David Tye, and so many more. I'm just as proud that so many of my family were at the show. Alongside my parents and Sean, there were the people who supported me for years – Auntie Betty and Uncle Jeff, who had put money into *The Orchestra* when I had desperately needed it. Auntie Monica and her husband Bryn, Uncle Ken and his wife Valerie, my relatives Michael and Annie O'Toole – the photographs and the memories just go on. It's traditional to end *This Is Your Life* in tears. I didn't stop for hours.

Oh God. Does going on *This Is Your Life* mean that your career is over? Is it like a Lifetime Achievement Award at the Oscars? Am I a has-been already? I had a bit of a wobble after the show. Had they wanted me on because they thought that if they waited any longer the world would forget my name? Was I never going to get back on television again?

At times like that you need to turn to your friends for comfort, reassurance and support.

'Biggins, you know you've really fucked up your career.'

That wasn't quite the comfort, reassurance and support I was after. Cameron Mackintosh was giving me what he thought passed for a pep talk. The only good thing about the conversation was its location. We had just had a wildly camp holiday in Las Vegas and were in the glorious first-class cabin of a flight back to London.

'What do you mean I've fucked up my career?'

'You've never lived up to your potential. There are a million things you could do that you haven't done. You should be playing Thenardier in *Les Miserables*, for a start.'

'Cameron, I'd love to play Thenardier in *Les Miz*.'

'Genuinely?'

'Come on, you know I would. Get me an audition.' So he did. But let me get to the end of the story before anyone cries nepotism or gay mafia.

The show was about to go on its first national tour and I was auditioned alongside the marvellous Rosie Ash. At first all went very well. 'Oh my God. You can sing,' one of the casting directors said.

'Of course I can bloody sing.'

And so, of course, could Rosie.

So we got a call-back and went through it all again. And again. Then again.

In total we performed for them eight times. Then they said no. I rang Cameron and went ballistic. 'How dare you have us strung along for so long. And not just me. Rosie, who's magnificent. She's been the lead in *Phantom* and all your shows. What more did you all want from us?'

'I can get them to send you a letter of apology,' Cameron began.

'I don't want a bloody letter of apology. I want a job.' And out of all this anger it suddenly looked as if I might get an even better one than I had ever dreamed of. One of Cameron's US partners had been particularly impressed at my auditions.

'You'll be in New York playing Thenardier by the end of the year,' he promised me.

But then he left the organisation for pastures new. My Broadway debut never happened. But maybe it was all for the best. Maybe working with such a close friend as Cameron wouldn't have worked. That's the problem with this business. It's as incestuous as hell. The more people you know the more likely you are to trip over them in one job or another. And the last thing I want to do is lose a friendship with someone like Cameron. We go back some 30 years now. We make up a wicked little trio with the agent Barry Burnett and call ourselves the Three Sisters. We all put on our best Dame Edna voices when we talk on the phone. And we do that almost every day.

I signed up for *Jack and the Beanstalk* in Cambridge over the millennium holiday – we did a show on the big night and then Neil and I headed to Kate and Kit's for the midnight celebrations. And in the new millennium the ups and downs of my life were as pronounced as ever before. There were times when there seemed to be very little work or money. And there were times when the parties were as lavish as they could possibly be.

On the work front I was to meet two legends in my next few jobs: Paul Scofield and Eric Sykes. I embarrassed myself in front of Paul and showed off a little too much in front of Eric.

Paul was starring in an incredibly prestigious Shakespeare series on Radio 4. I had some tiny part far behind in his wake. And he did make me just a little nervous. We rehearsed and recorded at the BBC's radio studios in Portland Place. And in the lunch hour I decided to take advantage of the location by popping into John Lewis. Of all things I needed a new pedal bin for my kitchen. Who says my life is all just about parties and glamour?

Anyway, when I dragged it back to Portland Place, who should be the only person sitting in the rehearsal area with his script but Paul. With my huge shopping bag I must have looked about as unsophisticated as it was possible to be. 'Hello,' I said, slightly nervous, trying to push my purchase out of sight.

'Hello, Christopher. And where have you been?'

There was no avoiding it. I had to come clean. 'I've been to John Lewis. To buy a pedal bin.' It was like the watermelon scene from *Dirty Dancing*. I was mortified at how small and pedestrian my life must seem. This man was my hero. He has turned down knighthoods. He's won Oscars. He doesn't bother about the shopping and domestic appliances. Fortunately my purchase did not seem to attract much more comment. Paul moved on to read a newspaper and I started to read through the script.

'Christopher. Can I look at your pedal bin?' this great actor suddenly asked, his voice booming around the rehearsal room.

'Of course you can.' I took the damn thing out of its bag, took it out of its box and set it on a table next to us. There was a long, excruciating silence.

'Christopher, you must have a ravishing kitchen,' was his equally loud verdict.

And with that we went back to our scripts.

I met Eric Sykes in Windsor when we had a three-week tryout for a revival of *Charley's Aunt*. Bill Kenwright was producing it. He is a man who has kept faith in me, and seen things in me, through some pretty lean times. On a wider scale he has also kept faith in theatre. Bill is one of the few producers to focus on straight plays. Some are good, some not so. But he keeps on producing them, right across the country. He employs so many people. And when I needed him most he carried on employing me.

No one earns much on a tryout of a new play or a revival. The money, such as it is, comes if we go on tour and if we make it to the West End. I was desperately hoping that we would hit the jackpot with *Charley's Aunt*. It's an old chestnut of a play. But I had a feeling that we would at least make the tour – because of dear old Eric's box-office clout.

He was in his late seventies in 2001. He could barely see and he could hardly hear. His wonderful assistant Janet Spearman, whom I'd known for years, was his eyes and ears. She would walk him from his dressing room to the stage. She would check his costume. She would check that every prop he would need was exactly where he would expect it to be. It was wonderful, heartening kindness.

And Eric himself? I would watch him from the wings desperate to work out how he'd got to be so good. I'd never seen technique like it. All I can say now is that he could somehow sense the audience. He had comedy running through his veins, he could feel when a laugh was going to come. He could adapt his timing to the idiosyncrasies of every audience. He was magnificent.

But he kept us on our toes. He was a perfectionist – at his level you have to be. He was very critical of himself, and when he felt it was necessary for the good of the production he certainly expected the best of others. At one point in the show I saw the opportunity for a cheap laugh from the audience. I've never knowingly passed up on a cheap laugh and I had no intention of starting then. Plus, of course, I wanted to show off a little in front of Eric and prove that I knew how to whip up an audience. I hope he approved of that, but I think he felt my cheap laughs were just that.

Sadly this wonderful production was to end with a tragedy. The marvellous Nyree Dawn Porter was in our company – the woman most audiences would always see as Irene Forsyte in *The Forsyte Saga*. She was probably the greatest hypochondriac I had ever met – and I loved her for it. We would all rise and fall in the dramas of her imaginary illnesses and afflictions. But in Windsor, as we prepared for our transfer up to the Theatre Royal in Newcastle, she was taking it to a new level. 'I'm not well,' she announced.

We all nodded, barely paying attention. This was hardly new.

Bill tried to calm her down. But she was adamant. 'I can't do the tour,' she said.

In the end he brought his own doctor to examine her. And, after a tip-to-toe examination, she was given a clean bill of health. But still she refused to come up to Newcastle. Nyree's understudy, Jane Lucas, was fantastic. She had little more than a day to rehearse but she was magnificent. She saved the show – and she wasn't alone. We had another understudy in a lead role that extraordinary opening night in Newcastle. An old pal of mine, Francis Matthews, was in the company and his wife was terribly ill herself as our transfer approached. As we left Windsor he too was excused in order to care for her. Wishing him – and her – all the best, we all went on stage up in Newcastle.

And we had a triumph of an opening night. Everyone

was word-perfect and the audience loved us. There were tears and cheers and dances backstage as we hugged and congratulated one another. But then, suddenly, the company manager appeared and hushed us down. Grim-faced and grey, he said he had sad news to impart. My hand went to my heart. Francis's wife must have died. My heart ached for him.

But that wasn't the news. It was Nyree who had passed away. Like the old joke about the inscription on the hypochondriac's gravestone – 'I told you I was ill' – she had been right all along. The girls were crying and we all felt terrible for having dismissed Nyree's fears. It was a devastating piece of news, right after the triumph of our big opening.

'Come on, come on. We must all stick together. We have to go out. For Nyree.' I took charge. We went to a nearby pizzeria. It wasn't exactly the Ivy or the Caprice but it was what we needed. In remembering Nyree we became hysterical, telling jokes and stories about her. It was cathartic and a fitting tribute to a colleague we sadly missed.

'Biggins, shall we go and see Barbra Streisand?' It was Joan Collins.

The answer, of course, was yes. Streisand was in town on her much-hyped live tour and Joan and I were thrilled to be able to call in favours and get some great tickets. But then we had a different, better offer. Prince Charles was hosting an evening for one of his charities at the concert and his office asked if we wanted to attend as part of that.

The answer, once again, was yes.

Joan and Robin had recently split up. They handled the

separation with charm and grace. None of us was forced to take sides. There was never a sense that you had to be a 'his' or a 'hers' friend in the new world order. Nor did any of us have to sit through recriminations or nastiness. It was the most grown-up of partings. But it was no less sad for all that. Joan's new beau, Percy Gibson, is a good man and is clearly good for her. But it was tricky for a while to adapt. I saw less of Joan as this new love got off the ground. So I was even more determined to enjoy our night with Prince Charles and the biggest diva in showbusiness.

We were all having drinks at the charity reception before the concert and when we talked to him it was clear that Charles was a little distracted. His dog had just gone missing and he was clearly very upset – making him, in my book, a sensitive and admirable man. Anyway, it was clear that the staff wanted us all to take our seats in the box, but Charles was still talking and of course Joan and I couldn't leave until he led the way. The whole room emptied before our conversation finally drew to a close. Charles then led us to our seats.

Later in the evening, after clips of the event had been shown on the news, my phone started to vibrate – thankfully I had put it on silent. 'Biggins, trust you to go and see a Barbra Streisand concert and end up on the news walking in with Prince Charles and Joan Collins,' was the gist of them all. But dear old Jenks in my first RSC production had taught me the benefit of making a great entrance. It's something I've never forgotten.

One thing about showbusiness, you never know when your next big break will come. I certainly hadn't expected mine to materialise in Manchester after the christening of Denise Welsh's son in 2003 (Denise was an old pal I'd met at a party years ago and we'd hit it off straight away). After the ceremony I got chatting to an exciting man called Brian Park who turned out to be the producer of *Bad Girls*. 'You must come and work for us,' he said. They were my seven favourite words.

'I'd love to.'

The show was camp and cult and preposterous. It fitted me like a glove.

What helped me ease my way back into prime-time television after a gap of something like a decade was the fact that I played myself. The idea was that I was the star guest at a charity presentation of a wheelchair for a fictitious charity that the scriptwriters had come up with.

I had a huge speech in the central hall of the prison as all the old lags, all the wardens and all the local dignitaries look on. Then, as I inspect the chair, the girls pounce on me, push me in it and wheel me away at speed. Which, I can tell you, isn't as easy as it sounds. Anyway, I end up held hostage in the prison greenhouse until their demands for better treatment are met. Ultimately, my character – me – agrees with their cause and joins it. We get drunk on gin they have made from an illegal still, we sing songs, I do a bit of Shakespeare and it's all an absolute riot.

Hopefully viewers liked it too, because I was asked back for a second episode, where I adopt one of the prisoners' kids. As usual, the behind-the-scenes story is one of plenty of laughs and a fair few new friends. Linda Henry in particular is a wonderful pal I might not know if it wasn't for HMP Larkhall. I hope I wasn't rusty on set – it was a long time since my last television show. But, as I say, it was a joy to play myself – or at least the *Bad Girls* scriptwriter's view of myself.

A dear friend is Sue St John. We both love technical things, like Sky Plus, gadgets and television shows. 'Are you watching this or that?' we're always ringing each other to ask. Her life's worthy of a book of its own – she was PA to Adnan Khashoggi, though she is irritatingly discreet about it. I was there on the sad day when her lovely husband Dick died.

Sue's sister was being wonderful, but one day on the phone I asked, as usual, if there was anything practical I could do. For once there was.

'There's something we need to collect from a chemist on Wimpole Street. Could you go and get it for us?' Sue asked.

'Of course I could. I'll be there with it within the hour.'

I collected the package and rang the doorbell. 'Here it is, Sue. But I won't stop.' I hated to intrude and knew I would speak to her on the phone later as I always did. But she wanted me to stay.

Poor, wonderful Dick. He had taken a turn for the worse – and there seemed to be death in his eyes and all around. I've been so fortunate in my life. I had rarely seen that look before. But it was unmistakable. In that awful atmosphere you learn new things about yourself. I learned that it helps to help. I made the teas and coffees and later helped lift Dick while we changed his bed. In my arms was a shell of the wonderful man I had known for so long. And I am sure he was as horrified as me. What the hell is Biggins doing here? he was probably thinking. I hope it made him smile inside.

Time was running out that afternoon. Dick's son was on his way over from America, but it turned out that his taxi had got lost. Somehow it seemed as if every second counted. Sue didn't want Dick to miss the chance to see his son. Finally, the doorbell rang. I raced to answer it, faster than I have moved in my life. I pushed Dick's son into the house and ran out to get his bags from the cab. Dick saw his son in his last moments, as I finally slipped away to leave the family together. Life can be short and is precious. That's the clear lesson I learned from Sue and Dick.

Now I don't want to end a chapter on a low point. So here's one last funny story from that era. I've been great friends of the Forte family for years and think all the sisters are particularly marvellous. Irene, married to the former American ambassador John Danilovich, is a particularly close pal. When the couple's 30th wedding anniversary approached, we all knew they would celebrate it well. We were right. They had five days of parties, events and functions in Washington DC. There were lunches, dinners, private tours of the White House and the Capitol. And on the final evening there was a black-tie dinner for 460 people, with Laura Bush as the guest of honour.

I was chatting to Irene when she saw a chance to introduce us. 'Come and meet the First Lady.'

So we crossed the room.

'Laura, meet Christopher Biggins. He's an actor friend of mine from London.'

'Nice to meet you, Christopher.'

'Lovely to meet you as well. We were at your house this

afternoon and I have to say we were very disappointed that you weren't there to make us tea.'

What possessed me to try to crack a joke with the President's wife? Especially a weak little joke like that? And especially when it appeared that Laura's sense of humour had deserted her that evening. 'Well, I'm terribly sorry, but I was out,' she said flatly.

As an embarrassed silence developed, I thought I saw a chance to create a distraction. Neil was just a few feet away from us, chatting to someone else.

'Neil!' I called out, far too loudly. 'Come over here and meet Barbara Bush.'

The whole room chilled. 'Laura,' she barked as she turned on her elegant heel. 'It's Laura.'

Neil never did get to meet her.

19

Back on Stage

I was 55 years old, I had been working since my teens and I had never fought tooth and nail for a role. I had never been convinced I had been born to play any particular part. I had never worried as much as people think you do if the good jobs don't come up.

But in 2003 I did have a rare sense of humour failure about the industry. The grapevine was buzzing with news that *Chitty Chitty Bang Bang* was about to be staged in a massive new show at the London Palladium. I was beside myself when I heard of the plans. *Chitty Chitty Bang Bang*! The London Palladium! And who better than me to play Baron Bomburst?

My old *I Claudius* co-star Brian Blessed, it turned out. Then Vincent Spinetti when Brian's initial run ended. I was devastated. I had put myself up for the role right back at the start, when I heard the earliest whispers that a production was on the cards. But they wouldn't even see me. I was having my Barbara Windsor moment. Oh, it's only Christopher Biggins, they must have been thinking. Too frivolous, too lightweight, too needy even? I have no idea what it was that counted me out – probably simple snobbery. Maybe the industry just didn't know that I could sing – just like the auditions people on *Les Miz*.

Yes, I was there as Herod in *Jesus Christ Superstar* at the Barbican. Yes, I had been there in the high-camp film version of *Joseph and the Amazing Technicolor Dreamcoat* (you were fabulous, Joan). But while I thought Brian was fantastic – however grim I felt, I wasn't going to miss that opening night – I was determined to keep the pressure on. So, when Vincent's run approached its end and a third cast rotation was due, I got my agent to call yet again. Finally she won me my audition. And in the summer of 2004 I won myself a chance to appear at the Palladium.

It's a huge stage. It's wide and it's deep and it reeks of history. On my first entrance in rehearsals I kept thinking of little Judy Garland, sitting on the edge of the stage and dangling her legs into the orchestra pit as she sang 'Somewhere Over the Rainbow'. On Argyll Street outside the Palladium, there's a board that lists all the huge stars who have performed there over the years. I had stood and read though that list endlessly over the years. Now I was finally on it. Christopher Biggins. Right there alongside the greats. Fabulous. Quite amazing.

Louise Gold was my beautiful Baroness and we made a marvellous double act, though I say so myself. We managed to bring the house down with 'You're My Little Chu-Chi Face'. And we never let it go stale. I loved adding little bits to give Louise and the audience an extra giggle. Everyone loved that. Didn't they?

'There's a note for you, Mr Biggins.'

The doormen would hand me envelopes or I would find one in my dressing room. They were from our choreographer, the terrifyingly good Gillian Lynne. She wasn't happy with my added extras. So I kept on having to apologise and promise never to go off script again. Then something funny would occur to me and off I would go. Once, I think, Louise and I ran 'Bombay Samba' for an extra six or seven minutes because everyone was having so much fun. The whole cast on the show were on top form. Dear Gary Wilmot, a fellow stalwart of the Regent's Park Open Air Theatre, was with us, and Jason Donovan and Brian Conley, and Scarlett Strallen as Truly Scrumptious, closely followed by Summer Strallen. We had Tony Adams, now a good pal, and Freddie Lees – so many lovely people.

Then, of course, came the Child-Catcher. My run started out with Alvin Stardust in this role, then we had little Stephen Gateley and Lionel Blair. Lionel, perhaps surprisingly, was the most terrifying of my trio. It was a tight ship. Robert Scott, our musical director, and Michael Rose, our producer, were fiercely professional. We had a compulsory warm-up before each show. I would mark out an area at the back of the stage for the oldies. We would gather there to do what the youngsters did. Well, most of it.

I was in the show for a wonderful 18 months. My bank manager loved it as much as I did. My dressing room was a joy in itself. It had a bed, a fridge, a kettle, a colour television and a telephone. It was like having my own little apartment right in the heart of London. I could have made my bank manager even happier by renting my house out for 18 months and moving in at Argyll Street. I'm sure I wouldn't have been the first to try it.

Long runs are tough. You need secret ways to keep it fresh. I would make eye contact with different members of the orchestra each night. I'd wink at the trumpet players. I'd blow kisses to the flautists. And they in turn had challenges for me. They would come up with words I had to slip into my performance. And not just easy, obvious ones. They seemed to use a thesaurus to find tough ones. But I'd do it, however little sense it made. I'd give it my all to win the bets.

While the show was good for my self-esteem, good for my career and a dream come true for my bank manager, it also did wonders for my waistline. I had to stay in shape. In one scene I had to lift Louise – and, bless her, even I, a best friend, couldn't call her petite. One night I lost my balance, she began to slip, I began to fall and we ended up in a tangled heap on stage. The audience howled with laughter, I'm pleased to say. Though I probably got another cross note telling me off the next day.

The New York-based writer and producer Bob Calleley is a dear pal. On a short break from *Chitty* I saw him in the garden at Orso in LA, where I was visiting Joan. 'What are you doing here?' I asked.

'I'm here for Angela Lansbury's 80th,' was what he said. 'Beat that' was what he so clearly meant. I couldn't. And, oh, how I wanted to go too. Angela is another icon and inspiration. But, however heavily I hinted about my availability, Bob didn't leap in with a 'plus one'. But he knew, of course he knew. He just wanted me to sweat a little. 'Oh. Do you want to come, Christopher?'

'Of course I bloody want to come.'

So off we went. It was a small party – really just for family. Bob had been Angela's producer in *Mame*, so it was clear why he was there. But how amazing, how extraordinary, that I had found my way there. So many times in my life I've found myself in places and with people that I should never really have met. My privilege has been to gatecrash some of the best parties in the world. The first person I spoke to at length that night was Jean Simmons – and what an adorable character she proved to be.

And Angela? She was just as charming and enchanting as I had hoped. She too had been on stage at the London Palladium and it was wonderful to hear her thoughts on all the classic musicals, most of which she had been in. For some reason Bea Arthur's face kept flitting through my mind as I left that golden party. What clever ladies these are, I thought. Angela, just like Bea, had ultimately taken control of her show, becoming producer and star of *Murder, She Wrote*. That's the way to get rich and really make your mark in the industry, I thought. And it was worth remembering that neither Bea nor Angela was a spring chicken when they hit television gold. I was rushing towards my sixties but I wasn't going to count myself out just yet.

I don't remember watching the first series of *I'm A Celebrity... Get Me Out Of Here* in 2001. But, like everyone else, I was well aware that it was a massive hit.

Like everyone else, I also thought that Ant and Dec were the perfect hosts for the show. They make it look so easy. But everyone in the industry knows how hard they work to look so good.

But would I ever see it first-hand? My agents got a call to sound me out for the second series, then the third. Apparently, I was on Ant and Dec's private wish list of dream contestants. But every year I had to say no. The show clashed with panto – and, trivial as that sounds, panto was still my bread and butter. By 2005 I had done some three dozen consecutive panto seasons and I was immensely proud of that record. Should I break it for a programme that could be a poisoned chalice?

In a youth-obsessed society, did it make sense for a man in his late fifties to lay his life on the line and be judged by the viewing public? I was convinced that people would far rather have a footballer or someone from a girl or boy band in the jungle. Being voted out on day one would be mortifying – and possibly career-ending. So every year I was secretly pleased that the approach from *I'm A Celebrity* came just after I had signed up for that year's panto. I don't break contracts, so this always gave me the perfect excuse for saying no.

And yet, and yet. A tiny part of me still liked the reality-television concept. When you're an actor people think they know you. But they really only know the roles you play. I could see the attraction of going on screen as myself. Telling my own story, not reading anyone else's lines. I hoped people might like me. I was sure I could entertain.

If I had been available, taking the plunge might not have been as hard as I'd thought because I had done a tiny bit of reality TV before. *The Entertainers*, for BBC2, was a fly-on-the-wall documentary where Neil and I were allocated a wonderful director, producer, cameraman and make-up person – all combined in the single wonderful form of a lady called Harriet Fleming.

I was a bit nervous about having my real life on film. And it was Neil's first introduction to television, so he was just as anxious. But it turned out to be such fun. Harriett followed us around as I did my year's panto in Cambridge, set up some other work, went to a string of charity events and generally tried to live and act just the way we would on our own. Neil was brilliant, coming over really warmly on screen, and we got plenty of positive feedback from friends, colleagues and strangers alike.

Tony Blackburn, Leo Sayer and Bernie Clifton were also being filmed for the show and they all agreed it had been a lovely experience. Reality TV wasn't so scary after all, we said. And I knew that *I'm A Celebrity* wouldn't be entirely uncharted waters if I ever signed up. It all still hinged on my availability.

The producers of *I'm A Celebrity* are, not surprisingly, clever people. You don't make a television juggernaut by mistake, after all. So in 2007 they found out when I normally sign my panto contracts and got in touch well beforehand. 'This is very early for us, but we didn't want to miss you again because you're right at the top of our list yet again,' they said. Flattery, of course, would get them everywhere.

And, because they spoke to me before I had a ready excuse to say no, I was forced to think more seriously about the idea. I had a long talk with my agent, Lesley Duff. I was soon to be 59. That's 159 in showbusiness years. I knew that people were taking me for granted. Good old Biggins, he'll always be around, they would think. We'll get him if the others all say no. But the others weren't saying no, so there wasn't exactly a queue to offer me great jobs. I'd not been on television much since *Bad Girls*, and that had only been for two brief episodes. Yes, I was in a very deep lull. I had panto, but I didn't have a pension. So I signed up.

Last year I had watched as David Gest, the man I felt had been a factor in causing further upset in my pal Liza's life, had come fourth. I had seen what this had done to his profile, career and no doubt to his bank balance. My target was to come fourth as well. If I could do that the whole adventure would be worth it.

'What do you mean you're not doing panto? Biggins, are you OK? Are you ill?' If I had a pound for every time I was asked this in 2007 I wouldn't have needed to go on *I'm A Celebrity* in the first place. People were genuinely perplexed. And such is the way of *Celebrity* that I couldn't put anyone's mind at rest. When the producers say 'top secret' they mean it. Blab and you're out. They make it clear that they have plenty of reserves signed up. So I, of all people, had to keep the secret. Agony, absolute agony.

'I'm making a film in Australia. It's an all-star cast and it's hugely exciting, but I can't give any more details,' was the lame excuse I finally settled upon. But pals who didn't buy it would soon get plenty more grist for the rumour mill. In September, some three months before the show's start date, I gave up the booze. In October I began a strict protein and vegetable diet. In November I started to eat next to nothing.

It paid off. I'm not sure really what was worse in the camp, the boredom or the hunger. But at least I was relatively ready for the latter.

I was able to show off my newly svelte form (in my dreams) in the hilariously organised photo shoot set up to promote the new series. Secrecy still reigned supreme. The contestants mustn't meet, so we were hustled around by production assistants in cars with blacked-out windows, rushed up and down corridors as their headphones buzzed with muffled instructions and requests. It was the closest I have come (so far) to a James Bond film. After the pictures I had my session with the show's psychologist. What a hoot. A lovely lady, Sandra, in Swiss Cottage. I loved being able to lie back and chat about myself. But one of her final questions brought me up short. 'How's your libido?' she asked.

'I beg your pardon?'

And so we got on to the subject of masturbation, the way you do. Apparently the only place to do it was in the dunny – which, of course, was the least conducive place for such an activity. As an aside, the men did all talk about this when we were in the camp – I'm not sure if it was broadcast. It seems that whatever we had said to the libido question from Sandra it wasn't an issue in the jungle. Forget waking up with a hard-on. We all said we didn't even consider sex once. I hardly thought of it. Maybe the final secret of the show is that they put bromide in the water.

'You're going into the show a few days after the other contestants. We want to surprise people.' This set-up meant I was flown to Australia on my own, which was lovely. The first two days I spent high up in the Meridian

Hotel on the Gold Coast and managed to get some sneaky intelligence from home. My minder didn't know I had an extra mobile phone in my bag. So, while we couldn't see any TV or log on to the internet to find out about the show, I could ring Neil to get some early warnings. At least I could until I was overheard, ticked off and had my phone confiscated. So I was left in the dark – just the way the producers wanted it.

Dr Bob was my key ally. He's a lovely man they should show more on the show. He runs through all the pitfalls, the dangers, the spiders. I thought back to the little boy in Salisbury who hated going to the outside toilet because of the spiders. Fortunately *On Safari* had given me a genuine interest in animals – even scary ones. So I thought I could cope.

'Walk sideways' is a key instruction for the jungle, for reasons I probably should remember. But Dr Bob and his team certainly don't pull any punches. Some of the things you're told before the show do freak you out. They make it very clear that it's a very real jungle and is more, not less, serious than it looks. If you think you're walking on to a safe, sanitised film set, the warnings about poisonous snakes soon put you straight. It's worst-case-scenario stuff and I think it was what caused Malcolm McLaren to opt out at the last moment. Maybe he, like me, thought it was all just a bit of a giggle at first. Dr Bob put us right. But I'm glad I didn't bottle out.

The madness of television is that you get the talk of doom in the most inappropriate surroundings. After my two days in the Meridian I was moved to the Versace Hotel. Yes, it's everything that the name implies. And it wasn't really me. All those bright colours. Everything ridiculously expensive. I defer to no one in my love of the good life, but I still don't think Versace style will ever be for me.

Three pairs of pants, two pairs of swimming trunks, and that's it. That's all you are allowed to take into the camp. All the other clothes are issued on the way in, along with a regulation bag of shampoo, conditioners, soap, toothbrush and toothpaste. You can take any medication you need – Janice certainly availed herself of that opportunity – but other than that you travel very light. You get up very early too. My entrance, with a Bushtucker Trial, was timed to be shown live in England, so it had to take place around dawn in Australia. First there was a drive of about an hour and a half to the camp in another van with blacked-out windows. Once there, we went through the magic gates to the compound – which have a worrying amount of barbed wire on them – and I was told to wait behind a bush.

It was there that I first heard the dulcet tones of dear Janice. Now, in one of our illegal, sneaky phone calls Neil had mentioned some mad American woman. But beyond that I had no idea who she was – or who anyone else was. Camera rolled, Janice hugged me and my first thought in the jungle was: This woman is fantastic.

Oh dear, oh dear.

20

The Jungle – and Beyond

My new best friend Janice lost a little of her shine straight away. I was on the show to get the job done. My attitude to most tasks is simple: I've done worse. So, if the boys want me to put my hand in a tree full of scorpions and snakes, then in my hand will go. Janice didn't see it quite that way. She chickened out of the first three tasks and handed the next over to me. It was the one with the gunge. Within ten minutes of my freshly ironed arrival on prime-time television, I was covered in fish skins. And I had swallowed a fair few of them too. Apparently, all my family and friends at home were screaming, 'Close your mouth!' at the television as my big moment arrived. For some reason I was looking up open-mouthed in excitement. Big mistake.

Next came the cockroaches, the ants or whatever they were.

And on it went. I reeked and could feel the creepy-crawlies creeping and crawling all over me as the trial went on. You don't get as much as a paper tissue to clean yourself up for an awful long time. In fact, you don't get paper tissues at all.

But at least I had Janice. Didn't I? Where the hell's she gone? Goggles on, I'm in the bug chamber looking for stars. One second ago Janice was right beside me. Now I turn and she's safely on the outside, directing operations next to Ant and Dec. I'll have to watch her, I thought as the bugs flew down my throat. Once again, Biggins, close your mouth.

With a batch of stars in my hands I gave my first interview as the gunge started to ferment all over me. Then it's about an hour to the main part of the camp. When I got there I found out that even then I couldn't have a shower. The recycling system and the fish scales couldn't mix. So I was led to the pond, where Marc Bannerman proved to be a real gentleman by helping. It was surprisingly cold and seemed ominously stagnant. But at least I had found a friend in Marc.

Meeting the others was all a marvellously exciting blur. I was just so thrilled to have made it through my first task and made it on to the show. Anna Ryder Richardson was the sole face I recognised – we had worked together years earlier and I knew she would be a treasure. She and Cerys Matthews helped me do my washing in the creek – and trust me, there's really no better sign of friendship than that in a wet, steamy jungle.

From the start I found out that life in the jungle was harder work than it looks, though maybe I only felt that as

I was three times as old as some of my campmates. But, still, it was a long way down to collect the wood and it felt a lot longer on the way back up. Dealing with the silence was my next big shock. With no radio, no television, no music, I nearly went mad. No wonder I barely stopped talking.

Cooking would have helped pass the time, if John Burton Race hadn't been so strangely insistent on taking it over. We weren't there for five-star food, after all, and taking turns would have been fun. But John's ego seemed to get in the way of that. He was my least favourite campmate.

The kiddies, Gemma Atkinson and Jason 'J' Brown, were adorable. They were like my children and since the show I've seen a lot of both of them. One thing they said had horrified me: that neither had ever been to the theatre. So afterwards I took them to my favourite, the Haymarket, in London. We saw *The Country Wife*, with Toby Stephens and my dear friend Patricia Hodge, and I hope they finally saw what all the fuss was about. 'Oh, they're so close!' Gemma whispered at me as the curtain rose. Just adorable.

In the camp, J and I both loved to find spiders, animals and insects. 'When you're in there, look for things. Make the most of the experience,' Dr Bob had told me back on the outside. It was great advice. When would I be in that kind of situation again? When would I ever have the opportunity or the time to see things like baby crayfish in a creek? It's to J's credit that he felt the same.

Seeing the poisonous spider under Janice's bed was a high point on several levels. I loved the fact that, of all the beds, this little predator had found that one. Same with the snake. We got the warning over the PA system (it was like being in Butlins or a remake of *Hi-de-Hi!*): 'Celebrities, be aware, there is a snake in the camp.' Well, we all knew that, didn't we, Janice? Seriously, we were all looking for something small. But it was a seven-foot carpet snake. And once more it was on Janice's bed. Funny that.

Cerys was as adorable as the kids. When it was down to the last five and they brought a guitar in we had our own personal Cerys Matthews concert around the campfire – a beautiful moment. She's far more talented than I might have thought. And I know now that she's got lovely parents and a wonderful family. She deserves another shot at happiness with someone great. Call me blind, but I hadn't spotted that Marc was a candidate for the role of romantic lead in Cerys's life. I'd liked him from the start when he had shown me the ropes and helped me get (relatively) gunge-free. As the classic good-looking young male in the camp, he was, in my view, a potential winner – especially as I think the public tends to reward a nice guy. But I'd missed the fact that in most people's eyes he was a love rat. It was a big shock that he was the first to be evicted.

What I liked about Rodney Marsh is that he himself didn't know how nice he was – or could be. Yes, he said some horrible, cutting things. And at first I didn't think that following them up with a joke or a high five could excuse them. At first I thought he was so awful it took my breath away. 'I don't have a heart,' he said at one point. But when I was told to read out the letter from his daughter (everyone had a letter from a loved one except me – mine, from Neil, was held back because I had failed a trial), he proved that he did. Funnily enough, Neil ended up getting on particularly well with Rodney's daughter when we all had dinner after the series. Rodney is a good dad and a good man. He shouldn't be afraid of letting his heart show a little more.

But the way he treated Lynne Franks in the camp? He should be (and indeed is) ashamed of that. 'Sorry, Christopher. You were right and I was wrong. I've tried to apologise to Lynne,' he told me when I was King of the Jungle.

I liked Lynne. Yes, she's tricky and can be difficult. But it still appalled me that when she was evicted Janice and Rodney headed down to the creek and didn't even say goodbye. Call me old-fashioned but that's just plain wrong.

Katie Hopkins, drafted in to replace Malcolm McLaren, was another surprise. Everyone was whispering that she was a total bitch. But I liked her. She had me in stitches with her stories. She's got two kids, and there's something childlike in her attitude to the world. Somehow I think she turns the bitchiness and the nastiness on and off like a tap to get publicity. I missed her when she was gone. Which brings me neatly back to Janice.

After the show Cunard very kindly asked me to speak on a three-week, round-the-world cruise on the *QE2*. As we moved regally from port to port I had plenty of time to think back on *I'm A Celebrity*. I also had time to watch all the tapes. So I finally saw what the viewers had seen. Janice was hysterical. She was entertainment, pure and simple.

At the time it wasn't always so funny, however. 'She's a professional reality-television star,' was how J described her to me. And so she is. She was in our show to win it. She came over as devious, dishonest, a monster. The uppers and downers she said she needed made every emotion even more pronounced. The crocodile tears and faux despair at everyone else's evictions were award-winning stuff. Many was the time when J and I could have killed her. But sometimes I did feel differently. We had a few very quiet chats about real life. She talked about her childhood, her dad, her bad times and her early days in the modelling industry when all anyone seemed to want from her was sex. That was the Janice I would like to have known. But throw in a third person – or a muffled cough from a concealed cameraman that reminded her of the cameras' existence – and the other Janice shot back.

I'll not forget the madness of her exit – the vitally important helicopter dash back to LA. Funny, but I'm sure that trip wouldn't have been so essential if she had been Queen of the Jungle in my place. But divas are as divas do.

'All I want is to be fourth.' That was all that ever went through my head. And as the days passed and my beard got longer and my stomach tighter I began to think I might make it. Knowing people are voting for you is quite wonderful. It makes me a little tearful to think of it, even now. But, oh, we worked for those places in the final few days. The best fun was the cyclone of a water game – it was like being hosed down at Shrublands Health Farm all those years ago. And there were just as many surprises. At one point I remember sitting on the stairs to catch my breath. I looked up and thought we had a new campmate. I swear it was Gollum. It was Janice.

As we went from the final six, to five, to four, I was beside myself with excitement. I would do anything to get further. Just as well.

I'll never forget the bacon sandwich on my food challenge. Or that glass of champagne with the strawberry. Or the chocolate cake, for that matter. But I wasn't ever going to give in. To be honest, it's all a bit of a blur. But I think the tapes prove that I ate the witchetty grubs, the crocodile foot, the three cockroaches and then the kangaroo penis, washed down with some poor sod's testicles. Chewy, if you want to know about the penis. Chewy and moist, if you're interested in the testicles. How I love it when people nod wisely when I say this and say that's what they thought. What you thought? What were you doing thinking about things like that in the first place?

Janice hugged me tightly when I won the show. A tad too tightly? It's just possible. But then the madness really began. The bridge, the best bits, the knowledge that it's over and you can finally get the mud from under your nails – it all floods into your mind at once. Running over the rope bridge, seeing Neil, knowing I had won. After all those days with less than a dozen people, you are thrown into a massive set of meetings and interviews. Then you scrub up and go to a party with 600 guests. No wonder I kept crying. I was in shock for days and days.

Neil and I flew home the day after the party. I just wanted to see friends and family. I wanted to know it was all real. But the air of unreality has hardly left.

Back in London I wanted life to carry on just as it had

before. So I went to the Ivy with Joan Collins. I got a standing ovation when I walked in – and was barely able to eat because so many people kept coming over to speak to me. I can't pretend I didn't love it.

'Did you know Daniel Craig voted for you?' the marvellous Lisa Tarbuck told me when I saw her that December. *Coronation Street*'s magnificent Helen Worth, a dear pal, said she had barely stopped voting. And strangers in the street came up to congratulate me each and every day. 'How did you do it?' people kept on asking. I have no idea. My only tactic was to be myself. I've been with Dame Judi at the RSC but I'm not that good an actor to play a part 24/7 for three weeks. All I could offer up was who I am. It is humbling and wonderful to think that so many people liked me enough to vote. Thank you.

And what else did I get out of the show? Boxing Day. My first at home in nearly 40 years. I'm back in panto again in *Cinderella* in Southampton for the 2008–9 Christmas and New Year season. But opting out, just that once for *I'm A Celebrity*, turned out to be the best career decision in many a year.

I think I may well have a pension at last. And I'm certainly being paid to have a lot of fun. I did chat show after chat show after *Celebrity*. But some were much more fun than others. I loved being on *Never Mind the Buzzcocks* with the dear Simon Amstell. 'You mustn't do it. They'll annihilate you. Don't you know what those kinds of shows are like?' my friends warned beforehand. But I knew what Simon was like. We had met years earlier when he was the up-and-coming host of Channel 4's *Popworld*. I did the voiceovers for the Top Five chart each week.

The Jungle – and Beyond

Simon told me I was a cult hit – and I so hope he wasn't just being kind. Anyway, despite the fact that the *Never Mind the Buzzcocks* regulars might as well have been talking Greek when they got on to all the latest people and bands, I managed to keep my head above water. Simon was a darling, just the way I knew he would be. But the show: it took us three and a half hours to get enough footage for a half-hour programme.

'I can't go on any more. I'm exhausted!' I screeched on camera as a fifth hour of filming approached.

Going on *Friday Night With Jonathan Ross* wasn't quite as much fun, though that wasn't because of its host. The problem, shock horror, was my fellow guest – Janice Dickinson. Janice came over as a bad loser. She was quite cutting in the green room – which, of course, is all part of the set on *Friday Night*. Stephen Merchant and Freddie Flintoff were as surprised as I was. And none of us could quite believe how someone who talked to me in the way that she did could have such a charming boyfriend. He was quite lovely.

Anyway, as the show went on Jonathan came to my aid. 'You can't say that. Biggins is a national treasure,' he said after one of her worst comments – most of which I think were cut before the broadcast.

'Darling, it's all done for the cameras,' she whispered at the end as we did some awful dance.

Perhaps. I just know she is very unlikely to be on my Christmas-card list any time soon.

I think I would have missed it if I hadn't done a panto at all that season. So putting one on for *The Paul O'Grady*

Show in December with so many of my best friends was a marvellous bonus. And that wasn't the only time I saw Cilla and Joan in that particular week. When I talk of the great divas in my life how can I forget Shirley Bassey? We had all been at her 70th – imagine! – at Cliveden House that week, camping it up with the best of them.

But back to *The Paul O'Grady Show*. Paul himself is, of course, a dear old pal. If anyone had told me, 20-plus years ago when Paul was facing the hecklers as Lily Savage in those dire south London pubs, that he would end up the best-loved and most popular presenter on teatime television, I would have had them committed. As if something like that could ever happen! But happen it has. And to the nicest man in the industry. Lovely proof that fairytales do come true, even for drag queens.

Talking of which, one more deserves a very honourable mention. Dave Lynne, another dear friend who lit up my life for a while. What a wonderful, generous man. If you saw him train up the ex-soldier in *Faking It*, you'll know what a gentleman he is – and what a great lady he makes when he's on stage. He is a brilliantly funny man. I've loved his appearances on shows like *The Weakest Link*. He should get so much more. What most people won't know about Dave is how charming his family is. He had wonderful parents, a great, characterful and endlessly amusing Jewish family. Good times all round. Good memories. And Dave is still a good friend today.

As I was writing those words in 2008, I realised that the approaching autumn was bringing my 60th birthday. My mother kept reminding me how much I cried when I reached 21. I thought my life was over back then. I think this walk – well, meander – down memory lane proves that it wasn't. And this walk (or meander) is far from over, as the next pages will show.

21

The Big Party

I was going to turn 60. I tried to hide from that horrible fact but there was no escape. Sixty! Where did all that time go? I still felt like a teenager, sometimes. Or at least I acted like one. But, reality was reality and it seemed that I couldn't fight the calendar. My 60th birthday was indeed just around the corner and I had two big choices. Choice number one, I could keep my head in the sand and celebrate very quietly at home. Or, choice number two, I could throw a party.

Guess what? I decided to throw a party – and not just any party. It would be a big, fat one. I decided to throw the 60th birthday party to end all 60th birthday parties.

I chose one of the grandest and one of my favourite hotels in London as the venue. The five-star Landmark Hotel in the heart of beautiful Marylebone. I drew up a guest list. I decided to keep my birthday a modest and an intimate affair. I would invite just 400 of my closest and dearest friends. No need to go overboard, after all.

The night was black tie, naturally. Posh frocks, for anyone who wanted to wear them, of course. And lavish from the start. We took over the hotel's vast, palm-filled atrium for a champagne reception. Then we moved on to colonise the Landmark's stunning ballroom for dinner. Sitting people down wasn't easy. The table plan had been hell. Placements are a nightmare. We had forty tables of ten. But who would sit where? Who would sit with whom? What about all the last-minute calls – can I bring a guest? Can I ditch my guest and bring someone better? Can I sit next to my wife? Can I sit next to someone else's wife? Can I sit a very long way from my husband? Yes, the pre-party questions went on and on.

But Neil and I did it in the end. We drew up that table plan. When the champagne reception was over we had our photographs taken with all our guests as everyone slowly trooped towards the dining room. We all sat down at our tables. And then the fun began.

The music came from off stage, outside the room. 'Get the party started,' the vocals rang out. It was one of Shirley Bassey's signature songs. But was it Shirley singing? I knew that it wasn't. I'd hired Lorraine Brown, the amazing look-alike and sound-alike who's been playing Shirley for years. And she was pitch perfect at my party, the way she always is. She sounded so right that night. So right, in fact, that everyone thought it was the real deal. 'It's Shirley!' came the cry! Everyone in the vast room applauded and roared their approval. And the cheers got louder when Lorraine finally strode into the room, microphone in hand, glamorous as hell and all guns blazing. She looked as good as she sounded. She looked exactly like Shirley. People were going bananas and I was laughing my head off.

Because by this point nearly 400 people were entirely convinced that it was Shirley. Joan Collins, who knows Shirley really well, thought it was Shirley. For a moment even I thought it was Shirley – and I'd made the booking.

Those crazy first moments set the tone for the whole night. It was stunning. And stunning fun. What was the meal actually like? I'm sure it was wonderful but I have no idea. After the first few moments I don't think I sat down once. I spent the whole night table hopping. I covered more ground than Paula Radcliffe. I should have worn running shoes. So who was there? Who wasn't? Apologies to anyone I forget. But alongside dear Joan we had Cilla Black, Barbara Windsor, Lynda Bellingham, Stephanie Powers, Denise Welsh, Claire Balding, Helen Worth, Jane Macdonald, Gloria Hunniford, Lorraine Chase and so many more lovely ladies. Among the most suave of men we had Tim Rice, Matthew Wright, Theo Fennell, William Hague, Jason Donovan who had shared my pain in his own *I'm A Celebrity* camp, and so many more absolute gentlemen. And of course so many other dear people I should mention now or should have mentioned elsewhere in this book and I apologise for being so muddle-headed that I don't have the memory or the space or the brains to mention them now. To you all, if you were there I adore you and I thank you for being part of my crazy, madcap life.

What time did the party end? I've no idea about that

either. Did I dance? Of course I danced. I sang, I laughed and I made merry. I cut the most beautiful cake – a jungle-themed one, complete with a rat made out of icing. I was 60. Sixty! I acted as if I was six. What a hoot.

But there's something we all come to know about a big party. It's the morning after the night before. It hit me hard, that time. I was exhausted. Never again, I said the day after. No more big parties. So much fun, but too exhausting, too stressful. It's the quiet life for me, I said. Until the next one, of course.

And I did have lots to do once the party was over. I was heading towards the end of my year as the reigning King of the Jungle. I had an endless series of interviews to do as the next show began to air – with Joe Swash pipping the amazing Martina Navratilova to the post to take my title. I also had a panto to put on.

It had been a wrench to miss out on panto in 2007. After such an unbroken run I'd felt terrible about opting out for my trip to Oz. So I was more than thrilled to head back to the Mayflower Theatre in Southampton to play Buttons in *Cinderella*. It wasn't always easy, getting back into the swing. As I've said so many times in this book, the world is changing. Those long, lovely weeks of readings and then rehearsals that I'd loved when I started out are a thing of the past. Now we have to ready far faster. It's still great fun, meeting the new crowd, catching up with old faces. But it's work. It's a lot to take in and to get right.

And would it all be all right on the first night? Would the crowd really care about a 60-year-old gay man from yesteryear? Sure, enough people had voted for me a year ago in the jungle. But I had to prepare myself for a reality check. I got myself ready in case they'd changed their minds, already moved on and no longer cared. Maybe they had all misdialled when they voted. Maybe I wasn't the one, after all.

But I needn't have worried. The audience reaction, show after show, matinee after evening after matinee after evening, was stupendous. The roars of laughter were priceless. There are some 2,300 seats at the lovely Mayflower, I believe. And box office records, it seemed, were there to be broken. So we filled those seats, night after night.

When I say 'we' I'm including the whole team who made my return to the stage so good. We had Ryan the Rat, all the way from my jungle, and a character everyone adored. We had Matthew Kelly, we had Stephanie Powers from *Hart to Hart* and we had an amazing cast and crew – plus a whole lot of high-energy, high-camp songs from *Wicked* to *Hairspray* to belt out from start to finish.

So after my one-year gap, Biggins was back. And he wasn't going away.

For in that first year I had as reigning King of the Jungle I realised that the role, and the title itself, really did change everything for me.

It's hard to explain now just how important that reality show title meant. It's hard to say what it did for this 60-year-old man. It opened so many silly and fun new doors. So many doors I thought would be closed to me, an oldie and a pantomime dame in a world where the young take all.

And what do I do when I see an open door? I rush right through it. I'm the fool that rushes in. So I was there, on *Pointless Celebrities*, having a hoot. I was there, on *Loose Women* again and again – how I love those lovely ladies.

How great that such a mix of people put on such a fantastic show.

I did so many other shows that year and in the years that followed. I love *The Wright Stuff* – because Matthew is a great host and because I don't just enjoy it: I always seem to learn things. I get a buzz from the banter and the mix of news and entertainment that we get to talk about and comment on.

I did plenty more as well.

I had a hoot on *Come Dine With Me* the following year – though I will officially confirm my naughty little secret. Because of technical reasons – the size of the lights and the cameras and so on – I couldn't use my own lovely house to cook my dinner. So the house you saw wasn't where I live. But I felt at home there, funnily enough. I was cooking for Edwina Currie, Julia Bradbury and the man always described as '*Hollyoaks* hunk', Philip Oliver who is, I'm very pleased to say, a hunk and a half in real life. We all had our ups and downs in all the kitchens and dining rooms. But guess who won? I did, I'm thrilled to say, getting to earn £1,000 for charity and to laugh my head off for hours on end as one culinary disaster followed another.

Would I have had this fun, and worthwhile gigs a few years ago? Probably not. Nor, I think, would have I got to play the voice of a plane in a kids' cartoon – a job that was even more enjoyable as my lovely partner Neil flew as cabin crew for years. Now I was the voice of a plane. It's like I was following him to work and haunting him, the poor lamb.

Then, in a typical jumble and in no particular order,

there is all the other fun I've had of late. Starting with *Strictly Come Dancing: It Takes Two*. I'd be on every episode of that show if they wanted me. So do just call. But seriously, it's a fun and fast slice of quality TV – don't let the 'takes two' label put you off. The team behind it work like mad to make it. But *Strictly* itself? I get asked, I'm flattered to say. But to appear on it? I couldn't. I don't want to be the next fat fool stumbling around the dance floor. I want people to laugh with me, not at me. Plus, I'm not sure I've got the stamina or the memory for all the steps. So many dear pals have been on the show. I've seen them get worked ragged. I've seen how much weight they lose – which is one advantage of going on, I suppose. But I've seen the worry lines on their faces. I've seen how distracted they are in the week before each live show. I've seen them desperately trying to remember everything they're taught. I've also seen that the contestants mean it when they say they don't want to let anyone down by messing up. There's a very peculiar pressure on that show. It's a huge team effort – and I'd never want to let that team down. Besides, who'd really want to dance with me? What would those lovely lithe ladies really think if my name came out of the hat next to theirs? They're an incredibly talented bunch. They deserve to dance with someone a little more graceful than me.

Anyway, my dance card was getting full even without *Strictly*.

As I say, these last few years it's all been a long whirl of fun, frothy stuff. It's been marvellous. I did *The Chase* with Bradley Walsh, which was mildly terrifying. I went for £70,000 for my charity. I didn't get everything right –

that's an understatement. But how lucky to be the person who can have some fun, can laugh like a drain, can hopefully entertain people – and can see a good cause get some cash at the end.

Moving on from Mr Walsh, I'm on and off the Alan Titchmarsh sofa as often as I can. I love chat shows, because I love to chat. So if I get a call for one of those then I'll probably take it.

But what calls me most, year after year, is good old panto.

That lovely first year back on the boards in Southampton was only the start. The next season saw me head to Plymouth to wear a ridiculous number of even more ridiculous frocks as Widow Twankey in *Aladdin*. The producers had something extra up their sleeves that year – we had 3D special effects so the audience had to put those big ugly glasses on that always remind me of – well, the big ugly glasses I used to wear way back, that I thought were so fashionable at the time. But how great to offer 3D at a panto. How great to be doing more, offering more and finding new ways to entertain. I've said it before and I'll say it to the end – but panto is vital. It is so often the very first show young kids ever see. It is the first time they ever go into what they probably think of as a stuffy old theatre. If we can keep it alive, if we can inspire and entertain those kids, then they'll come back. And theatre stays alive. So a 3D genie of the lamp? Bring it on.

We sold a lorra lorra tickets in Plymouth. And we sold a lorra lorra lot when I got back on stage the following year to play the narrator in a travelling performance of *The Rocky Horror Picture Show*. We started off in Belfast and went who knows where. What a great show that one is as well. Another 'entry' show that can get people into theatres for the first time and show them that us old thesps know how to have a good time.

Aladdin was back later that year in Wolverhampton where I decided to channel my inner Ann Widdecombe as Ms Twankey. My abiding memory of Wolverhampton that year? Some 1,200 people screaming: 'Don't touch the prawn balls! Leave the prawn balls alone!' at every performance. If you were there, you'll know how much fun that was!

Move forward a little bit and I was back as Mrs Crusoe in *Robinson Crusoe* in Cardiff in 2011. I got some more fabulous frocks to play Sarah the Cook alongside Basil Brush in *Dick Whittington* in Plymouth in 2012. Then the merry-go-round continued as I joined Bob Carolgees in *Jack and the Beanstalk* in Hull the following Christmas and New Year. And every time it still felt great to be back in that saddle. Because for all my jokes and jollity I was taught and brought up to be professional about work. If I make a commitment I stick to it. And it's clear I'm committed to being in panto.

And you know what? You never know what else might crop up along the way. Such as the film version of Ray Cooney's *Run for your Wife* – where I played a gay fashion designer with Lionel Blair as my boyfriend. That old farce (the play, not Lionel) is a hoot of course. Filming it wasn't always easy. But we got and give a lot of laughs.

So through all of these post-*I'm A Celebrity* years there was so much to enjoy. So many good times to be had. So much of life to grab. I'd thought, as this second wave of my life's madness started to build, that the joy would last forever. I'd thought that the good times were here to stay. I'd thought that I would carry on laughing for the rest of my time.

But it turned out that in very many ways I was wrong. For throughout these otherwise joyous years, life was going to get in the way. It seemed that a new world of sadness was always waiting in the wings. There were dark clouds on the horizon and so many tears to be shed. So many lives were going to get colder in these sad, sad years. For so many of us, everything was about to change.

22

Sad Days

It's hard to pinpoint when exactly it began. It's hard to say when I first felt it and knew it. But somehow, sometime, it was clear that the shadow of death was being cast over some of the most wonderful people in my life. So many of the men and women I loved and admired and respected were to be taken from us all. Too many of them. And they were being taken far, far too soon.

One of the first was a great girlfriend of mine, Pam. She died at just 52, of cancer. She had been an actress, a voice teacher, a therapist and a dear, dear pal. She was so young. It was such a shock to lose her. So hard to be without her in the years ahead. And her loss was only the start.

For with Pam's passing it felt as if the call was out for Neil and me to attend so many funerals. I have had the grim task of trying to add it up. And I found that in the next few months and years more than 60 of my friends were to die. *More than 60*. It was frightening. Sobering. Terrible.

Of course I could explain some of it. I could put some of it down to my age – as I got older so too did many of my friends. So departures from the stage were inevitable. I could also put some of it down to my large circle of friends. When you know and love so many people it will again be inevitable that a certain number will leave you. But 60 people? In such fast succession, in really such a short period of time?

Anna Nicholas was one of the next to leave our stage. She too had been such a firm friend. She had been beautiful. She had everything. She had a wonderful husband, two beautiful children, grandchildren, friends, money, all the things we should need. We'd met so long ago. We'd played together in *Connecticut Yankee* in Regent's Park Theatre. We'd connected and never lost our connection.

Her passing was somehow slow and sudden at the same time. As well as all the other times we'd meet up we had a tradition. We would always meet at New Year, at panto. Wherever I was, whatever role I was playing, Anna and her husband Graham would always come.

But that one year they didn't come. I played that full season in Hull without seeing her. She told me the family had bought a new dog that couldn't be left. I was furious. Because of course I hadn't known that the dog wasn't the reason. The dog was an excuse. Anna used it to cover up how fast her health was declining. She didn't want people to know. And she wanted to try and shield us all for a little bit longer.

As I'd not seen her in Hull we arranged to meet for

lunch in London when *Jack and the Beanstalk's* run was over. We booked a table at the glorious Delaunay restaurant on London's Aldwych, where we planned to exchange presents.

Anna cancelled. She told her husband: 'Biggins won't like this.' And then, so very soon afterwards, she died. That simple, funny phrase was one of the last things she said.

A few painful years have passed now. I have still got Anna's husband and her children as my friends. But oh how I miss the lady herself.

And oh how I miss Lynda Bellingham. We had been friends for more than forty years. We had been so close. She had been so brave. It's not for me to repeat the story of her terrible battle with colorectal cancer. Her marvellous book, *There's Something I've Been Dying to Tell You*, does that better than I ever can. Her decision to walk away from some of treatment to spare her family the pain of seeing her suffer is one I can't forget and can only admire. Her loss, so soon, was so awful.

I was proud to be part of her funeral, as well as of her subsequent memorial service in London. And I tried to bring something I knew Lynda would have wanted to both occasions – a bit of laughter.

My dear old 90-year-old mother had given me just the line to use at the funeral. We had been speaking on the phone just beforehand. My mum had asked me what I was up to. I told her I was going to Lynda Bellingham's funeral.

'Oh the poor girl. Where is it?' she had asked.

'Crewkerne.'

'Oh it's lovely,' my mum had replied. 'I was stationed there in the war. She'll love it there.'

I told the story at the funeral. It got a big laugh. It was what we all needed in our grief that day. And a big fat round of laughter was what Lynda would have wanted.

I tried to help strike the same note at the memorial that was held later, in London. I was asked to speak just before her dear husband Michael Pattermore. I tried to lighten the mood, to disperse some of the clouds. 'Every actor longs for a full house,' I said, to that very full house. Then I turned to her two sons, Robbie and Michael, boys who had grown up to be fine young men. Fine young men who I wanted to see smile, on this saddest of days.

I turned to them. 'I was there the night she met your father. He was the most handsome man in the room. It was a toss-up which of us was going to ask him for his phone number. So think about it, boys. If Lynda hadn't got in first I could have been your mother,' I said. I saw their smiles then. We all cry, still, about Lynda's loss. But we smiled too, which is what she wanted us to do.

There was more of the same as the guests talked and remembered Lynda afterwards. I was talking to another Lynda, the author Lynda la Plante. 'She's out-sold you,' I told her, as the sales figures for that most moving book, *There's Something I'm Dying to Tell You*, were quite rightly going through the roof. All our tears turned, somehow, to laughter. Again, it was just what the Lynda I had loved would have asked for.

But what is so truly sad is that these first few funerals were only the beginning. I say I added up 60 of them. But in truth I think begin to lose count now of all the sadnesses in those years.

There was another of my very dear girlfriends, Jeannie,

who walked into the shadows in these months. Her son-in-law had a massive stroke at just 52. He was paralysed, brought to hospital in an air ambulance – another extraordinary charity, by the way. And in the awful aftermath the other terrible lesson is how far tragedy spreads, how many people it can affect – and of course how quickly all our lives can be changed.

In what felt like a series of grim, sad times, it seemed as if everything was there to remind me of the people I had lost. It couldn't be avoided, even at work. I found that out in a big blast from the past when the 40th anniversary of *Porridge* approached. Forty years! Can it be that long, I asked? Yes it could. Forty years. Gold, the lovely retro channel beloved by old timers like me, decided to do a three-part documentary about it. It was lovely to catch up with old faces and to remember good, old times. But, of course, very few of the original cast are still around, so there were still more shadows of the past to stride through. Ronnie Barker and Richard Beckinsale were gone, of course. And so were so many more. But the work – our work – lived on. *Porridge* had been voted one of the greatest sit coms of all time. I'd been in it. And I was still there to tell the tale.

Of course I don't want to dwell too much on these gloomy thoughts. Sadness can be the stuff of life, after all. All of this is bound to happen, as the years pass. All you can do is hope that when your number is called you will have lived the life you wanted, loved the people you could and left the world with more than you took from it. And, of course, to have laughed as much as you can. So I'll move on now with one last story of a funeral service where I did, again, try to bring memories of joy to all the tears.

It was the memorial for Jimmy, the pianist at Joe Allen restaurant in London's theatre land. He had been there since day one. Everyone knew and loved Jimmy. We gave him a wonderful memorial in St Paul's Church, the actors' church in Covent Garden. I'd reminded us all of the fact that Joe Allen's owner at the time, Richard Polo, never really liked it when people sang over their supper.

'You have to tell people not to sing. It's policy,' he'd told Jimmy. But that had been easier said than done.

So at Jimmy's memorial I reminded everyone of the night the much-missed Elaine Stritch had been in for a late-night supper. She had got up from her table, gone to the piano and begun to sing.

Dear Jimmy had asked her to stop. He'd told her to stop. He'd said she had to stop. But she didn't stop. So he got desperate. He played his final card. 'The only people who can sing are the ones who've shagged Joe Allen,' he declared.

'I have. Play on,' this very grand dame had declared in that legendary, raspy voice.

23

Saying No!

In showbusiness we say the show has to go on. I say something a little different. I say the panto has to go on. And so it does. After *Jack and the Beanstalk* in Hull Neil and I took our usual holiday to recharge our batteries and prepare for the year ahead. Neil still flies the flag, with British Airways, and it is nice to fly in style. I'm torn, sometimes, between an urge to explore, and a need to lie flat on a sun lounger doing nothing after a long run in panto. But we normally get a bit of both. We love grand old cruise ships as well. I'm lucky enough to be invited to give talks on many of them – and what a wild and fun bunch some of the passengers can be. Talking about old times and old shows while the oceans glide by is quite wonderful.

And sitting back a little, while life glides by, is just as nice. I realise that at my grand old age I've learned to say an important new word. It's the word 'no'. It's actually a great word. You don't use it when you're young. When you're starting out in your career – in any career – you can never say 'no' to any job. You never know if it will be the one – the one that changes everything and propels you where you really want to go. And you never say 'no' because you're terrified that every offer of work might prove to be your last. So you swallow your pride, your reservations, your doubts and you say 'yes'. That's why I've said 'yes' so often and to so many jobs that might have inadvertently taken me in the wrong direction or pushed me on to a road I didn't want to follow.

But today I have the courage to use the other word. 'No,' I'll say. It's vital to learn that word as you get older. I often look around when Neil and I are together. We've got a wonderful home, a wonderful life and we know wonderful people. We should live in it, really live in it. We should enjoy it. And we should enjoy all the others pieces of good fortune we get. Which of course includes our chance to travel. One last word on that. If we're not flying far then I'm not proud. I'll sit at the back of the plane if I have to. But if it's long haul then I'm not as keen on the cheap seats. I've seen plenty of flying carpets in panto. And I do like a flying bed when I travel!

The other beauty of learning the word 'no' is that it means more when you say 'yes'. If I sign up for something now it's because I really want to do it – not because I've nothing else to do or because I think it could be a useful means to an end.

So when I was invited to be on *Celebrity Masterchef* I went back to my old ways and gave them a resounding 'yes'. The world thinks I'm always darting from theatre to restaurant and back again. People think I eat out for England at The Ivy or the Wolseley or some other celebrity haven every night. But in reality I love to cook. I'm as happy as Larry in my little kitchen. I love rustling up a storm, knowing the people I love will soon be eating and laughing around the table next door.

So when I was asked about *Celebrity Masterchef* I said yes straight away. I knew I'd love it. But what I didn't know was how tough or terrifying it would be. Forget eating kangaroo penis or whatever else it all was in the jungle. Cooking odd ingredients in front of the *Masterchef* team is the biggest bush-tucker challenge of all.

When you sign up for shows like this you're told they can be a big commitment – though I knew that if my soufflé deflated I could be out on my ear after the first week. But I wanted to do it anyway. And I wanted to make it well past the first week. Funnily enough I prefer the idea of cooking for 150 to cooking for just two. I live big. So I cook big. I like to throw it all together and hope for the best. So I thought the crazy extra challenges in *Celebrity Masterchef* would suit me. I was as excited as a little boy at Christmas. And the show didn't disappoint.

We started off in a big studio somewhere out in west London. Lots of people think we know who the other contestants will be beforehand. But we don't. I had no idea who I would be cooking with – it was just the same as turning up in Australia for *I'm A Celebrity*. They really do keep their secrets, the producers and crew on these shows. But they do like throwing surprises, so a tiny flash of worry did cross my mind at one point. Surely Janice

Dickinson couldn't be here as well? My nemesis. In a kitchen full of knives and pots of hot oil. It wouldn't end well, I felt. So surely they wouldn't risk that.

And they didn't. And this is what I love about shows like *Masterchef*. They choose nice people! They don't set things up in the hope of conflict. And my team was fantastic. I was there with the likes of Tina Hobley, Kiki Dee, Jason Connery, Charlie Boorman, Jodie Kidd and Sophie Thompson. So many other great people would join us as the show went on. But I was thrilled to be with such a lovely bunch from the start. But could I cut it in the kitchen?

I got really, really nervous as we all waited to walk into the kitchen area. The work spaces with cookers and fridges and so on were waiting for us. As was the box of ingredients, all covered up. Oh, and the judges, of course, at the end of the room, standing there like, well, real-life judges in some awful court of cooking law. I think I wanted to die, not cook, at that point. I'd forgotten how to boil an egg. But there was no going back.

We get a very, very quick welcome. Then they say what they want us to cook. We get to look in the box. And we're off. On your marks! Go!

I lifted the lid to see what was in store for me. I was transported back to the jungle. Lots of raw fish. Lots of food that, when raw, looks a little bit scary and a whole lot unappetising. The octopus tentacles, the prawns all the other bits of cod, halibut and all. It was like a bush-tucker trial without Ant or Dec. So what to do? What to make?

I decided to be a true Brit. I would keep it simple. I went for fish and chips. But I tried to do it really, really well. I double fried my chips and the judges seemed to like them. Phew. I could wipe away those beads of sweat. And I could start to laugh. We all laughed, when it was all over. Lovely Jason Connery had gone mad. He had cooked every last bit of his pile of fish. Talk about an over-achiever. His plate was piled so high he could have fed us all.

As the weeks pass and the show goes on you really get into it.

Our first big set-piece occasion took us to the London School of Music by the Albert Hall to cook for 150 hungry students. Kiki had gone, sadly, and I was alongside the terrific Tina. Things didn't go entirely to plan. We began to run out of food, for a start. But the students were fantastic.

So I stayed in the competition for at least another week. Wonders will never cease. Jason had gone – and oh boy was he competitive so he hated it, poor lad. Tina had gone too.

And the surprises kept on coming. We were cooking in a real-life restaurant for one show. We were all set up and to go, ready for the off – when the lights went out! The hotel had lost all its electricity. We stood stock still and waited. The wonderful woman in charge did a lot of shouting and screaming at people and in the end the power was back. And so it began. I burned my hand then on a hot pan. There is so much danger in real restaurant kitchens. They are so small, so crowded and so hot! How I respect all the people who have cooked every meal I have ever eaten.

We had little and large alongside us by then: Wayne Sleep and Jodie Kidd. We had Sophie Thompson, Emma's sister who had been such a wicked *EastEnders* villainess. Not so in real life. I fell in love with that girl. The funniest sense of humour. And the fun went on.

For the next big show we were all taken to Stratford in a bus – oh the glamour of showbusiness. It was the year of Shakespeare's 450th birthday, if you know what I mean. We were off to the farm where his mum had been brought up, Mary Arden's Farm, a working Tudor farm today. And we weren't alone. There were about a hundred Shakespeare fans, all in fantastic, costumes, waiting for a birthday banquet. A birthday banquet we had to cook in a field kitchen using only ingredients that were around in the 16th century. Oh, and it was boys versus girls for a bit of added zest.

It turned out to be the funniest day ever. The boys and I went for risotto from pearl barley, old-fashioned food from that period. And yes, you've probably seen the episode. So you'll know that, yes, I stole things from the other team. All is fair in love and kitchens. Didn't Shakespeare say something like that?

Then we moved on to do afternoon tea in Richmond for the lovely ladies of the WI. That was one of my favourites. I love afternoon tea. And the WI. And then, at the semi-final stage, I made a mistake. We had to pick something that meant a lot to us. And I thought back to my childhood when my Aunty Vi had made trifle. She'd taught me how to make it, and to make it properly, all those years ago. So her trifle meant a great deal to me. And I made it. I made my own custard and really tried to get the details and the extras right.

The crew adored it, I'm thrilled to say. But the judges?

Saying No!

They thought it had been too easy. I'd finished first, I think. So they had seen me loafing around a bit when I was done and the others were still creating. So off home I went, feeling it was a little bit unfair. Should I have chosen to cook something complicated, even if it hadn't meant as much to me?

But I'd been thrilled to get so far. And I was thrilled that funny girl Sophie won. And I'm even more thrilled I've been asked back as a judge for the next series – and hopefully for many more shows after that. I've eaten some quite disgusting food from some of the poor contestants. But how I love the good stuff.

Later that year the only way was Essex for me. I was off to Southend to play in *Peter Pan* – for the very first time. Mad, really, after all my pantos, that I've never been in this most famous one. But it's not got a part for a big, loud dame in a crazy dress. So we re-wrote it. We turned Mr Smee into a very sexy (some may disagree) Mrs Smee. We wrote in ten different entrances and exits for me. We found ten different madly over the top costumes for me to wear for each and every entrance – the giant, multi-coloured cupcake on my head being a big favourite.

We were at Cliff's Pavilion on the sea front. And I was there alongside anther stellar, talented cast, including one David Hasselhoff. What a lovely man he proved to be. And oh, what a show. We broke all box-office records in Southend. We did phenomenal business. And we had fun – even though the people in charge tried to stop me.

Some of that illicit fun began right at the start. I decided I wanted to wear a red swimsuit and do a Pamela Anderson, *Baywatch* thing to sort of take the mickey out of my co-star. Of course I did. It was David Hasselhoff. He was going to be Hoff the Hook. I had to make fun of him. So I had to do it.

But our producer said no. He said David wouldn't like it. You can't do it, he said. David doesn't like to be sent up.

Nonsense, I thought. Everyone likes to be sent up. So I did it anyway. I got the fabulously talented costume people to run me up a vast red bathing suit. I got my mad hair and madder make-up done. I had some pictures taken on my phone.

And then I decided to show them to the Hoff, whom I had really only just met. As I did so, I did hold my breath a bit. Had I made a massive miscalculation? Would this Hollywood star prove to be as humourless as some of the other Hollywood types I've met (Janice Dickinson, for example)?

But guess what? David almost fell over laughing. He loved it. The Hoff doesn't like to be sent up? Nonsense. He's an old pro. He knows what works. So we put it in the show. That vast red swimsuit was one of my ten big costumes. And we got the biggest laughs of the night, every night. We got wave after wave of laughter and goodwill. We sailed away on that laughter for the rest of the night. Everyone left the theatre on our high. *Peter Pan* was panto magic in Essex. I was thrilled to have finally added it to my list of productions.

And the Hoff and I have become real friends. He's one of the good guys. He even got me a cameo part in one of his new TV shows, a series he was making for Dave. The run was long and as draining as ever. But it was a good one. And as the show came to the end in Essex I came to the end of my latest contract with Qdos, the people who put on all the good shows. I thought long and hard about what to do at that point. Then I signed a new contract. I signed up for another three years, starting with *Aladdin* with Blue's Simon Webbe at the Theatre Royal Nottingham for the 2015–2016 season. That three-year commitment will take me through to my seventieth birthday, I realised. At which point I would probably be getting to old to be the dame and to play the fool. I'll think again when we get there. But my feeling now is that it will be the time to take a panto bow at seventy. A final bow, to retire and to say goodbye, goodnight and thank you for some amazing panto memories.

In the meantime, I am still available for work, darling. Aren't we all? I'll listen to any proposals, I'll consider it all. But I must admit that one thing I don't think I'll do as much of in the future is pure acting. I'm losing my interest, after all these roles and all these years. To be more specific, I just hate learning lines. It's so dull, so dreary and I struggle so hard to do it nowadays.

There are ways around this. They say Marlon Brando never learned a line in his life. You can find ways to manage it, places to read things from and ways to cover it up. But I don't want to get into all of that. I can't take the pressure any more. If I can't learn the lines then I shouldn't be saying them. It's only fair to give the role to someone who's got the brains.

And there's a little bit more. I've turned into one of those old fools who bangs on about the olden days. But in the olden days it really was different. When you did TV or theatre back then you had fun. You had time and you had rehearsals, for a start. We'd turn up for a show. We'd meet up, cast and crew. We'd talk, we'd work and sometimes we'd make lots of mistakes. But we'd get it by the time we did the take or took to the stage for real.

Now there's no time and precious few rehearsals. You're expected to turn up knowing all your lines, your cues, your role. You won't necessarily know who your fellow cast members will be. But you're supposed not to care. You just turn up, do it, and go home. No room to get to know people. No room for laughs. I think of all those life-long friendships I have made in long, lovely rehearsals over the years. I don't make them now because it's wham, bam and thank you, man. And we all move on, with barely a goodbye.

One more moan? There's so little money nowadays as well!

What other industry has seen pay slump so far, so fast? Lots of them, I suppose. Lots of us have seen our workplaces change for the worse. I'm not too out of touch to think actors are special. And I know how lucky I was to be signed up in the good old days. I think back to the days when Cilla and I would get it all – new frocks and shoes and jewellery for her each show, new handmade suits and handmade shirts and handmade shoes for me. We'd have cars and handsome chauffeurs ready to pick us up and take us anywhere each night. And we'd get something like £5,000 an episode, thirty long years ago when that kind of money went a very, very long way.

So I'm happy to star with the autocue nowadays. I can read words that are put in front of me. So if it's a studio-based show, I'm there. Or a panel show or chat show where I can be myself, ad lib and just say what I think. I'm there for that. Radio? I'm there for that as well. *There's Nothing Like a Dame* was great fun. Taking over from lovely Lisa Tarbuck for two hours on Christmas Day was hard, but a hoot.

And when lots of work does come in I do have a brand-new secret weapon that sees me through it.

It's that at the grand old age of 65, I think, I did something I never expected. I gave up alcohol. I gave up the booze and I've not looked back. Why did I do it? Two reasons, really. One was in my subconscious. Over the years I realised I'd been seeing what alcohol did to so many people I had loved. I'd seen so many people aged by addiction. Killed by addiction, for some sad souls.

Then I had a clever wake-up call when I had a regular health MOT one year.

'How do you want to die?' I was asked.

'I'm sorry, what?' I replied, unsure whether I was being offered a specific menu of choice.

'Do you want to die peacefully in your own bed at a grand old age? Or do you want to die a whole lot sooner, dribbling away in a hospital bed and being looked after by strangers?'

I said that the first option sounded a little bit nicer. He said he couldn't guarantee it would work out that way. But that there was a simple way to improve my odds.

'Give up drinking,' I was told. It was as clear and simple as that. So I did. Why make a fuss? Why not get on with it? And I don't miss it at all. I sleep better. I'm not as tired. Without any hangovers I have more energy.

Yes, I had a chink of a champagne glass last Christmas.

A sip of red wine at a special Easter lunch. But that's it. We threw the most amazing party for Neil's 50th birthday a few years ago. It was on the top of Soho House, the private club in the East End of London closest to our home. It has a swimming pool on the roof, just like something out of *Sex and the City*. The day we had Neil's party was gloriously sunny and boiling hot. Dozens and dozens of slim, hot, young people were draped around the pool in their part of the club. And in the outdoor area on the other side of the doors from the pool you could find us – dozens and dozens of hot (literally hot, due to the sun) older people, not all of us as slim as we once were. But I bet we had a better time on our side of the fence. We laughed more. We let it go more. It's another lesson of age. Don't get so worried about what others think. Dance like no one's watching, or whatever the phrase is. And, as I said, don't feel you need to drink to enjoy the moment. I didn't drink at Neil's party. And I enjoyed every moment.

So if you're getting on a bit, if your energy levels are dropping then join me. Give up the booze. Give it a go. It worked for me. I'm not going back now. I need every ounce of energy I can get. Life is for living. I need to keep at it.

Another thing I do like doing nowadays – and what I thrive on – are charity auctions. They're oxygen to me now. And they can spring some real surprises – like the one I did in the height of *Top Gear* madness in 2015.

I got drafted into the cause by Nick Allot, Cameron Mackintosh's talented right-hand man. He asked me to help out at a big auction at the Roundhouse in Camden, north London. The Roundhouse charity, which does so much for disadvantaged youngsters, is such a great cause.

It was always going to be a totally worthwhile night. But it turned into a media whirlwind because sitting right there, on my top table, was one Mr Jeremy Clarkson, who was the man of the moment after being suspended from *Top Gear* after reports of him lashing out at a producer on location. Or something. I can't say I'd read that much about it, if I'm honest.

I can't say I ever really got Jeremy Clarkson either. I don't watch the programme. I'm not a petrol head, or whatever they are called. My big question about cars used to be: What colour is it? Now it's likely to be: Is it easy to get in and out of? So I'd not expected to bond with the man behind the show – and nor, to be fair, had I expected him to bond with me. But you know what? He was enchanting company. He was open and charming and philosophical about the demise of his show. On the other side of our big round table his lovely girlfriend told my lovely Neil exactly what had gone on – you'll have to ask him for all of that information. And as we were all getting on so well I decided to see if I could gee Jeremy up for a final lot to raise some extra cash.

'Will you offer anything for the auction?' I asked, right before I went up to the stage to get it going.

He would and he did. He said he would offer up a seat for what he declared (with a fair few bleeps required if you listen to it online) his last ever lap on the *Top Gear* track in Guildford, I believe.

And it got better. Nick Mason, the Pink Floyd drummer, was on our table with his wife Nettie as well. It turns out he owns some rare gazillion-pound car that again I'd never really heard of. But we added it in to the lot.

I did my very best auctioneer job of whipping up the crowd. I made sure everyone knew how important this charity was. And how great this particular lot would be. Then the bids started to fly. In the end we came down to two – two generous souls with deep pockets, bidding against each other for that final lap with Jeremy.

I knew by then that we were on target to make lots of vitally important money for the charity. And I thought: What a shame only one of these bidders can write a cheque. So I stopped the auction for another quick word with my new friend Mr C.

'Can you do the last lap twice?' I asked, not quite sure how all these things work.

'Of course I can,' said Mr Clarkson.

So both our bidders won. And all the disadvantaged kids won.

Those last-minute lots got us around £430,000. On the night overall we raised an incredible £1 million and more came in from an online auction that had been running alongside us. In the current climate that was big, big money. It was far more than anyone had expected. And it was all going to a good, good place.

So I'll do charity auctions all the time. I don't need to learn lines for them. I can play it by ear. And, sometimes, I can do what I did with Jeremy Clarkson and add a little to the sale list as well. I do that with dear Joan Collins all the time. She's always offering up lots for charity sales. I took advantage of that a while ago when I bumped into Elizabeth Hurley at a bash. 'I want to ask you a favour,' I told her. She tried to hide it, but I am sure her face fell. Mine always does, when I hear those words.

'I want to auction you and Joan Collins for Stonewall,' I said.

'Yes,' Elizabeth said, without a moment's hesitation. And I knew then that this auction would raise a lot of cash as well. Dinner with Joan and Elizabeth? Who wouldn't bid for that? Especially as Joan's life was about to get even more exciting. She was about to join my club. She was going to be made a dame.

24

There's Nothing Like Another Dame

You don't get made a dame every day. I get made-up as a dame every year. But that's a little bit different, of course. So when Joan Collins was given the real honour by Buckingham Palace it was party after party after party. Of course it was. It's Joan. I know we were all hoping the ribbon would be bestowed by the Queen, who Joan has met so many times over so many years. In the end it was Prince Charles who officiated at the Palace. And what an honour, what an occasion.

The day itself had dawned freezing cold and horribly windy for Joan – more worrying for her Philip Treacy hat, as it turned out. And Joan was on fine form when she and her family arrived at the Palace gates, where her husband Percy realised he didn't have photo ID on him.

'Will you vouch for this man?' Joan was asked by the Palace guard.

'Well, I'm not sure I'd go that far, but he is my husband,' she replied, before being waved through with a smile.

After all the pre-party parties we then had a big dinner on the day itself. Some 110 of us got together at the grand old Claridge's Hotel in London. Percy looked fantastic in his HMS *Dame Joan* sailor's hat. And we were all in fine voice – which was important as there was a lot of singing to come.

Percy kicked it off, starting with the first verse of 'There's Nothing Like a Dame'. I was allocated the second verse. Then a whole gang of others took us to our rousing, possibly not entirely pitch-perfect, conclusion. Though we were all laughing too much by then to care. There were so many lovely things said, of course.

'Well, Joan, welcome to the club. It's taken a hell of a long time for you to get here. I've been a dame for forty years,' was how I started off my little speech.

And, seriously, Joan has been a great, great friend over the years. She's a hoot, of course. But it's not just that. She's also good at sharing friends and people. She's generous with her time and with her friends. She mixes people up, she leaves them to get along with each other and make friendships of their own. So many of the jaw-droppingly famous people I've met, I've met through her.

What did I do after Joan was made a dame? I went off to watch a bit of telly. It's funny, that as the years go by everything comes back around in the end. Such as *Poldark*, of course! That new man, Aidan Turner, he's gorgeous and he's great in the role. The whole show was a lovely return to form for the Beeb. I particularly loved the fact that Robin Ellis, the original Poldark, was given a chance to return to his show. Robin was great in the cameo they wrote for him as the judge. And I got some fun out of it as well. Lots of us from the original series were invited on to telly to talk about it. The BBC took me down to Cornwall to talk from there. I relived my time as the dastardly Ossie Whitworth – a delicious and wonderful part. It was a lovely day out, Aunty Beeb, thanks so much.

While it would take a lot to get me back on stage night after night on a very long-running show, I do still enjoy going to the theatre. I will walk out, at the interval, trying to be subtle, if it's really poor. But it rarely is. Mostly I sit there, even if I don't like the material, marvelling at how much talent there is in the cast, the crew, the whole creative industry. Too much talent, I could say. Too few jobs for them all. Too few opportunities.

For my part I'm happy with short-term or one-off gigs, of course. One of those came up in early 2015 after I was chatting to Barry Satchwell Smith. They were putting on a one-off performance of the Stephen Sondheim show *Follies*, which I love. It was at the Albert Hall, which I also love. And it was to star all sorts of people that I love. There were two lovely Anitas – Dobson and Harris – in the cast. There was Ruthie Henshall, Roy Hudd and Russell Watson. My old mate Stefanie Powers from panto was there with other stellar Americans such as Lorna Luft, Betty Buckley and Christine Baranski. Craig Revel Horwood was directing and I was cast as the compere. I had about ten lines. Even I can manage that, I thought. And it was a magnificent event. Just two performances, a matinee and an evening show. What a joy.

Talking of old mates like half the cast of *Follies*, one of mine has been through the mill lately. I met Katie Hopkins back in the jungle. She was fresh from *The Apprentice*. Even then she was tough and direct and feisty. Some people didn't like that. I did. And I respected her for two things. One for speaking her mind and two for making her living. I don't know this for sure. But I think she realised that there is a niche in being controversial. I think she realises that it can pay. And she's got kids. She has a family. She needs to earn a wage so she works it. It's controversial, what she says, writes and tweets. It's lost her friends. It's been said that I've been shunned by some for sticking up for her. But I do stick up for my pals. I always have and I always will. That's what friends are for. It's not all about the good times and the fun, frothy stuff. I learned early on that loyalty and honesty can mean everything when the chips are down. I've had my share of controversies.

Over the years I've been attacked for admiring Margaret Thatcher – though I still believe a grocer's daughter, a girl from nowhere who made it to the very top of the tree, should be a role model, not a pantomime villain. She never deserved the hatred and the vitriol that was and is thrown at her. I love my country. I am proud to be British. And I think we need to applaud those who work hard, pull themselves up and beat the odds. I've also taken some blows over a hundred other things over the years. I didn't leap out and give a 100 per cent backing to gay marriage – and I was all but called a traitor to the gay cause. And that's me, the man who rode through London on a red Routemaster bus stuffed with family and friends after Neil and I became civil partners. I am not a traitor to any cause. I'm true to causes. And I'm not ashamed of going against the crowd.

I'm unashamed about admitting one other fact about my life today. It's that deep down I've started to enjoy staying in! And that's not something the old Biggins would have said. I love my telly, now. We've got a vast 54- inch screen at home now. I can lie in bed and watch hour after hour. Sky+<NB plus sign, no space> is my favourite gadget in the world. I love the big American series, the box sets, the long-runners. But I'll try it all. Pals and I ring each other to tip each other off about the next best thing to watch. We have marathon viewing sessions when we try to catch up on something we've missed. I love it. What else is good? *Gogglebox* is terrific! I love that show. I was on one of the shows being watched by the chosen viewers one week. How strange is that – to watch yourself as other people are watching you, if that makes sense? If you know *Gogglebox*, you'll know the viewers on it, so it'll come as no surprise that Leon didn't like me. The others whooped a bit though, which was great. I met the two boys from Brighton at a charity event. They are just as funny in real life as they are on their sofa on telly, I'm pleased to say.

I'm even more pleased to say that I myself popped up a few times in the advert break on shows like *Gogglebox* around then as well. Or at least I made myself heard. I was chosen to be the voice of Morrisons the supermarket. It was a marvellous job. I'd forgotten how much lovely money you could get on a gig like that. I had a great team who made it all so easy and so much fun to record. And I know, getting on for a decade since *I'm A Celebrity*, that

I owe that show for getting me the job. I so treasure this second chance, this new wind of opportunity I've been given. So do I get bored talking about bush-tucker trials and the like? Not at all! Why would I? It was a hoot then, it's a hoot now. So I talk about it a lot at corporate speaking events and award ceremonies. I love all of those. I can play off the crowd, I can be myself, make people laugh and sometimes even make people think. I wonder if I might also inspire or help some people. I have, I realise, become a poster boy for second chances and for the merit of plugging away, year after year. I'm also the proof that you don't have to be one-size-fits-all to succeed in our wonderful, open and increasingly tolerant country. The 60-year-old gay man who won a telephone vote proved that. We should all be proud of that. Round of applause. We truly should be proud.

The other lesson I'm keen to teach, though, is about stress. It's part of life. It can't be avoided altogether. But I've become a little scared by it. With the passing of so many dear friends in the past few years, from so many causes, I've thought about this a lot. Unnecessary stress really does seem to kill. So I'm trying to focus less on working and more on living.

Neil and I want to spend more quality time in our lovely house, where the walls are covered with pictures and where every picture tells a story and shares a memory. We're doing ordinary things there, to set us up for the future. New windows, a new roof, some solar panels. It's not glamorous, it's not exactly showbusiness, but it's good. I've also bought a flat to rent out, at the top of a building looking out over the Olympic Park in Stratford, just a little east of our home. It's hopefully going to generate a little income for the future that might take the pressure off. I've got my state pension now, of course. I can get a bus pass, so I'm told; I might even use it one day.

And I do have a great example of how to live long and well. My dear old dad passed away a few years ago, lost to cancer of the bowel in another very grim time. But my dear old mum is over 90 and still going strong. We had a big birthday bash for her in Salisbury when the big day came. She has terrible arthritis but is as bright and funny as a button. She's gregarious. She loves people. That's a family trait, of course. My brother Sean and I visit a lot. She's in a very social area. Moving to a quiet country cottage would never work for her. She needs people around her. We all do, at any age. But we need it most of all when we're older, I think. Twice a week my mum gets a taxi to a local luncheon club where she sees even more friendly faces – and we can see the good it does.

Funnily enough, I try to do my bit on this score as well. I'm chairman of the theatrical arm of the charity Age UK along with so many other honours. I'm genuinely honoured when people ask me to help a charity or good cause. I don't have millions in the bank. But I've been given so much by life. If I can give back then I will.

In the meantime I do have one other thing I want to do more of. I want to travel more. Neil and I want to sail the Atlantic on the *Queen Mary*. I can't imagine a better trip than that. We also plan to see Vietnam and the Mekong Delta. And so much more.

And every time I sit back and think about my life I think of all my marvellous memories. So many stories haven't yet been told. I would have needed something the size of a telephone book to get them all in. To all those dear friends and incredible characters I apologise. You might not have been mentioned, but you have not been forgotten. Making friends and keeping them has been the great joy of my life. That's the real lesson I'd teach to anyone who wanted to learn from me. Forty years on, I still adore the reunions we have for the Bristol Old Vic Theatre School. And I still see old faces from Salisbury Rep.

Theatre people are like family. We're thrown together seemingly at random. We live cheek by jowl on productions. We go through some extreme ups and downs. But when the chips are down we'll fight like dogs to support our own. So many people have helped me at the very few low points I have had in my life. And it's not just material help I've needed sometimes. It's the invitations to get on and to go out. To be at that next first night, charity party or birthday bash. Meeting one person always leads to another.

What good is sitting alone in your room, as someone once sang?

None at all. So that's why I do still have plenty to do. There's a play I sometimes dream I might direct. It's called *Out Late*, by Tim Turner and it explores the lives of a doctor and his wife in their sixties. The focus is on the husband, who falls in love with a young, handsome patient. But the role of the wife is just wonderful. And who better than me to find a wonderfully strong woman to play it? I can think of so many dear friends and talented actresses who should get the chance.

There's also a film I sometimes dream of making. It's

The Orchestra. I've known that play almost all my life. Sometimes it feels as if it was only last month that I was in my charity shop black tie at the first night of that play in Bristol. Sometimes it feels as if it was only last week that I directed it in a nightclub in Leicester Square in London. Sometimes both occasions feel as if they were a thousand different lifetimes ago. But that play still moves me. And it's got even more roles for strong, powerful women. I'd relish the chance to cast that.

In the meantime, I'll throw myself into every opportunity that comes my way. I know I've had an incredible, charmed life, full of extraordinary events and larger-than-life characters. I've been to places very few Oldham boys get to see. Not all my reviews have been good and not all my career decisions have been right. But I've never stopped having fun. And what do I hope for most in the years ahead? Really just for three simple things. More time with my friends, more laughter and more of the same.

Every day that I have thought back on my life I've remembered more marvellous memories. So many haven't yet been told. I would have needed something the size of a phone book to get them all in. To all those dear friends and incredible characters, I apologise. You might not have been mentioned but you've not been forgotten. Making friends and keeping them has been the great joy of my life. That's the lesson I'd teach to anyone who wanted to learn from me. Forty years on, I still adore the reunions we have for the Bristol Old Vic Theatre School. And I still see old faces from Salisbury Rep.

Theatre people are like family. We're thrown together seemingly at random. We live cheek by jowl on productions. We go through some extreme ups and downs. But when the chips are down we'll fight like dogs to support our own. So many people have helped me at the very few low points I've had in my life. And it's not just material help I've needed. It's the invitations to get on and go out. To be at that next first night, charity party or birthday bash. Meeting one person always leads to another.

What good is sitting alone in your room, as someone once sang?

None at all. So that's why I've still got plenty to do. There's a play I would love to direct – it's called *Out Late*, by Tim Turner, and explores the lives of a doctor and his wife in their sixties. The focus is on the husband, who falls for a young, handsome patient. But the role of the wife is just wonderful. And who better than me to find a wonderfully strong woman to play it? I can think of so many dear friends and talented actresses who should get the chance.

There's also a film I'd love to make – it's *The Orchestra*. Sometimes it feels as if it was only last month I was in my charity-shop black tie at the first night of that play in Bristol. Sometimes it feels as if it was only last week when I directed it in the nightclub in Leicester Square. Sometimes both occasions feel as if they were a thousand different lifetimes ago. But that play still moves me. And it's got even more roles for strong, powerful women. I'd relish the chance to cast that.

In the meantime, I'll throw myself into every opportunity that comes my way. I know I've had an incredible, charmed life, full of extraordinary events and larger-than-life characters. I've been to places very few Oldham boys ever see. Not all my reviews have been good and not all my career decisions have been right. But I've never stopped having fun. And what do I hope for most in the years ahead? Really just three simple things: more time with my friends, more laughter and more of the same.

25

A Last Word
for Cilla

It was a sunny Sunday morning in early August. I had
plenty of time before I met some friends for lunch so I
was able to relax. I'd made myself a pot of lovely coffee
and I was sitting in my kitchen with a stack of Sunday
papers. I love the Sunday papers, even if what I read
sometimes horrifies me. But it's part of my routine when
I'm at home. I'd be lost without them.

So there I was, radio on, sun shining, coffee in hand,
papers in front of me, all was well in my world.

Then my phone rang.

And then everything changed.

It was a reporter from the *Daily Star* who I've known
for years. He lives in Spain. He's on the celebrity beat. He
always knows the gossip. But why would he be ringing me
– on a sunny Sunday morning?

He said it, very fast. 'Have you heard? Cilla's had a heart attack.'

'That's ridiculous,' was all I could think to say. I asked him how he knew. He said he'd heard it from someone else. He wanted me to confirm it.

I couldn't of course, because I kept going back to what I'd just told him. It was ridiculous. It was stupid. Too ridiculous and too stupid to even consider. I'd spoken to Cilla just over a week ago. She had the usual cracks and creaks, the way all us oldies do. But nothing more. She'd actually started some new painkillers for her arthritis and she was doing well. It was helping. So she'd been getting ready to go to Spain when we talked. We'd made plans for her return. She'd not been to our old haunt, the refurbished Ivy restaurant, since it re-opened a few months ago. So we'd made a date to go in September. She'd also talked of us taking another, longer holiday in the New Year. 'When you've finished your panto you and Neil must come back to Barbados with me,' she'd said. So she was planning a long way ahead. A heart attack? It didn't seem real. It couldn't be real. But I had to know.

I rang Cilla. Her phone rang and rang. No reply.

I sat in my kitchen. I could feel my pulse racing faster. Could this actually be true?

I rang Robert, Cilla's son. Again there was no reply but I got the tone that said he was overseas – in Spain with his mum, I was sure. I made one last call. I rang Martin, a former producer on *Blind Date* and one of Cilla's loyal 'walkers' she'd go to theatres and parties with after Bobby's death.

'Have you heard anything about Cilla?' I asked.

He hadn't. But he said he'd try Robert too. I sat back. It was nearly midday and the sun seemed harsher now.

I got ready for my lunch, half distracted and totally convinced there should be something else I should do, someone else I should call.

Then I got in my car. It was still such a lovely day so I had the roof down as I motored towards the West End. I was joining two friends at the Ivy. So, of course, that kept my mind firmly on Cilla, and the date I had there with her next month. A heart attack? Ridiculous, I kept saying. Ridiculous.

My phone went again as I approached Covent Garden. I answered it on the hands-free. It was my dear friend Nichola. She told me the news straight away. 'Cilla's dead,' she had said flatly.

I almost crashed the car. I screamed out loud. I gasped for air, suffocating. Gripping the wheel and looking in the rear view mirror I managed to get the car to the side of the road and I stopped. Was I on a yellow line, a double yellow or a red line? I didn't know and I didn't care. Cilla's dead. Two words. The worst of words.

And this time I had to believe them. This time it wasn't ridiculous. I thought, suddenly, of all those other people I had lost in recent years. All those friends, all those faces who had left the stage too soon. And the exodus wasn't over. Now Cilla was dead too.

'How? Where? What happened?' The questions flooded out of me as I spoke, still hands-free, into what must have looked like thin air.

It was a heart attack, the words came floating back to me. We might know more later on.

The call ended and I sat in my car at the side of this busy central London road. I felt horribly vulnerable with the top down. But nothing seemed quite real. And as I tried to get my breath, to gather my thoughts and to decide what to do my phone rang again. It wasn't going to stop that day, or the day after that.

The first call was from Joan Collins. She was in the South of France. Moments ago she had heard something on the radio. Was it true? I told her all I knew. We were quiet for several moments, not speaking, not ending the call. If we didn't speak, then maybe it wasn't happening. But it was. We talked of the last time we had both seen and spoken to Cilla. We talked of the plans we had both made with her. The dates in our diaries. The fact that we couldn't understand or comprehend this.

I then called my partner Neil, of course, who was in Hong Kong for work and we just talked of how much fun we'd had last time we'd all caught up with Cilla.

So many other calls flooded in that day. I spoke to Paul O'Grady, another of Cilla's loyal, loyal pals. I spoke to John Madejski, the tycoon and Reading football boss and a dear friend of Cilla's. I spoke to Cliff Richard from his home in Portugal. All our conversations were awful, strange. We went round in circles, disbelieving, uncomprehending. With Paul a rush of reminiscences flooded out. I reminded him of the time we'd all been with Cilla at her place in Spain just after his heart attack. The doctors had told him to stop smoking, of course. He said he would. But as I sat in the sun with Cilla one long, hot afternoon I swear I smelt cigarette smoke. Paul, we guessed, was having a sneaky ciggie round the corner.

'He won't listen to me any more,' I told Cilla. 'You'll have to tell him.'

So she had. In that no-nonsense voice that always came from the heart. She'd told Paul off the way his mum might have done, or his teacher, or his doctor or, of course, as his friend. And that was what we had all lost, a true, honest friend.

Between phone calls I headed home. I'd agreed to speak about Cilla on the radio and ITV were sending a car for me at 5.00 the following morning to talk on TV as well. I'd agreed in a daze. I wanted the world to know what a wonderful woman we had lost. And I wanted the distraction as well. If I was talking then I couldn't be thinking.

By the afternoon of the Monday I'd had between two and three hundred calls, texts and emails. And I'd noticed something. The people closest to me knew that Cilla and I had been like an old married couple sometimes. So they were asking after me. Was I OK? Could they do anything to help me? It was so lovely. But of course none of this was about me. As I knew later that same afternoon when I spoke to Robert.

I told him I was so very, very sorry. And he told me he didn't think his mum had suffered. But he had. I soon learned that he had. As we spoke I realised he was in shock, as we all were. He couldn't yet take it all in. Cilla had arrived at the villa that weekend – later we'd see a photo of her posing with fans at Malaga airport, ever the star, looking fabulous in leopard-skin.

She had a lovely sun trap off her bedroom – there was nothing my Cilla loved more than the sun – and she'd been there when he'd shouted to her in the afternoon. 'I'm going to do some shopping,' he'd yelled.

Cilla hadn't replied, he told me. But that was normal. She had music on a lot and we all knew her hearing wasn't great. She hated wearing the hearing aid she'd been given – so most of the time she didn't use it. I smiled, in spite of the sadness, as Robert told me this. Cilla's poor hearing had been a real problem lately. It was isolating her from people – because she wasn't as keen on crowded, noisy places and she wasn't as comfortable on the phone.

'You're the only one I can ever hear, Biggins,' she had told me. My foghorn of a voice had its uses. So we'd spoken on the phone a lot.

'Love you lots,' was what I'd boom at the end of all our phone calls.

'Love you more,' was what she would always reply.

But back to that awful Monday, talking to Robert. He told me he'd got the shopping. He'd called upstairs on his return but had thought his mum was probably sleeping. He'd had a swim then he'd gone to wake her. He tried the door after knocking on it and getting no reply. It was locked. Again, we both knew that wasn't unusual. Cilla had often been in the villa on her own. She locked doors behind her. Who wouldn't?

But Robert had known, then, that something was wrong. So that poor boy had had to smash down his mother's door, terrified of what he'd find on the other side. What he'd found had been Cilla, on the ground between the balcony and the bedroom. We talked for a little longer. Then we said goodbye.

'If there's anything I can do... ' I'd said at the end of the call. The same thing people had said to me. It's the circle of kindness. The reminder of simple humanity.

Robert told me his brothers, Jack and Ben, were on their way and said he'd call if anything changed. I hung up. I sat back. I thought back thirty years to those crazy, unrepeatable days when it had all begun for me and Cilla. I thought of the first time we had met, when we had been work colleagues on the biggest prime-time show on ITV. We could have stayed work colleagues and gone our separate ways when the cameras stopped rolling. Instead, for some magical reason, we had become lifelong friends.

I'd been up in Newcastle working when ITV super-producer Alan Boyd asked to meet me. He had taken me out to dinner. Marvellous. And he had put that amazing proposal to me. 'We want you to co-star with a big star for a huge new Saturday and Sunday night show on ITV,' he had told me. He ran through the ideas they had for the programme. It was pure showbusiness. It was entertainment every step of the way. It sounded quite extraordinary. And they wanted me to be on it! I was so incredibly excited, dazed, confused and thrilled that I agreed without even asking the vital question – who would I be appearing alongside?

'Don't you want to know who else is on the show?' he'd asked at the end of the meal.

'Of course!' I'd said.

'Cilla Black.'

I nearly fell off my chair. I nearly fainted. I'd grown up listening to Cilla Black. She was wonderful. She'd had this amazing career, she had dominated the pop charts. And after taking something like ten years out to raise her family – well done Cilla, for that, I say – she'd just come back with a bang. She'd been a guest on *Wogan* and she'd been a sensation. She'd been funny, fantastic and utterly charming. She'd romped away with the whole show. I'd seen it. I loved her. And back then, the likes of Alan and David Bell at ITV knew light entertainment backwards. It was in their blood. They knew a star when they saw one. They knew Cilla was a star. So they'd cooked up the idea for *Surprise Surprise*.

I met Cilla for the very first time as our first proper rehearsals approached. I'll admit it. I was terrified – of her, of the show, of everything. But you know what? Cilla and I had a big, warm hug and I realised she was nervous too. The show was a huge deal for both of us. And somehow, maybe without words, we knew we'd support each other. We'd help each other. We could tune in to what we were both thinking. Without words, under the lights of a burning hot stage, we could communicate. The vast, big-budget prime-time show with its live studio audience would never be easy. But we'd do it together.

And there were three of us in the marriage, of course. For Bobby was always there. The rock that Cilla's life stood upon. Dear, wonderful, Bobby. He was there every step of Cilla's journey. When she was on a stage, he was in the wings. When she was at a meeting, he was at her side. When she was having her hair done, he was in the hairdressers too! It worked so well, that marriage. They were two people who really did exist as one – Cilla hardly ever carried money, because Bobby was always there for everything. So that's why, so many years later, Bobby's illness hit Cilla so hard. I remember visiting him at their home in Denham once, when the cancer was really taking hold. For some reason I can't remember, some in-joke we'd enjoyed at the time, I had brought him a six-foot tall inflatable plant. He'd laughed so much as we all blew it up that he'd had to go and have a lie down.

Cilla had been so vulnerable after his loss. She'd never been on her own. I remember the day he died. Somehow we had got her home. We gave her a drink. We respected what she wanted and left her alone. And later that night she had called me. She had been in a terrible state. 'Biggins, I don't know how to feed the dogs,' she had cried. Bobby had looked after everything. But Cilla had been strong. She had that Liverpudlian grit. In the end she picked herself up. She made an amazing recovery.

Years later, we all had mixed feelings when ITV announced it was making *Cilla*, a TV drama out of her life. I thought it was wrong. I thought it was disrespectful. Sheridan Smith was amazing in the role, by all accounts, and I know lots of people asked what Cilla thought about seeing herself portrayed on screen by someone else. But this wasn't what bothered Cilla. What hurt was seeing Bobby portrayed on screen by someone else. Maybe the writers, the producers and others didn't think of that. But that was the thing that could hurt the most.

Today, with Cilla gone, I can focus on the good times. I'm so proud of her three boys, Robert, Ben and Jack. They're men now with lives and families of their own. Cilla loved being a grandmother. What a life. Two amazing careers, as a chart-topper and as a TV mega-star. And as a wife, mum, grandmother and true friend to boot. Not bad, for a hat-check girl from Liverpool. And the good times? They include her 60th birthday. She had thrown a big party at her house in Denham with a marquee and lots of her favourite Dom Pérignon. What do you buy Cilla Black as a present? We'd all scratched our heads. Then someone had come up with a very naughty idea. We'd bought her a Rampant Rabbit. And if you don't know what that is, then you're not alone. Cilla didn't either. She opened it, long after the party guests had gone at about 4am, with her dear pal Pat and her housekeeper Penny at her side. She'd screamed with laughter when she realised it was a sex toy. And she made us laugh about it for years – because she told us he had put it, still in its box, never used, in her bedside table. It was seen there, years later, when she had been burgled and her room had been turned upside down. 'Forget the jewellery. I bet that's the one thing they remember finding beside Cilla Black's bed!' she hooted.

So goodbye Cilla. Yes, she really had said those things about 75 being the perfect age to go. We all make jokes and say things like that, us oldies and crumblies. The thought of me living another 30 years fills me with horror sometimes. We want a break from the aches and pains sometimes. But 72 was too, too soon.

Cilla, I remind myself, will be in heaven now, reunited with Bobby and with a glass of champagne in her hand. So many other lovely people are there too. And Cilla, like so many of the others, lived life to the full while she was here. I had her friendship, I have my memories and I've learned her lesson. Grab every opportunity, take every chance and enjoy every moment. They won't all work out the way you want them to. But if you don't try you'll never know. And

A Last Word for Cilla

if you try and fail you should at least get a story out of it. You should get a memory and a fair few laughs before you dust yourself down, pick yourself up and start all over again. Make the most of every sunny day. That's what Cilla taught me. So that's what I'm doing today.